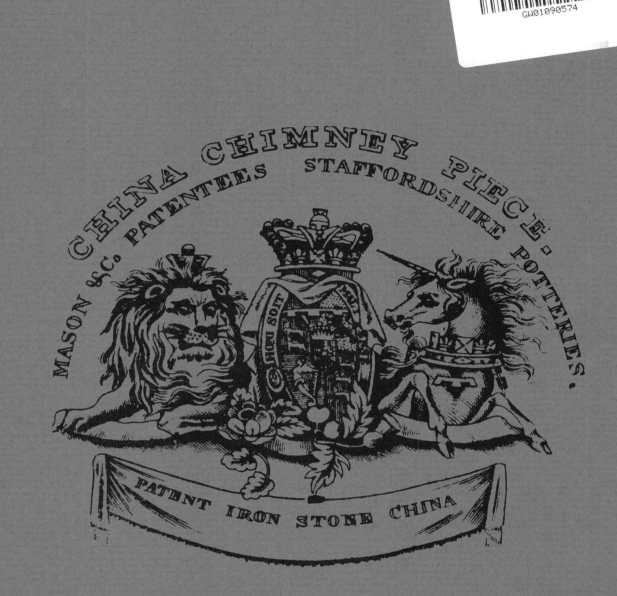

CHINA CHIMNEY PIECE.

MASON &Cº. PATENTEES STAFFORDSHIRE POTTERIES.

HONI SOIT

DIEU ET

PATENT IRON STONE CHINA

Colour Plate 1. Representative pieces from a Chinese hard-paste porcelain teaset, hand-painted with the 'Pagoda' pattern which was much copied by the English manufacturers. The gilt enrichments were added in England. c.1775. Such Oriental porcelains stocked Miles Mason's London retail shop and greatly influenced his later products when he became a manufacturer. Godden of Worthing Ltd.

Godden's Guide to

MASON'S CHINA AND THE IRONSTONE WARES

Geoffrey A. Godden F.R.S.A.

Godden's Guide to

MASON'S CHINA AND THE IRONSTONE WARES

Geoffrey A. Godden F.R.S.A.

The Antique Collectors' Club Ltd.

This is a revised and enlarged edition of the book
first published in 1971 by Barrie & Jenkins

ISBN 0 902028 86 3

British Library CIP Data
Godden, Geoffrey Arthur
    Godden's Guide to Mason's China and the Ironstone Wares.
    1. Porcelain, English — England — Staffordshire — Collectors and
    collecting
    2. Ironstone — Collectors and collecting
    I. Godden's Guide to Mason's China and the Ironstone Wares
    738'.0942   NK4210.M3

            Published for the Antique Collectors' Club
            by the Antique Collectors' Club Ltd.

            Printed in England by Baron Publishing
            Church Street, Woodbridge, Suffolk.

Why not join —

The Antique Collectors' Club

The Antique Collectors' Club was formed in 1966 and now has a five figure membership spread throughout the world. It publishes the only independently run monthly antiques magazine *Antique Collecting* which caters for those collectors who are interested in increasing their knowledge of antiques, both by increasing the members' knowledge of quality as well as in discussing the factors which influence the price that is likely to be asked. The Antique Collectors' Club pioneered the provision of information on prices for collectors and still leads in the provision of detailed articles on a variety of subjects.

It was in response to the enormous demand for information on 'what to pay' that the price guide series was introduced in 1968 with the first edition of *The Price Guide to Antique Furniture* (completely revised 1978), a book which broke new ground by illustrating the more common types of antique furniture, the sort that collectors could buy in shops and at auctions, rather than the rare museum pieces which had previously been used (and still to a large extent are used) to make up the limited amount of illustrations in books published by commercial publishers. Many other price guides have followed, all copiously illustrated, and greatly appreciated by collectors for the valuable information they contain, quite apart from prices. The Antique Collectors' Club also publishes other books on antiques, including horology and art reference works, and a full book list is available.

Club membership, which is open to all collectors, costs £7.95 per annum. Members receive free of charge *Antique Collecting,* the Club's magazine (published every month except August), which contains well-illustrated articles dealing with the practical aspects of collecting not normally dealt with by magazines. Prices, features of value, investment potential, fakes and forgeries are all given prominence in the magazine.

Among other facilities available to members are private buying and selling facilities, the longest list of 'For Sales' of any antiques magazine, an annual ceramics conference and the opportunity to meet other collectors at their local antique collectors' club. There are nearly eighty in Britain and so far a dozen overseas. Members may also buy the Club's publications at special pre-publication prices.

As its motto implies, the Club is an amateur organisation designed to help collectors get the most out of their hobby: it is informal and friendly and gives enormous enjoyment to all concerned.

For Collectors — By Collectors — About Collecting

The Antique Collectors' Club, 5 Church Street, Woodbridge, Suffolk

Contents

List of Colour Plates

Preface

This book, whilst based on my highly successful and popular earlier work *The Illustrated Guide to Mason's Patent Ironstone China* which has been out of print since 1976, is not a mere reprint of that work.

Whole sections have been rewritten to take account of new information, and this edition now includes two completely new and important chapters. The early Mason porcelains made in Staffordshire were hardly touched on in the earlier book, whereas Chapter Three of this edition amply makes up for the earlier omission with its lengthy discussion of the high quality and decorative Mason porcelains. Many helpful new illustrations have been added and the present book has been completely redesigned to incorporate illustrations in the text. This revised and enlarged book will completely supersede the earlier *Illustrated Guide* and will be even more helpful to the collector, student, dealer or auctioneer.

The extended coverage is unique to this new book, ranging as it does from the Chinese porcelains in which Miles Mason dealt in London in the eighteenth century, through his Liverpool porcelain manufacturing partnership, into Mason's ventures in Staffordshire where he produced some of our most interesting English porcelains early in the nineteenth century, to the world-famous Mason's Patent Ironstone China introduced by Miles' eldest son Charles James Mason in 1813. The coverage extends further to list well over a hundred of Mason's contemporaries who sought to produce these popular durable Ironstone-type wares which were exported far and wide giving pleasure and long service to all users. Probably more of these Ironstone-type wares were exported to North America and other overseas markets in the nineteenth century than any other type of English ceramic.

Today collectors vie for the self-same pleasure of acquisition, though nowadays it is the beauty of the products and the interest in them which makes them so desired, rather than acquisition for everyday use. Yet there must be many articles of Mason Patent Ironstone China made before 1840 which are still in use. How decorative those 'antique jugs' of the 1822 sale (see page 161) still look on an oak dresser or filled with flowers on a table and, of course, earthenwares in the same tradition — often based on the old shapes or added patterns — are still being made today in Staffordshire by Mason's Ironstone. It is interesting to learn that this present-day firm (formerly Ashworth) is now a division of Josiah Wedgwood & Sons Ltd., and that in 1810 our Miles Mason offered to make porcelain for sale in Wedgwood's London showrooms. Today Mason and Wedgwood are equally famous and wares bearing their time honoured names are displayed and sold side by side. The tradition lives on and some of the present day products — the antiques of the future — are also featured in this work.

This book is dedicated to all Mason collectors and users. It seeks to make the study of Mason's porcelains and Ironstone wares all the more enjoyable and fulfilling.

Geoffrey Godden,
Worthing, West Sussex.

Acknowledgements

Very many kind collectors, dealers and auctioneers have assisted in the preparation of this book over a lengthy period, but firstly I wish to record my gratitude to the late Alfred Meigh for his pre-war research into the history of the Mason family and their various Potteries. His unpublished manuscript passed into my hands after his death and it was this which first prompted me to enlarge upon his work.

I am also indebted to Reginald G. Haggar for his generous help over many years, to Mr. J.S. Goddard, of Mason's Ironstone China Ltd., for his interest and for his kindness in permitting me to examine the early Mason copper plates which have been passed down to the present firm. I am also grateful for much help and encouragement received from Mr. and Mrs. A.E. Grove, Mason collectors.

My appreciation to Christie, Manson & Woods Ltd., and to Phillips, Son & Neale Ltd., the well known fine art auctioneers, is two-fold: to past directors for preserving the early nineteenth century catalogues of Mason's Ironstone wares sold by them in 1818 and 1822, and to the present directors for permitting me to make full use of the material.

Other interesting material has been obtained from contemporary records housed at the Guildhall Library; India Office Records; the National Newspaper Library and the Public Record Office and I gratefully acknowledge the help I have received from their officers and staff. I have also received much help from Francis Baxendale, Dr. G. Barnes, Christopher Gilbert, Derek Harper, Bevis Hillier, Christopher May, Bill Saks, Cyril Shingler and Alan Smith.

The illustrations have been taken from specimens in the possession of individuals, firms or museums, and their names are recorded at the end of the book. I am most grateful for their generosity in permitting me to reproduce their treasures. In most cases these illustrations were taken by Mr. A. Whitcomb of Walter Gardiner, photographers of Worthing. I regret that I do not have records of the names of other photographers who have contributed their talents but I acknowledge their help.

Chapter One

Miles Mason, Chinaman

IN THIS FIRST chapter I wish to record the very brief details we have available on Miles Mason's early life and then to explain something of his stock as a London 'Chinaman' or dealer in china ware.

It is also interesting and relevant to learn how the stock of Chinese porcelain was purchased via the bulk importations of the English East India Company and to judge why and when this vital source of stock dried up. To set the scene.

In subsequent chapters we will learn what steps Miles Mason took to remedy the situation in the 1790s and subsequently extended his trade into Staffordshire where he and his sons were to produce superb porcelains and the now world-famous Mason's Patent Ironstone China in the nineteenth century.

Miles Mason was born in December 1752, the son of William Mason of Dent in Yorkshire. He is said to have worked first in the Bank of England, a statement that cannot be confirmed, but in London he certainly struck up a friendship with Ruth Farrar, whose father Richard had been an important Chinaman or dealer in the imported Chinese porcelains with premises at 131 Fenchurch Street, London. By 1763 Richard Farrar must have been of some considerable standing for in that year Richard Farrar & Co. supplied General George Washington (later the first President of the newly formed United States of America) with a ''complete sett of table china fine blue and white numbering fifty seven pieces''. This was almost certainly a Chinese blue and white service — the staple of Farrar's trade.

Richard Farrar had died in May 1775, leaving over £30,000 in trust to his daughter, who was then only nine years old. Miles Mason subsequently married her in August 1782, and took over the old established business, probably in about September 1783, when he joined the Glass Sellers Company. According to the local Sewer Rate records the business was in Miles Mason's name by at least September 1784.

In the past it has been stated that Richard Garrett joined Richard Farrar in 1772 but a minute in the records of the English East India Company shows that they had been in partnership from at least August 1769 and were then purchasers of Chinese porcelains sold at the Company's auction sales of this commodity: ''The request of Messrs

Plate 1. Representative pieces from a Chinese porcelain dinner service of the type which were imported into London in quantity prior to 1792. The basic plate and tureen shape was copied by the Masons in the nineteenth century. c.1775. Earle D. Vandekar, London

Farrar and Garrett to be allowed for breakage in a lot of chinaware bought by them at the Company's candle''.

When Miles Mason began his career as a Chinaman in London in the early 1780s there were relatively few English porcelain manufacturers able to supply the retail trade. There was, of course, the Derby factory with its own retail showrooms, as well as the Lowestoft factory — in the main catering for its local markets and not seeking to compete with the London trade; the New Hall partnership in Staffordshire was in its early days, the partnership having been formed in 1781; the Worcester Company was rather in the decline and was bought up by Thomas Flight in 1783, but it too had its own retail outlets; whilst Thomas Turner's Caughley porcelain works, which was founded in about 1775, also had its own London wholesale warehouse.

The great majority of the London Chinamen's stock comprised Chinese porcelains and this is precisely why they were called Chinamen.

This Chinese porcelain was imported in bulk by the Honourable East India Company which enjoyed a State monopoly on the

Plate 2. A Chinese export market porcelain dinner service plate of the type sold by the London 'Chinamen' or retailers in the second-half of the eighteenth century. c.1780. Godden of Worthing Ltd.

18

Colour Plate 2. Representative pieces from a Miles Mason teaset showing the 'Boy in the Door' subject which is an outline print coloured in by hand. c.1804-08. Teapot 10½ ins. long. Godden of Worthing Ltd.

19

importation of goods from the East and these bulk imports were sold at huge auction sales, which for china ware were normally held twice a year. These auction sales were wholesale ones catering for the dealers (not individual retail customers) who purchased bulk lots and then divided them up into individual pieces or made up saleable sets.

The Company's bulk order in the 1776 season for example included no less than 168,000 blue and white cups and saucers and 35,000 dinner plates. Coloured teasets cost the Company a mere 12s., or 60 new pence, per set which then comprised two teapots (of differing sizes), a slop bowl, a sugar bowl and cover, a milk jug, a tea canister and cover, two plates, twelve tea bowls and saucers and twelve coffee cups. A typical Chinese blue and white teaset is shown in Colour Plate 1 with other related standard items shown in Plates 6, 9 and 10.

Plate 3. A Chinese export market tureen from a dinner service of the 1780s showing typical formal floral designs of the period. Godden of Worthing Ltd.

The large dinner services cost £10 for the richly enamelled designs, which sounds expensive until one looks at the standard make-up of these Chinese dinner services which comprised:

2 large soup tureens, covers and stands
4 smaller do.
8 salad dishes
2 deep square salad dishes
4 sauce boats and stands
18 flat platters, in six sizes
72 dinner plates
36 soup plates
24 side plates
24 'water' plates

A total of 210 pieces costing 1s. a piece including the large tureens!

The blue and white wares were cheaper still. No wonder our own porcelain manufacturers could not compete with the Oriental imports, especially in the production of dinner wares, bearing in mind all the troublesome plates and platters which gave so much difficulty in the firing. No wonder, too, the London Chinamen were so dependent on the Company's imports of Chinese porcelain. Typical Chinese porcelain dinner wares of the 1775-85 period are shown in Plates 1-5 and their shapes and general styles of decoration are reflected in Mason's later wares.

In the 1777/8 season the English East India Company imported no less than *348 tons* of Chinese porcelain, all to be sold in their bulk auction sales to dealers such as Miles Mason.

However, one must make the point that all was not plain sailing. At times the market was glutted with these bulk imports and trade was bad. For example in January 1779 the Company's agents or 'Supracargoes' in Canton reported:

> As the orders this year received from the Honble. Court [of Directors] give us reason to suppose that China ware is not now an article in so high demand as some seasons past we have come to the resolution not to make any contract for the ensuing year as the quantity we have remaining will . . . be sufficient to load eight ships . . .

Nevertheless, in October 1781 they contracted with their Chinese agent Exchin for 1,200 chests of china ware ''the patterns to be new''. It is interesting to see how in the 1780s the amount of tea imported into this country rose to staggering figures — in the 1786/7 season the Company ordered eighteen million pounds of tea; by 1798 over twenty million pounds were ordered.

It is also of interest to see the Conditions of Sale under which Miles Mason and his colleagues purchased their stock. In 1787 for example we find recorded:

> Resolved that 1732 lots of China ware more or less be declared for sale on Tuesday the 4th December next at 11 oclock.
>
> That the following articles be inserted in the Preamble of Sale and at the head of the China ware sale books . . .
>
> That every buyer who shall be declared the best bidder for any lot or lots at this sale pay one tenth part of the value thereof within twenty days afterwards [this was called the Deposit] and shall make good the remainder of the purchase

Plate 4. A Chinese export market tureen from a large dinner service. The design is rather crudely painted in underglaze blue but is of a popular type which inspired many English copies. c.1785. Godden of Worthing Ltd.

money on or before the. . . [left blank in the Minute] without discount.

That no lots of china ware sold at this sale shall be divided or parted whilst the same shall remain in the Company's warehouses but shall be cleared and taken away as sold whole and entire without breaking bulk and that the China ware is to be taken away with all faults and none to be refused or allowance to be made on any of the lots on account of any pieces being cracked or broken or on pretence of not answering the sample, differences of figure, painting or blistering, discolouring, cracks in glazing, want of glazing, snipped or rubbed edges or on any other account or pretence whatever. . .

The reference to the items "not answering the sample" serves to remind us that most of the bulk lots were sold in their packed state, sight unseen by the trade buyer who had only a sample piece and a written list of the contents!

Perhaps then it is not surprising that in October 1788 Joseph Lygo the manager of the Derby factory's retail shop in London reported back to William Duesbury in Derby: "In the India House sale this week I am informed out of more than eighteen hundred lots there was not five hundred sold. . ."

But at the same time this retailer also lamented that trade was "very dead".

Two years later Joseph Lygo wrote another letter which helps to prove that the Chinese blue and white porcelains undersold our own porcelain factories — even the Caughley or 'Salopian' wares which are not renowned for their great quality; indeed one forms the impression that Thomas Turner's main concern was to compete with the Chinese imports by mass-production techniques such as printing his designs in underglaze-blue from copper plates. Yet he apparently lost the race. In August 1790 Joseph Lygo reported:

I have been to the Salopian Warehouse to enquire about the wash-hand basons and jugs blue and white, they have got 4 common ones only and the price is 10/6 each. Chamber pots they have none, and have not made any for some time and the reason is foreign Nankin ones are so much cheaper than theirs.

The term 'Nankin' was used at that period in England to describe all Chinese porcelains decorated in underglaze-blue, rather than in over-glaze enamel colours.

Much play has been made by other writers of the very high rates of duty levied by the Government on the imported wares, rates which forced Miles Mason and presumably other Chinamen to seek other types of porcelain to sell in their shops or even, in the case of Miles Mason, to undertake a porcelain manufacturing enterprise himself. The fact is, however, that the rates of duty had almost nothing to do with the situation which was to lead to Miles Mason producing his own porcelains. As I have shown, the imported wares compared in price very favourably with our English porcelains.

The basic trouble was that in December 1791 the Court of Directors of the East India Company decided to cease their bulk importations of Chinese porcelains.

Miles Mason was right in the centre of events, not only because he was an officer of his City Company — the Glass Sellers (there being no China Sellers Company) of which he was Renter Warden in 1791/2, Upper Warden in 1792/3 and Master in 1793/4, but also because he

Plate 5. A Chinese export market dinner service platter painted in underglaze blue. Such services would have been sold by Miles Mason and other London dealers. c.1780. Godden of Worthing Ltd.

and some of his colleagues had in effect been cheating the Company at the sales. It is probable that this cheating by the dealers caused the Directors of the East India Company to stop all imports of the troublesome china ware.

I now can record the situation as told in the Company's minutes of the period.

The troubles arose from the Company's auction sale held in December 1787, the very auction from which I have just quoted the conditions of sale, but the first intimation of action by the Company is contained in a letter dated 28th December, 1787, written by four London Chinamen of which Miles Mason was one of the signatories:

> To the Hon. the Court of Directors of the United East India Company.
> Honble. Sirs
> ''We the undersigned Buyers of Chinaware at your sale having applied in the accountants office as usual to pay Deposit on the goods bought have received for answer that there were orders given to take no Deposit. Wherefore we pray your Honours that we may be heard upon the matter.
> December 28th 1787.
>
> James Shaw for
Isaac Akerman and self
Samuel Corbessor [? — this
name is illegible]
Miles Mason.

The Court of Directors acceded to the request to meet the china dealers and the Court Minutes report the occasion in the following manner:

> On reading a letter from Mr. James Shaw and several other buyers of china ware dated this day (December 28th 1787) signifying that they have not been permitted to pay their deposits in the usual manner and praying to be heard upon the matter.
> Mr. Shaw and the other buyers were called in and acquainted by the Chairman that under the circumstances in which the sale was conducted on the part of the buyers, the Court consider the sale of the lots in question to be void.

Plate 6. A Chinese hard paste porcelain saucer-shaped dish, hand-painted with the extremely popular Pagoda or Broseley-Willow design which was copied by many English potters, including Miles Mason. c.1780. Diameter 7ins. Geoffrey Godden, Chinaman

It would then appear that the Company sought to take the dealers to court over their conduct, for in June 1788 the Company's minutes record:

> On reading the request of Sundry dealers in china ware offering to the Court a subscription to the charity for the Seamen's Widows of £100, instead of continuing the prosecution carrying on against them.
> Resolved that the Secretary do write an answer to the said letter that the Court have not instituted the present Proceedings from resentment or any personal private motives but as a matter of Public justice to correct an abuse which they have reason to believe has long existed very highly detrimental to the Company. They therefore conceive it absolutely incumbent upon them to continue the Legal Proceedings.

Still the matter continued, and on 21st January, 1789 it was resolved that:

> The prosecution now carrying on against the buyers of china ware for a combination be stayed on their acceding to the following requisitions viz.
> That they relinquish all claims to the china ware bought by them at the Company's sale of that article on 11th December 1787 and that they pay to the Company the sum of five hundred pounds to be applied in such manner as the Court (of Directors) shall think proper to direct...

However, Miles Mason and his fellow dealers declined to accept this offer and on 29th January, 1789 the complaint was heard on the Kings Bench and was reported to the Directors of the East India Company in the following words:

> The Company's Solicitor reported that the motion for making a rule absolute for an information against the China Dealers... came on in the Court of Kings Bench yesterday when although the offence was admitted and the china dealers refused to comply with the terms offered by the Company, the Court was pleased to discharge the rule, under the idea that as the combination complained of was at an end and the Parties had expressed contribution for their offence it was not a proper case for the Court to interfere by such a prosecution as was applied for...

The offence was of course the ancient one of forming a 'combination' or 'ring' of friendly parties who would agree not to bid against each other, so depressing the auction price by lack of full competition. In this case the dealers would not only have purchased the Chinese imports at a lower figure but, because all the extra charges and taxes were calculated on the hammer price, these extra costs too would have been reduced. Under most ring agreements the items purchased by the private combination are then auctioned in private between the parties concerned in what is known as a 'settlement', the difference in price between the original hammer cost and the later private settlement bid being divided between the combination concerned. The Directors of the Company were probably correct in their assumption that the practice had been carried·on over many years.

Plate 7. A Chinese export market punch bowl painted in a typical style suited to the European market. Such bowls would have been a standard line with the London china dealers. c.1775. Diameter 9ins. Geoffrey Godden, Chinaman

The troublesome question of conditions of sale continued to concern the East India Company, and in April 1789 the Committee of Warehouses submitted the following suggestion:

> ...that although it would be very desirable to carry into effect the new regulations as to the sale of china ware yet under all the circumstances of the case, it may be proper to comply with the request of the buyers and revert to the former mode of sale...and should the Court concur in this opinion the Committee mean to establish such regulations for conducting the business of Ringing out as may best tend to prevent any improper practices in future.

It was "Resolved that this Court do agree in opinion with the Committee".

The china dealers were by now probably feeling very relieved that the Company's Court case had failed at its first stage and felt that they had gained a victory over the Directors but, as we shall see, it was to prove a very hollow victory. The Directors obviously were not now well disposed towards the china dealers who they felt had been cheating at their sales and defrauding them their full profit on the imported Chinese porcelains. They perhaps began to wonder if it was worth all the expense and bother.

The Directors of the East India Company often complained to their agents in Canton regarding faulty or badly packed porcelains. One such letter read:

> We think it necessary to repeat, we continue to sustain very heavy losses by the china ware being much false packed, that is to say the goods have come of a variety of patterns, where they should all have been alike... In some cases there have been so many patterns and so very different from each other that they could not possibly have been put up to sale in sets...

With this in mind, coupled with the troubles with the trade buyers at the Company's auctions it is perhaps not all that surprising that in December 1791, after more than a hundred years of trade in Chinese porcelains, the Directors of the English East India Company suddenly decided to cease their bulk imports. Leaving not only the London dealers in the lurch but also their Chinese china ware merchant.

The Company's agents in Canton reported back to London in the following terms:

> We have lately had an application from Exchin our late china ware merchant to afford him some relief from the loss and inconvenience he has sustained by the discontinuance of that article of the Honble. Company's investment.
>
> It appears by the Honble. Courts instructions on that head, that the Select Committee were directed to send home no more china ware than they had existing engagements for and accordingly it was discontinued in the year 1792, there being then no exciting contracts.
>
> The plea urged by Exchin is, that although no contract was made at the close of the season 1791, the then President of the Select Committee encouraged him to make a quantity under the presumption that it would be wanted, but as no china ware was ordered that year, it has been upon his hands ever since, till this time that his losses and misfortunes have compelled him to have recourse to the Honble. Company for relief. The amount of china-ware is about 60,000 Tales.

The above letter was dated Canton 14th May, 1795, a point which underlines the distance in time between the Directors in London and their agents in China. Indeed it would seem that the London china dealers did not know of the decision to stop the bulk imports from China for over three years! This was probably due to the large amounts already ordered and on voyage back to England and because the Company's warehouses held such large stocks. The amount left on Exchin's hands was some £20,000 worth — a truly huge quantity of porcelain at the prices then current in Canton.

On 28th January, 1795 the London dealers wrote to the Directors of the Company ''expressing their hope that the trade in that article may be continued by the Company''. In March the following Minute was written by the Company's clerk:

> The Committee of warehouses in a report dated the 11th instant, now read, stating that the reasons urged by the dealers in china-ware in their memorial read in Court the 4th ultimo are not sufficiently forcible to induce the Committee to recommend to the Court to depart from their former resolutions as to the non-importations of china-ware, and that with regard to the china-ware now on hand, application be made to the Lords Commissioners of the Treasury praying that the period for allowing the drawback on the same may be extended for two years from the expiration of the usual period.
>
> Resolved that this Court approve the said report.

This recommendation to extend the period of 'drawback' makes the point that much of the ware sold at auction and purchased by the dealers was subsequently re-exported by them and that on the exports

Plate 8. A humble Chinese export market saucer painted with a design which was copied by the Wolfe-Mason partnership at Liverpool, see Plates 34 and 35. c.1790. Diameter 4¾ ins. Geoffrey Godden, Chinaman

Plate 9. A Chinese export market teapot hand-painted in underglaze blue with the much copied Pagoda design. The gilt enrichments were added in England before sale. c.1790. Godden of Worthing Ltd.

they were able to reclaim or drawback the initial import taxes. However, this drawback was only permitted up to three years after the porcelain was first imported. Now, however, only old imports were being sold and the three year period of grace was running out — hence the application to the Treasury to extend the period to five years, an application which was granted. London was a great centre of international trade and Miles Mason would no doubt have shared in the export market.

Application to extend the period of drawback was not the only request recorded in the Company's records. Reading between the lines of the following letter from Miles Mason we can judge that money was short and that trade was slow: "Letter from Mr. Miles Mason requesting the time for his paying the deposits on china ware bought by him at the present sale may be extended for two months" (Minute dated 27th March, 1793).

Now that the East India Company had declined to reconsider the question of recommencing the bulk imports, the dealers themselves sought to find ways to bring china ware into this country where the Company enjoyed its State monopoly in all trade to and from the East. On 1st April, 1795 we find minuted:

Letter from Mr. Miles Mason requesting to know on behalf of the dealers in china-ware, upon what terms of Freight the Company will permit their officers to bring that article as a flooring for tea.

In former times the china ware had been considered by the Company to be vital cargo, being both water resistant and heavy to make the vessels 'sailworthy', to use the contemporary term. Yet in the reply to Miles Mason's letter the Company now put forward the reason for turning down the request that the heavy china ware was not now required. Even if it was no longer strictly necessary it must have been beneficial and, of course, the Company would still have taken its percentage. It seems therefore that the real reason was the Director's attitude to the dealers after their 'combination' had been brought to light — they wanted no more truck with the china ware dealers.

I record the Director's reply to Miles Mason's request, as it seemingly forms a landmark in the manner of stowing cargo on the returning East Indiamen:

> The Committee of shipping in a report dated the 7th instant [7th April, 1795] now read stating that they have taken into consideration a letter of Mr. Miles Mason requesting to know on behalf of the dealers in china ware upon what terms of Freight the Company will permit their officers to bring that article as a flooring for tea and as the ships are dunnaged with Deals and it is by no means requisite to floor the tea with china ware the Committee think it unnecessary to enter into consideration of the terms upon which the officers in the Company's service might be allowed to import china ware. Resolve that this Court do approve the said report.

A suggestion for a new method of stowing the teas was put forward in December 1787, but in fact the old method was continued, the heavy china ware was packed in cases below the lightweight teas — the Company's excuse was a lame one as is evidenced by its own documents.

As a matter of history I quote extracts from the Company's Minutes to remind present-day readers that in the 1790s England had been at war with France from the beginning of 1793. Some of our vessels were lost with the Company's cargo, but on the other hand prizes were taken and their goods sold in the Company's sales found their way into our china dealers' shops. But of course the war greatly affected our export trade and Mason and his fellow dealers no doubt found the times hard.

In November 1795 the following was recorded:

> Request of the buyers of China Ware that the Court will accede to the sale of the china ware in the *Etusco* prize ship for home consumption agreeable to the prayer of the petition from the buyers to the Lords of the Treasury. (This sale was agreed to.)

> Letter from Major General Clarke dated the 23rd September 1795, advising the surrender of the Cape of Good Hope to His Majesty's Forces on the 16th of that month.

The Company obviously had an interest in the successful conduct of the war in which their vessels were very much concerned and the Directors voted the then considerable sum of £10,000 to the ''Rt. Hon Rear Admiral Lord Nelson on account of victory over the French Fleet near the mouth of the Nile on 2nd & 3rd August, 1798''.

Although the Directors ceased to order their bulk imports of china ware in 1791, and had declined to let the china dealers arrange their own imports through the Company's officers, it is still true that Chinese porcelains were being imported into London after 1791. This was made possible through the 'Private Trade' allowances of the ship's Captain, officers and crew. But this permitted 'Private Trade' was strictly limited in quantity and all such pieces still had to be sold at the Company's auction sales.

Very full details of these 'Private Trade' imports are given with other facts on the importation of Chinese porcelains in my standard book *Oriental Export Market Porcelains* (Hart-Davis, MacGibbon, Granada Publishing, London, 1979) and in this present résumé it is only necessary to state that as a general rule the private imports consisted of the more individual articles, including all the armorial porcelain, the crested and initialled pieces made to special order, but not the masses of standard dinner wares and teawares formerly imported in bulk by the Company for sale in their wholesale auctions.

I propose to close this brief coverage of the English East India Company's importation in Chinese porcelain at the year 1801, when the trade had dwindled to almost nothing, and at this point, two important, interesting and relevant extracts from the Company's archives are worth noting. First, a Private Trade sale notice:

> Resolved that the undermentioned goods be declared for sale...
> Private Trade China ware on Friday the 15th November 1799...and that the buyers be informed that they are to pay on such part of the above China Ware as may be cleared for home consumption, the Customs Duty of £109-8-6 per cent agreeable to the Act of the 39th Geo 3rd Cap 59 [of 1799].

This was of course special war-rate of tax but one that came into effect some eight years after the bulk imports had ceased and some four years after Miles Mason had started to take steps to produce his own English porcelains (and earthenwares) to fill the void left by the Company's decision of 1791. The special tax was in fact lowered by over half in 1803, but by now the quantity of Chinese porcelain imported into this country was extremely small being only 'Private Trade'.

Plate 10. A Chinese export market covered bowl and stand hand-painted with the Pagoda pattern but with gilt enrichments added in England, see page 30. c.1790. Diameter of stand 7½ ins. Godden of Worthing Ltd.

My second extract shows how, by March 1801, the Company's trade in china ware had dropped to such an extent that ships' owners had to supply their own kentledge to make the vessel sailworthy on the homeward voyage. For more than a hundred years the Chinese porcelains had formed the heavy flooring below the teas, but now we have the situation ''. . . that the owners of the *Lord Duncan* be required to provide a sufficient quantity of Iron Kentledge to be sent out by the direct China ships or to engage to provide an equal quantity of metal in China to ballast the ship on her homeward voyage.''

By this date however Miles Mason was himself a manufacturer and the decline of the Chinese imports suited his purpose very well — the main competition was now of little consequence. As a china dealer he had learnt well what the public wanted — serviceable decorative porcelains — and now he sought to provide it adding tasteful up-to-date English designs.

Apart from the facts already recounted we know very little about Miles Mason's life as a Chinaman in London, but certainly he was a leading member of his trade at a very vital period, in the mid-1790s. Llewellynn Jewitt in his *Ceramic Art of Great Britain* (Virtue & Co., London, 1878) quotes from a 1797 Mason invoice (the present whereabouts of which is not known) listing blue dessert services, each of which comprised a centre piece, six dishes, two cucumber tureens, covers and stands and twenty-four plates, oval and round baking dishes, oval and square salad dishes, basins, egg cups and 'Nankeen spitting pots'. These last mentioned articles would certainly have been of blue and white Chinese porcelain, as may the other items but they might also have been of English manufacture, either Staffordshire blue printed earthenware or Caughley porcelain.

The letterhead on this now missing invoice could well have been of the utmost interest, perhaps listing the various types of ware in which Miles Mason traded and the date of establishment for the shop which was obviously of long standing as Robert Farrar, the father of Richard Garrett's partner Richard Farrar, was admitted to the Glass Sellers Company in 1718. He moved to Fenchurch Street in 1741 and was master of the Company in 1753/4.

This 1797 invoice may also have stated that Miles Mason enamelled or gilded wares to special order — as several of his fellow dealers undoubtedly did, for much of the Chinese blue and white imports of the 1790s, especially the teawares, bears gilt borders and other enrichments added by the individual dealers in London. The teaset shown in Colour Plate 1 is such an English gilt Chinese service, as are the pieces shown in Plates 9 and 10.

The point about these sets is that the dealers all stocked very much the same assortment of Chinese porcelain, imported in bulk by the East India Company and sold at their sales. In order to lift one's stock and add a little refinement the London dealers added gilt enrichments to their own sets making them just a little different to those which their competitors were selling. Often, but not always, one finds the English gilder's tally-number or initials added inside, or near, the foot rim of the main pieces such as the teapot.

Apart from his china shop at 131 Fenchurch Street Miles Mason reputedly entered into a partnership in 1796 with James Green and Limpus of Upper Thames Street. This firm seemingly was mainly concerned in wholesaling Staffordshire earthenwares. At this period Mason had learnt that the Chinese imports were about to all but dry up and he was no doubt attempting to diversify. Now that he had two London outlets, his next step was to produce wares to stock these premises.

Chapter Two

Miles Mason's Manufacturing Partnership at Liverpool

ALMOST THE ONLY evidence that Miles Mason — the London Chinaman — was engaged in making porcelain at Liverpool comes from the announcement made on the termination of the arrangement in June 1800. The following notice then appeared in the *London Gazette* and in *Williamson's Liverpool Advertiser*.

> Notice is hereby given that the partnership heretofore subsisting between Thomas Wolfe, Miles Mason and John Luckcock and established at Islington, Liverpool, in the County-Palatine of Lancaster, in the China manufactory, under the firm of Thomas Wolfe and Co. is this day dissolved by mutual consent.
> Witness the parties hands this 7th day of June 1800.
> > Thomas Wolfe
> > Miles Mason
> > John Luckcock

The first-named signatory Thomas Wolfe, was the practical potter with the all-important know-how and, as stated in the notice, the three partners traded as Thomas Wolfe & Co. Miles Mason may well have invested money in the partnership and given the concern the advantages of an established outlet in London, largely replacing the earlier porcelains which were formerly stocked.

John Luckcock (or Lucock) was a talented modeller who, according to Simeon Shaw in his *The Chemistry of Pottery* written in 1837, had undertaken work for Flaxman. However, the so-far identified products of this short lived partnership do not display the talents of, or indeed

Plate 11. Two unglazed 'wasters' from the Liverpool factory site worked by the Wolfe-Mason partnership in the 1796-1800 period, showing parts of the blue-printed Pagoda design copied from Chinese imports. City of Liverpool Museum Service

the need for, any great modeller. They are simple tablewares, mainly teawares.

It must be assumed that Miles Mason took no part in the day by day running of this Liverpool porcelain producing partnership; his business was in London selling the products. However, a Liverpool directory of 1800 does list 'Miles Mason, China Manufacturer, Upper Islington' and he next appears in the Liverpool records in 1816 when he is described as 'Miles Mason Gentleman at 44 Mill Street'. The description ''Gentleman'' signified that he had retired from commerce!

The porcelains produced by Thomas Wolfe & Co. are unmarked and I owe my modest success in identifying the porcelains to Mr. Alan Smith who, in 1968, discovered a quantity of porcelain 'wasters' on the site of Wolfe's factory in Upper Islington, Liverpool. In general style it is clear that the fragments are of the 1790-1800 period and there seems no doubt that the finds do in fact relate to the Wolfe-Mason-Luckcock partnership, and not to any of the other Liverpool porcelain manufacturers.

Alan Smith's finds were first published in a paper he read to the English Ceramic Circle in March 1971, which was published in that Circle's *Transactions,* vol.8, part 2, 1972. In it Mr. Smith illustrated some of the all important factory 'wasters' (Plates 11, 19, 24, 28 and 37), but at that time he was only able to show one blue-printed teabowl and saucer (Plate 28) which matched his finds. I will, in a moment, discuss an extended range of porcelains which I believe link with these finds and which were made by the Wolfe-Mason partnership. These or similar wares would have been sold in Mason's London shop.

First, however, I should outline the history of this Liverpool factory and in doing this I have to draw heavily on Mr. Alan Smith's researches. There had been a pottery on the site as early as the 1740s, originally for the production of tin-glazed earthenware; later, by the 1780s, the Penningtons had a porcelain works there and wasters of this period were also found by Alan Smith.

In February 1790 the works were leased to Thomas Wolfe who seems also to have dealt in Staffordshire earthenware, for the Liverpool directories from 1787-96 list him as a dealer in Staffordshire wares:

1787 Thomas Wolfe, Potter & Staffs Warehouse, Dukes Place.
1790 Thomas Wolfe, Staffs merchant, 45 Old Dock.
1796 Thomas Wolfe, Staffs & China Warehouse, 45 Old Dock.
1800 Thomas Wolfe, Staffs & China Warehouse, 45 Old Dock.

Thomas Wolfe was certainly not alone in selling Staffordshire earthenwares in Liverpool. In the 1790 period there were at least six Staffordshire warehouses in Liverpool, a fact which reminds us of the importance of the port of Liverpool to our export trade and also that the Staffordshire Potteries were now conveniently linked to Liverpool by relatively trouble-free water transport — river and canal.

The 1796 directory is the first to list Thomas Wolfe as a china manufacturer at 2 Islington and in this year the vital partnership between Wolfe, Miles Mason and John Lucock was set up. When Wolfe's lease of the works was renewed on 1st March, 1798 the premises were described in the following manner:

> . . . all that parcel of land with the China Works and other buildings thereon erected situate on the North side of Upper Islington in Liverpool, bounded on the East by a common passage and on the West by houses fronting St. Ann Street and at the back or North side by buildings the inheritance of the said Thomas Wolfe, containing in front to Upper Islington aforesaid in a broken line 233 feet 3 inches and running in depth on the East and West sides severally 75 feet and at the back or North side 229 feet 6 inches.

Various plans of the Pottery and photographs of the site as it appeared in 1971 are included in Alan Smith's paper.

The original pottery was enlarged in 1798. The sale notice in Gore's *General Advertiser* of 22nd May, 1800 then described the premises as: ''. . . all that new erected China Works with steam engine and dwelling house at Upper Islington''.

The final act in Miles Mason's china-making venture in Liverpool is neatly set out in the *London Gazette* of 5th July, 1800, which I have already quoted at the beginning of this Chapter.

Before proceeding to identify the porcelains made by this partnership in Liverpool (wares made at least in part to stock Miles Mason's London china shop), it must be recorded that at the same time Miles Mason was a partner in an earthenware producing works at Lane Delph in the Staffordshire Potteries with George Wolfe. This concern traded as 'Mason & Wolfe', and this partnership too was terminated in July 1800 when, in the official notice published in the *London Gazette,* Miles Mason was described as ''of Fenchurch Street in the City of London, china merchant''.

No marked examples of Mason & Wolfe's Staffordshire earthenwares have been recorded but their productions most probably followed the fashion of the day and would mainly have comprised blue transfer-printed earthenware (termed pearlware) which before 1800 still consisted of mock-Chinese styled landscape designs. These Staffordshire blue-printed earthenwares of course undersold the porcelains and were in great demand, especially for dinner and dessert services (most teasets were still in the more delicate porcelains). These Mason & Wolfe earthenwares were no doubt supplied to Miles Mason's London shop and were especially welcome there now that the supply of Chinese porcelain had all but dried up. The invoice which Llewellynn Jewitt had in his possession in the 1870s, and referred to in Chapter One, noted blue dessert services of centre piece, dishes, tureens covers and stands and plates; these sets, and such other objects as the oval and square salad dishes, could well have been Mason & Wolfe's own make of Staffordshire earthenware, although other items such as ''Nankeen spitting pots'' were clearly of Chinese origin.

The task of identifying the pre-July 1800 Liverpool porcelains depends solely on the factory wasters discovered by Alan Smith. Unfortunately these key wasters are almost devoid of helpful handle or spout shapes and only one knob was discovered. However, the mass of often very small broken cups and saucers shows clearly that most of the wares were decorated with underglaze blue printed designs in the manner of the hand-painted Chinese blue and white, so called 'Nankin' porcelains which had been imported in bulk by the English

Plate 12. A detail from a Wolfe-Mason blue-printed teapot showing characteristic features of this version of the Pagoda design. These are, at A: long windows in central, zigzag wall; B: figure entering pagoda; C: two figures crossing bridge; D: mast-like object on top of pagoda. See page 36. Geoffrey Godden, Chinaman

East India Company before the cessation of this trade in 1792, see page 26.

The most popular of these blue designs I termed the 'Pagoda' pattern when writing of the Caughley porcelains, although Mr. Haggar refers to the same design as 'Broseley-Willow'. Slight variations of this blue Chinese design are to be found on nearly every make of English porcelain (and earthenware) from about 1780 into the nineteenth century. It pre-dates the famous Willow pattern and in its time was just as popular. Liverpool versions of the 1796-1800 period are shown here in Plates 12-21, whilst the later Mason versions made in Staffordshire are shown in Plates 40-49, 127 and 128. Examples of the hand-painted Chinese originals are shown in Plates 6, 9 and 10.

Noteworthy features of the Wolfe-Mason version of this design are the tall (often five storey) dark Pagoda-type building, the figure in the open doorway, the unshaded zigzag wall inset with various windows and the bridge with two figures approaching the main island. I have refrained from writing 'to the right' or 'to the left' as the whole design was sometimes reversed. Although probably more than twenty English porcelain factories produced their own version of this standard design, all used slightly different engraved copper plates. Once the collector has successfully identified a key piece from any one factory he should be able to identify other pieces from the same original source. A complication is, however, occasioned by the fact that the different pieces in a teaservice would have been printed from different copper plates according to the size of the object — obviously the large print required for the teapot would not fit the teabowls or the coffee cups! Nevertheless the main points of the design will be constant, in any one factory.

Let us therefore commence our study of these Wolfe-Mason Liverpool porcelains with a selection showing this basic printed Pagoda design. First, in Plate 11 I have shown two unglazed saucer fragments from the factory site. Next, Plate 12 shows a detail of the print as it appears on the body of a finished teapot.

Turning our attention to this basic print we can at once pick up various salient features which will be constant over this class and which link with the factory wasters. Firstly, at A, the two pairs of long windows in the central zigzag wall — the detail of these is quite intricate with the upper two-thirds showing closer window panes than the lower portion. Secondly, at B, the door or archway shows a figure entering the pagoda, posed in the unshaded half of the arch, while another figure is approaching the steps. Thirdly, at C, two figures are crossing the bridge towards the island and the rear figure is carrying under his arm a long narrow object. Note that all the Chinese figures are devoid of facial features. The rather tall narrow mast-like object at the top of the pagoda, D, is also noteworthy, differing as it does from the same feature on other versions of this standard design.

Now we can trace these features on a selection of teawares. The teapot shown in Plate 13 is of a basic oval plan but with vertical fluting of the type found on the so-called silver-shape New Hall teapots of the same approximate date, indeed very much the same shape can be

Plate 13. A Wolfe-Mason porcelain teapot bearing their version of this popular design (see Plate 12), with a knob shape found on the factory site. c.1796. 9½ ins. long. Geoffrey Godden, Chinaman

found in the output of several factories of the 1790-1800 period, for the Miles Mason-Thomas Wolfe partnership was producing up-to-date fashionable shapes. However, the spout and handle form is here unique to the class of porcelain under review and the knob shape matches the only teapot knob to be found on the factory site. Here we have a Wolfe-Mason teapot seemingly of the 1796-98 period which matches in shape as well as in the added printed design wasters from the factory site. The body moulding can perhaps be seen better in Plate

33, where the shape is decorated with a simple enamelled design that does not totally cover the moulding as this printed design does.

The elegantly shaped creamer or milk jug shown in Plate 14 probably represents the shape made to match the teapot in Plate 13 and is a very rare early form; the printed design is the standard Wolfe-Mason version although in this case it is reversed so that the pagoda is on the right rather than the left.

The teapot in Plate 15 is larger than that shown in Plate 13 and although of the same basic form the oval plan is more regular and the vertical fluting is much less pronounced. Note, too the simpler spout form. The printed pagoda design is identical with all other Wolfe-Mason examples but in this case it is embellished with an elegant gilt festoon border and other gilt enrichments.

This teapot was purchased with the oval and fluted covered sugar bowl shown in Plate 16 and is visually linked with it by the same gilt border. The noteworthy feature of this covered sugar bowl is the new knob form, which may be likened to a flattened fleur-de-lis motif. The printed pagoda is, as can be seen, the standard Wolfe-Mason version.

The teapot in Plate 16a is a very recent purchase of mine being part of an almost complete service bearing the Wolfe-Mason version of the Pagoda pattern. The basic handle and spout form match that shown in Plate 15 except that we here have the flattened fleur-de-lis knob as found on the sugar bowl just described. This teaset does not have the slight concave ribs or flutes in the body, a constant feature in the tea-wares previously shown, so that we here have a further basic type. This set also included the creamer or milk jug form also shown in Plate 16a, and seen again in Plates 25 and 26 bearing a different design.

The teapot shown in Plate 17 is of the same basic oval vertically fluted body shape as that shown in Plate 15, but here again we have the flattened fleur-de-lis knob matching the covered sugar in Plate 16 and the teapot in Plate 16a, and now we find a simple handle without the

Plate 14. A Wolfe-Mason Liverpool creamer of a form which would have accompanied the teapot shown in Plate 13. c.1796. 4½ins. high. Geoffrey Godden, Chinaman

Plate 15. A Wolfe-Mason Liverpool teapot bearing this partnership's version of the Pagoda pattern, with gilt enrichments added in the style of the slightly earlier Chinese wares. c.1796-98. 10ins. long. Geoffrey Godden, Chinaman

Plate 16. A Wolfe-Mason Liverpool sugar box from the same service and with the same gilt border as the teapot shown in Plate 15, but with a new knob form. c.1796-98. 5½ ins. high. Godden of Worthing Ltd.

Plate 16a. A Wolfe-Mason Liverpool teapot and creamer with the standard version of the Pagoda print. c.1796-98. Teapot 6¾ ins. high. Godden of Worthing Ltd.

thumb rest. This teapot forms part of a teaservice in which each piece has the same gilt leaf-and-berry border, a service apparently made and sold at the same time and therefore of great value to the collector as it shows a representative selection of contemporary shapes. The same gilt border design also occurs on the teapot shown in Plate 16a but painted in a different position.

Regarding these gilt borders, which serve at least to link different pieces of the same service and sometimes even to identify pieces from the same factory, it is not always the case that these gilt enrichments were added at the manufactory. In many cases they were added by the dealers, particularly the leading London merchants such as Miles Mason, to lift their own stock above that offered by others who might have similar pieces without the gilt enrichments. Of course, a tastefully

gilt set would be more costly than the plain blue-printed equivalent but they also sold better.

The London china dealers had also embellished the Chinese blue and white pieces which they purchased from the bulk East India Company sales. This is probably how the fashion started, for twenty or so dealers would all be stocking the same basic Chinese teasets, of the same pattern and forms, all purchased from the same source. The larger more enterprising dealers therefore employed gilders to add their own individual gilt borders. Such gilding could quite easily be fired in a small muffle-kiln on their own premises. The Chinese teaset shown in Colour Plate 1, has been treated in this way as have the Pagoda pattern Chinese teawares shown in Plates 9 and 10. Miles Mason, with others, seemingly continued the practice when stocking his own Liverpool-made porcelain.

Returning to the teawares matching the teapot shown in Plate 17, and embellished with the same border. The oval fluted covered sugar is exactly the same as that shown in Plate 16 except that it bears the gilt border to match this teapot. A trio of saucer, teabowl and coffee cup is shown in Plate 18. The teabowl has been turned to show the reverse side of the print which on these smaller items is extremely cramped.

The added gilt border occurs inside the cup and teabowls. The cup handle has a slightly relief-moulded oval panel at the top which in this case has been gilded — in the illustration this appears as a dark area.

A complete service of this type would probably have comprised:

Teapot and cover
Teapot stand
Sugar bowl and cover
Slop bowl
Creamer or milk jug
2 saucer-shaped plates
12 saucers
12 handle-less teabowls
12 coffee cups

Some of the more expensive sets may have boasted a tea canister and cover and a small spoon tray, although both these objects were almost out of fashion by the mid-1790s and I have not as yet found examples which I could claim as Wolfe-Mason.

I have already illustrated in Plate 14 a creamer, which I regard as being of an earlier shape than this teaset although it does bear the same gilt border. I show in Plate 19 another jug form which is more in keeping with the shapes of this teaset although in this case it does not have the same gilt border. Yet it does serve again to link this class to the Wolfe-Mason factory at Liverpool as the two unglazed fragments shown with this jug were found on the factory site. This handle form is very reminiscent of the later Staffordshire Mason porcelains, as is the whole jug shape (see Plates 42 and 44).

The gilt border featured in Plates 14, 17 and 18 links also with the covered sugar bowl shown in Plate 20 which, as can be seen, also bears the Wolfe-Mason version of the Pagoda pattern. I think there can be

Plate 17. A Wolfe-Mason Liverpool teapot with the standard version of the Pagoda print and with a knob form matching that shown in Plate 16. c.1796-98. 10ins. long. Godden of Worthing Ltd.

Plate 18. A Wolfe-Mason trio of saucer, teabowl and coffee cup bearing the standard Liverpool version of the Pagoda print and with a gilt border matching Plates 14 and 17. Brown line edging to the foot rims. c.1796-98. Godden of Worthing Ltd.

little or no doubt of its Liverpool origin although it is the only example I have traced of this plain oval form and with this knob form. The teapot would also have this shape of knob. In style this shape must be very near the termination of the partnership in July 1800 and I regard this shape as the latest example of Wolfe-Mason's Liverpool porcelain that I have traced with this standard blue-printed Pagoda pattern (but see my remarks on the teapot shown in Plate 38).

Before progressing to discuss other designs found on site wasters, some general remarks on the type of porcelain employed by this Liverpool partnership would be relevant. It is heavy, compact looking and of the type which has recently been called hybrid hard-paste, though not as hard as Chinese, Plymouth or Bristol true hard-paste porcelains. An analysis of a piece from the teaset featured in Plates 14, 17 and 18 has given the following interesting result which I have tabulated together with the result given by a piece of Chinese porcelain of the same period. The two results almost exactly match — as do many of the Wolfe-Mason printed copies of Chinese designs.

	Wolfe-Mason c.1798 %	Chinese c.1795 %
Silica	70.4	70.2
Alumina	24.6	24.2
Potash	3.4	3.1
Lime	.9	1.4
Iron Oxide	.24	.90
Phosphoric acid	.2	.1
Lead Oxide	.15	.12
	99.89	100.02

These analyses were carried out for me by Dr. Alwyn Cox of the University of York.

The main pieces of a teaset are thickly potted, although teabowls, cups and saucers can be quite trimly made. The glaze is hard-looking, liberally applied and somewhat prone to bubbling. The most noteworthy feature of many pieces and of factory wasters, is the brown line painted around the edge of the foot rim. This feature often occurs on teabowls, cup, saucers and plates and can be seen clearly in Plate 21. This brown-line edging is an interesting feature copied from the Chinese imports, a point which prompts the question — were these Liverpool porcelains being made to be passed off as Chinese?

At this point, before finally leaving the blue printed Pagoda pattern, I should introduce a cautionary tale. A year or so ago my heart almost stopped when, while walking through the famous Lanes in Brighton, I suddenly saw in a shop window my heart's desire — a complete Mason Pagoda pattern teaservice, see Plate 22. Here were the pointed oval knobs to the teapot and sugar, the oval creamer with the characteristic handle form, the teapot stand, a waste bowl, the two bread and butter plates and a complete set of teabowls and saucers and coffee cups. As I love to record photographically such complete sets to establish the relationship between shapes, here was a service I just had to buy.

However, this set turned out to be too good to be true. The body is certainly of the same hybrid hard-paste type but the potting is rather trimmer than the Wolfe-Mason pieces, the glaze is rather thinner and is devoid of any bubbling and the blue is rather brighter. Also the quality of the engraving is rather superior, the finished appearance

Plate 19. A Wolfe-Mason blue-printed Pagoda pattern creamer with two matching unglazed wasters from the factory site. c.1798. Creamer 4¹/₁₀ins. high. Wasters — City of Liverpool Museum Service

being crystal clear as you may be able to see from the group photograph, Plate 22. Indeed too good to be true.

In my initial excitement I missed the basic point that the Pagoda print was not the Wolfe-Mason version. Look at the similar oval sugar box shown in Plate 23, which in this case has been turned slightly sideways towards the camera. Compare this new version with any of the pieces shown in Plates 12-20, in particular with the covered sugar shown in Plate 16. Firstly the two figures on the bridge are facing each other, not walking towards the island. The zigzag wall is of a different form and has only two windows which are square and without shading. The door or archway into the pagoda is also of a different unshaded appearance and there is no second figure approaching the steps. Finally, the central spire on the top of the pagoda is not as slender and tall as it appears on the Wolfe-Mason porcelains or on the wasters from that factory site.

Here we have a most interesting teaset from another factory, one contemporary with the Wolfe-Mason venture in the last few years of the eighteenth century and which was following these Liverpool shapes very closely — particularly in regard to the knobs and jug forms. I regret that at this moment I cannot suggest which factory made this most attractive trimly potted teaset. A potentially interesting point is that this version of the print occurs on both porcelains and earthenwares so we are looking for a manufacturer of the 1795-1800 period who made both bodies.

Because of its complete state this teaset affords an object lesson, for if we examine closely the different shapes which go to make up the set, which has almost certainly remained intact since it was made some 190

Plate 20. An oval sugar box and cover bearing the Liverpool version of the Pagoda pattern and a gilt border matching Plates 14, 17 and 18, but with a new knob form. c.1796-98. 5¼ ins. high. E.H. Chandler Collection

Plate 21. A Wolfe-Mason Pagoda pattern coffee cup turned up to show the typical brown painted line around the foot rim emulating the Chinese technique. Geoffrey Godden, Chinaman

Plate 22. Representative pieces from a blue-printed Pagoda pattern teaservice which does not exactly match with the Wolfe-Mason Liverpool porcelains. c.1795-1800. Geoffrey Godden, Chinaman

Plate 23. An oval sugar box and cover from the service shown in Plate 22, compare the print with that shown in Plate 16. c.1795-1800. 5¼ ins. high. Geoffrey Godden, Chinaman

Plate 24. Two unglazed 'wasters' from the Wolfe-Mason Liverpool site, including the only knob form to be discovered. City of Liverpool Museum Service

years ago, we find that no less than eleven different copper plates were employed to transfer the main pagoda decoration and each one of these copper plates differs in some respects from the other. You may be able to see from the group photograph that the windows in the zigzag wall differ, or the men on the bridge differ — some carry objects, others do not. When making comparisons of blue-printed designs we should take care to compare like with like, this oval sugar bowl with another sugar bowl, this teapot with those shown, for example, in Plates 12 and 17, and so on. Yet in no instance does the engraving on this complete tea-set match with a Wolfe-Mason example or with any of the site wasters.

A further warning, some pieces I have traced with this non-Wolfe-Mason version of the Pagoda pattern also bear the Chinese-style, brown-line edging to the foot rim, underlining the similarity between the two types.

This is the place to record a further Wolfe-Mason underglaze blue print of the Pagoda type. This print appeared on several biscuit (unglazed) wasters found on the factory site which included a coffee cup with loop handle, an oval teapot stand and the oval cover to a teapot having a knob similar to those shown in Plates 13 and 15, plus many saucers, etc. Two of these wasters are reproduced in Plate 24. To date the only completed piece that I have found of this seemingly rare pattern is the creamer shown in Plates 25 and 26. This version of the popular Pagoda pattern is not as satisfactory as that already discussed and this rare version may be the earliest, superseded by the more common.

Here the border is a wide Chinese diaper design with a dagger or portcullis-like edging. The main building is only three stories high, two

Plate 26. The front view of the creamer shown in Plate 25. Compare with site waster, Plate 24 left. Geoffrey Godden, Chinaman

Plate 25. Side view of a Wolfe-Mason blue-printed creamer. The design linking with site wasters. c.1798. 4½ ins. high. Geoffrey Godden, Chinaman

Plate 27. A coffee cup and saucer showing a rare Wolfe-Mason blue print. Compare with Plate 28. Geoffrey Godden, Chinaman

long, low windows appear in the zigzag wall, no second figure approaches the steps and the first of two figures crossing the bridge is carrying a small umbrella-type object. In this case the blue is rather darker than that on the wares previously discussed.

The basic creamer shape will be found to bear other Wolfe-Mason designs (see Plate 16a), the inward-facing thumb rest at the top of the handle and the spreading foot are noteworthy features found on other pieces of this class.

Turning to a completely different blue-printed design but one which does link with one unglazed waster found on the factory site, we have the coffee cup and saucer shown in Plate 27. Here we have a pavilion-like structure with two figures standing in the centre of the design, which I take to represent a man presenting a pot of flowers to a lady.

Plate 28. A teabowl and saucer shown with a 'waster' found on the Wolfe-Mason site. City of Liverpool Museum Service

The border is noteworthy, comprising an outer criss-cross, basket-like design with an inner ring of formal four petal flowers seemingly strung together with a ribbon. The reverse side of this design, the secondary print, is shown on the coffee cup as well as on the very crazed teabowl shown with a site waster in Plate 28. The Wolfe-Mason glaze does not normally craze like this.

To date I have only traced cups and teabowls and saucers of this design but complete sets were obviously made and this print should occur on all Wolfe-Mason shapes.

A variation of this design is shown in Plate 29, but here both figures are facing the pavilion, neither holds a pot of flowers and the inner border is different. This design is printed in underglaze blue and is on an extremely hard-looking body and glaze. Whilst it must be admitted that no waster of this design was found on that small part of the site excavated, I regard this as a Wolfe-Mason print, a view which may be clinched when this design is found on known and identifiable Wolfe-Mason shapes.

However, two complications arise with the design. Firstly, a hand-painted version occurs on Chinese export market porcelain, such as the teabowl and saucer shown in Plate 30. No doubt this Oriental original served as the source for the Wolfe-Mason printed pieces, a point that reflects on Miles Mason's earlier trade in the imported Chinese porcelains. Secondly, at least one other English firm produced this design in a hand-painted version. I have pieces on known John Rose of Coalport oval teaware shapes and have found Coalport-Caughley wasters bearing this pattern on that factory site. Remember the Wolfe-Mason examples are printed, not painted.

At least one other blue printed Chinese-type scenic design was made by this Liverpool partnership, as is evidenced by the unglazed half tea-bowl found on the site by Alan Smith and reproduced in Plate 31. I have not as yet traced any finished example to match this waster but complete tea services must have been made.*

Before leaving our consideration of the blue-printed pieces, the point should be made that all these designs were often touched up with hand-painted blue washes, especially to fill up the foreground and to merge in the sides of the design where the cut out transferring paper would leave an unsightly straight line or break-off point. However, this hand-painted touching up must not be taken as a sure sign of a Wolfe-Mason origin, as it was a standard practice at most factories.

The two plates shown in Plate 32 illustrate just how closely the Wolfe-Mason blue and white porcelains could emulate the Chinese originals. The smaller plate is the Liverpool copy, and in the quality of the potting and the painting it is superior to the Chinese. Admittedly I can offer no firm evidence for a Wolfe-Mason attribution but the body is of the same hybrid hard-paste type and it matches very well all the pieces previously discussed, both in general as well as in workmanship. The only basic difference is that this is the first piece I have featured that is entirely hand-painted, not printed.

* At a recent Mason's Collectors' Club meeting a coffee cup of this pattern was displayed; it bore a simple loop handle, as the example shown in Plate 27.

On turning these plates over one sees just how close the Liverpool copy is; the foot rim is in the Chinese chamfered manner with a sunk central recess, not a European added foot rim, and the edge of the foot rim has been painted to emulate the standard Chinese finish. If Miles Mason was seeking to stock his shop with English imitations of the now lost Chinese imports his partners in Liverpool were serving him very well.

Plate 29. A rare Wolfe-Mason blue-printed tea-bowl and saucer. Hand-painted versions occur on Chinese porcelain, see Plate 30, and on Coalport porcelains. c.1798. Diameter of saucer 5¼ ins. B.M. Broad Collection

Plate 30. A Chinese teabowl and saucer hand-painted in underglaze blue with the same design as the Wolfe-Mason example shown in Plate 29. c.1790. Geoffrey Godden, Chinaman

Turning to identify the enamelled patterns produced by the Liverpool partnership we have two guidelines:
Factory wasters.
Shapes identified with the help of known blue prints.
Unfortunately only three enamelled shards or factory wasters were found on the site bearing overglaze enamel decoration. This reflects a

47

Plate 31. An unglazed blue-printed teabowl 'waster' from the Wolfe-Mason site illustrating a rare design. City of Liverpool Museum Service

fact of life for, on any site, the blue and white wasters will greatly out-number the enamelled pieces for the simple reason that the enamelled decoration was added to already fired and glazed wares and relatively few losses occur in the last process when the overglaze enamel decoration is fired at a relatively low temperature.

The teapot shown in Plate 33 matches in form the example shown in Plate 13 with the version of the Pagoda print which in turn matches fragments from the factory site. Indeed, this enamelled design shows the moulded form to better advantage than the blue printed example. The knob form also matches the only knob waster discovered by Alan Smith, see Plate 24.

The added enamel decoration is of the type one might expect, reflecting the type of decoration on so many of the Chinese teasets which had been imported into England by the East India Company

Plate 32. Right, a Chinese hard-paste dinner plate with, left, a Wolfe-Mason copy painted in rather a neater style. c.1798. Diameter of English plate 8ins. Geoffrey Godden, Chinaman

from about 1770 to the 1790s when the Directors ceased their bulk importations. This general style of decoration was copied by several other English manufacturers, notably the New Hall partnership in Staffordshire. I cannot record the present whereabouts of this teapot but it was sold by Phillips, the London auctioneers, in August 1972.

The oval teapot with wide facets shown in Plate 34 is available in our reference collection in Worthing and it is part of an interesting part service which I purchased in Brighton a few years ago. Alas there were no cups and saucers, nor a covered sugar bowl, but the four pieces I did capture had apparently always been together and all bore the same enamelled design, yet the moulded surface treatment was of three different types illustrating the types of forms available at one factory at one time. There was the wide faceted teapot and waste bowl, a spiral fluted creamer and a half-fluted small bowl with vertical fluting running only halfway down the body. These pieces are shown in Plates 34-36 and it is probable that at the same period these basic shapes were also available in a plain unfluted form (the plain version of the spiral fluted creamer is represented by the blue-printed example shown in Plate 25).

Plate 33. A rare Wolfe-Mason teapot enamelled with simple floral motifs in the style of the Chinese export market porcelains. c.1795-98. 9¾ ins. long. Phillips

Plate 34. A Wolfe-Mason faceted oval teapot enamelled with the basket of flowers design seen on the Chinese saucer shown in Plate 8. c.1796-99. 9½ ins. long. Geoffrey Godden, Chinaman

The added design is one found on Chinese export market porcelains (see Plate 8) and on the porcelains of several English manufacturers. It is, for example New Hall's pattern number 171 and is called the 'basket pattern'. Fortunately two of the three enamelled wasters found on the Wolfe-Mason site are of this design and one shows a particularly good example of the central basket motif. This shows an interesting feature not present on the New Hall version nor on most other pieces which I have examined — the basket has a false bottom — that is the red enamelling of the basket stops short of the bottom giving a thin white area or border to the basket. This is apparent on all the related pieces shown in Plates 34-36, although they have perhaps been painted by different hands. It is difficult to generalise over these simple hastily-painted designs, worked in all probability by young apprentice

Plate 35. A selection of Wolfe-Mason tewares, part of a set purchased with the teapot shown in Plate 34, and showing different basic body mouldings. c.1796-99. Creamer 4¼ ins. high. Geoffrey Godden, Chinaman

painters, but this basket feature seems constant to the Wolfe-Mason examples and one painter at least neglected to add stems to the flowers, as can be seen on the teapot and the large faceted bowl.

In regard to the smaller bowl, Plate 35 left, it should be noted that the fluting is regular. I make this point as other factories, including Caughley and Coalport, issued similar half-fluted tewares but in their examples the distance between the undulations is not regular. However on the evidence of factory wasters, our Liverpool partnership also produced this uneven division of fluting, see Plate 37.

The spiral fluted creamer to this part set also offers some object lessons or warnings: pay very close attention to shape. At first glance it might be taken that the two creamers shown in Plate 36 were from the same factory. The example on the left is the Wolfe-Mason example whilst the other is from another factory producing much the same type of tewares.

Plate 36. Two spiral fluted creamers of slightly different forms, the one on the left being a Wolfe-Mason example. Note the double line at the bottom of the painted basket. c.1796-1805. 4¼ ins. high. Geoffrey Godden, Chinaman

The non-Wolfe-Mason jug on the right is of a softer body, the flutes are smaller, numbering twenty-one against nineteen around the body of the Liverpool example. The shoulder dips far more than the Wolfe-Mason example and the thumb rests at the top of the handles show slightly different forms, the Liverpool one showing a tendency to turn forward. Curiously enough although the basket motifs on these two examples are vastly different both painters neglected to paint the flower stalks! Indeed there may be a connection for the design on the right hand example is Miles Mason's pattern 22 on his later Staffordshire porcelain, see Plates 56 and 57, and this may be a true Miles Mason example.

The remaining enamelled waster found on the factory site shows a simply painted Chinese-type export market floral border motif with scattered floral sprays painted on part of a spiral-fluted saucer. Several spiral-fluted wasters of cups, teabowls and saucers were found on the factory site (Plate 37) but I have as yet been unable to discover any

Plate 37. Two unglazed 'wasters' from the Wolfe-Mason factory site at Liverpool showing as yet unidentified teaware shapes. Cup 2½ ins. high. City of Liverpool Museum Service

complete examples which I would accept as Wolfe-Mason porcelain, excepting, of course, the creamer shown in Plate 36 left. The great trouble with the teabowls and saucers is that practically all English factories of the 1790-1810 period were making very similar spiral-fluted tewares.

It would seem that no Wolfe-Mason porcelain of the 1796-1800 period bears any form of mark, nor do pattern numbers occur. However, the shapes shown in Plates 13-19, 25 and 33-35 should enable other tewares to be identified and the characteristic features of the known prints may well enable other Liverpool porcelains to be identified, such as dessert, dinner wares, mugs, jugs, bowls and the like.

It is not now known why the two partnerships were dissolved in 1800 (see page 32). Perhaps Thomas Wolfe wished to retire, for he does not seem to have carried on the Liverpool factory, or perhaps Miles Mason wished to start up porcelain manufacture on his own account, which he was soon to do in Staffordshire. Certainly his participation in this Liverpool partnership is a vital and interesting link between Miles

Plate 38. An oval, fluted teapot decorated with gilt and blue enamel sprays. Perhaps of Wolfe-Mason manufacture on account of the similarity with the sugar box knob shown in Plate 20. c.1800. 10¾ ins. long. Geoffrey Godden, Chinaman

Mason the London china dealer, as detailed in Chapter One, and Miles Mason the porcelain manufacturer, the subject of the following chapter, and the products of this Liverpool concern formed a vital part in stocking his London premises with saleable items, mainly in the style of the slightly earlier imports from China.

Obviously the Liverpool partnership enjoyed other outlets and helped to establish a large trade probably including overseas customers whom Mason was pleased to cater for once he had established his own factory.

Much study remains to be carried out on these Liverpool porcelains and I trust this chapter will stimulate others to seek out other examples matching in shape or added pattern the porcelains illustrated here which are in the main pieces available for study. There are still many unanswered questions. For example did the Wolfe-Mason partnership produce the tasteful and well-potted teawares, of which the teapot is shown in Plate 38? The knob is very similar to that found on the sugar box shown in Plate 20, a piece which bears the Wolfe-Mason version of the Pagoda blue-print. If this set turns out to be from our Liverpool partnership what other superb wares await identification. Where are the jugs, the mugs and other standard shapes of the 1795-1800 period?

It should be pointed out that the porcelains here ascribed to the Wolfe-Mason-Luckcock partnership at Liverpool in the closing years of the eighteenth century and linked with factory wasters, do **not** bear any relation to the class of porcelain tentatively attributed to this partnership by Dr. Bernard Watney in the second of his two linked papers delivered to the English Ceramic Circle in March 1959 and published in that Circle's *Transactions*, vol.5, part 1, 1960. The views Dr. Watney put forward then have since found their way into several standard reference books as statements of fact, but in my opinion Dr. Watney's porcelains are earlier than hitherto believed and they seem to be of Staffordshire rather than Liverpool make. Certainly, they do not link with Miles Mason. I illustrate in Plate 39 a small selection of these non-Mason porcelains to illustrate the type I dispute, and a summary of my thoughts on this class is published in *Collectors Guide* June/July, 1979.

Plate 39. A tea canister, creamer and bowl of a type of porcelain previously attributed to Wolfe & Co. of Liverpool, but which does not link with the porcelains discussed in this chapter. Tea canister 5ins. high. Geoffrey Godden, Chinaman

Chapter Three

Miles Mason,
Staffordshire
Porcelain Manufacturer

IT IS NOT known how quickly Miles Mason set up his first porcelain producing factory in Staffordshire after having terminated his Liverpool partnership in June 1800. He had to close his London retail shop in Fenchurch Street as well as make arrangements with his fellow dealers to sell his new products. Reginald Haggar has suggested that one of his principal outlets was Abbott & Mist of 82 Fleet Street. Abbott's accounts, which are preserved in the Dorset County Record Office, show that this partnership dealt with very many potters of the period and the first reference I have been able to trace relating to Miles Mason is dated 11th September, 1802 and is for 'goods' to the value of £50. The entries remain in Miles' own name up to 1807 but in February there is the first reference to the expanded title 'M Mason & Son'.

However, the first real evidence for Miles Mason's new Staffordshire porcelain does not appear until the publication of his now famous advertisement in the *Morning Herald* of 15th October, 1804:

MASONS' CHINA

It has hitherto been the opinion, not only of the public, but also of the manufacturers of this country, that the earths of these kingdoms are unequal to those of foreign nations for the fabrication of china. Miles Mason, late of Fenchurch Street, London, having been a principal purchaser of Indian [Chinese] porcelain, till the prohibition of that article by heavy duties, has established a manufactory at Lane Delph, near Newcastle-under-Lime, upon the principle of the Indian [Chinese] and Sève [*sic*] china. The former is now sold only at the principle shops in the City of London and in the Country as British Nankin. His article is warranted from the manufactory to possess superior qualities to Indian Nankin china, being more beautiful as well as more durable, and not so liable to snip [chip] at the edges, more difficult to break, and refusable or unitable by heat, if broken. Being aware that, to combat strong prejudices with success something superior must be produced; he, therefore, through the medium of his wholesale friends, proposes to renew or match the impaired or broken services of the nobility and gentry, when by a fair trial or conjunction with foreign china, he doubts not that these fears will be removed, and in a short period the manufactories of porcelain, by the patronage of the nobility of this country, will rival, if not excel, those of foreign nations. N.B. The articles are stamped on the bottom of the large pieces to prevent imposition.

The significant points contained in this interesting advertisement are that by 1804 Miles Mason had left London and had 'established a

54

manufactory at Lane Delph', that his wares were apparently marketed under the name 'British Nankin' and that the larger pieces bore an impressed mark 'to prevent imposition'. The description British Nankin does not, incidentally, appear to have been first introduced by Miles Mason at the time of his October 1804 advertisement, for it was used some two and a half years earlier by Thomas Brocas in connection with Coalport porcelains (see my book *Coalport and Coalbrookdale Porcelains,* Barrie & Jenkins, London, 1970).

The reference in this 1804 advertisement to an impressed mark would seem to refer to the standard 'M. MASON' mark rather than the words 'British Nankin', for no pieces bearing this description have been recorded. The description was used, however, by Mr. Phillips, the New Bond Street auctioneer, in the same year as the above-quoted advertisement:

> A Table Service of blue and white china, British Nankin, containing 18 dishes in sizes, 2 soup tureens and stands, 4 sauce tureens and stands, 1 salad dish, 4 sauce boats, 4 vegetable dishes with covers, 4 baking dishes, 6 dozen meat plates, 2 dozen soup plates, 2 dozen pie plates and 2 dozen cheese plates.

This seemingly complete and perhaps new dinner service was sold for £15 4s. 6d. as lot 37 on 6th July, 1804.

Although the advertisement mentions that 'The articles are stamped on the bottom' the reader must remember that this applied only to 'the large pieces' and that articles such as cups and saucers were never marked — indeed some of the large pieces such as teapots often do not bear a mark!

It is interesting to note that in 1804, nine years before the patent for Ironstone china, Miles Mason was fully aware of the desirability to make strong durable china, not liable to 'snip' or chip, and that he was fully aware that the public wanted gay goods in the tradition of the earlier 'Nankin' ware which had been imported from China. This important knowledge of the market had been gained from his earlier experience as a London Chinaman, or retailer of pottery and porcelain — experience that was to be of the utmost value in later years, for the Masons were primarily concerned to give the public what it wanted: inexpensive strong, durable, useful wares painted in gay, cheerful patterns or in less expensive ranges decorated with underglaze-blue designs still in the style of the eighteenth century Chinese porcelains. In Staffordshire he still continued to produce the Pagoda pattern but from different copper plates.

The pre-1800 partnership between Miles Mason and George Wolfe had operated on the site of the Victoria Pottery (later worked by James Reeves). It appears that Mason continued operating there for a map incorporated in J. Albut & Son's Staffordshire Directory of 1802 records 'Mason & Co' on this site. These works were advertised in the *Staffordshire Advertiser* on 9th November, 1805:

CAPITAL POTWORKS
TO BE LET
and entered upon at Martin-mas next.

All these compleat set of Potworks situate at Lane Delph in the Staffordshire Potteries, now and for several years past occupied by Mr. Miles Mason, as a china manufactory, together with an excellent modern sashed House and necessary out buildings, adjoining thereto...

The use of the word 'china' rather than earthenware is interesting. As I do not know of any marked Miles Mason (or 'M. Mason') earthenware, it may perhaps be presumed that the early Miles Mason productions were confined to porcelain.

Be that as it may, the works were apparently not let, for in April 1807 they were advertised for sale by auction, the description stating that the works were then 'in the tenure and holding of Mr. Miles Mason'. The full description reads:

> Lot 1. All that eligible, complete, and new erected set of Potworks, and dwelling-house thereto belonging, situate at Lane Delph aforesaid, now in the tenure and holding of Mr. Miles Mason; and also a piece or parcel of Land, marked and staked... The above potworks are advantageously situated not only for coal, but also for water, there being a constant run of water through the land above mentioned commanding a ten feet fall capable of working a small mill, which will be very useful for grinding Potters' materials...

After vacating the Victoria Pottery at Lane Delph, Staffordshire, Miles Mason moved to a factory, later known as the Minerva Works at Fenton, which coincidentally had previously been worked by Mason's former partner John Luckcock. The first available rate records in which Miles Mason is listed at these Fenton premises (which were owned by Thomas Broade) cover the period August 1807 until November 1812. The next available Fenton rate record relates to April 1815 and shows the same works under the name of George Mason — Miles Mason's son. In the rate records of April 1817, the premises are listed as 'void'. In subsequent rate records, Felix Pratt & Co., are shown in occupation.

There were, however, two separate factories worked by the Masons from July 1811 to 1817 — the Minerva Works mentioned above and the Bagnall factory. The rate record of July 1811 shows 'Miles Mason & Son' as the occupiers of Sampson Bagnall's pottery at Fenton, but from 1812-16 William Mason's name is given. From 1817-22 the works reverted to Miles Mason in name; but it is likely that, in practice, Miles' sons Charles and George were managing the works. They certainly continued there after their father's death; and in 1816-18 directories Miles Mason is recorded as living in Liverpool, not at Fenton. He is believed to have retired from active work in the pottery in June 1813 leaving his two sons George Miles Mason and Charles James Mason to continue the enterprise. The later fortunes of the sons will be told in subsequent chapters.

Although Miles Mason may well have made agreements with various retailers to stock his wares before leaving London and setting up as a porcelain manufacturer in Staffordshire, he was not above returning to London seeking outlets for his goods. There is an interesting letter in the Wedgwood archives being a 1810 report made by Thomas Byerley, manager of the Wedgwood showrooms in London, to Josiah Wedgwood II in Staffordshire:

> Mr. Mason of Lane Delph is in town and called upon me, and in the course of conversation said that we should sell immense quantities of china here, if we had it and that he should be very happy to make it for you. His china is, I believe, very good and he has great orders for it. I only submit it for your consideration, whether you think it would answer, if Mr. Mason were to manufacture the china and you were to have it enamelled at Etruria.

The suggestion was not taken up but it may have served as an idea to Wedgwood, for within two years he was producing his own bone china.

I propose now to discuss and illustrate a representative array of Miles Mason's Staffordshire porcelains. I will deal with these wares under different headings — teawares, dessert wares, dinner wares and lastly other objects such as vases.

TEAWARES

It is difficult to be sure of the chronological sequence of shapes; teapots bearing early pattern numbers are not necessarily the first forms issued, as the pattern numbers may have been allocated later. The most common early enamelled design (see Plates 67-69 and Colour Plate 2) does not in my experience bear a pattern number, furthermore popular designs were almost certainly issued over a number of years so that the same design can be found on different shapes. Standard blue prints were not allocated pattern numbers — when these numbers do occur on blue and white wares they relate to the added gilt borders. I propose therefore to deal first with the blue-printed teawares to establish some of the key shapes. The enamelled patterns will be discussed later.

Initially, I must explain that the early examples are of the hybrid hard-paste body favoured by many English porcelain manufacturers in the approximate period 1790-1810. This has a slightly grey surface appearance and is not unlike the porcelains produced in the 1790s by the Liverpool partnership. It is not a bone china, which was to appear later, probably in about 1806. This early Mason body stood up well to recent refiring tests at a temperature approaching 1,400°C, and using this means the body seems harder than the New Hall porcelains of the same period. In general the pieces are rather thickly potted and the translucency can consequently be rather poor.

A fragment from a Mandarin pattern teaset (Colour Plate 2) gave the following analysis:

	%
Silica	63.46
Alumina	26.76
Potash	3.25
Soda	1.79
Magnesia	1.76
Lime	1.28
Ferric Oxide	.04

This early hybrid hard-paste body does not contain any bone ash.

In discussing the blue-printed teawares we should recall the words of the 1804 advertisement where Mason claimed that two types of his wares were based 'upon the principle of the Indian [by which he meant Chinese] and Sève [Sèvres] china.' As all the late eighteenth century blue and white Chinese porcelains were called 'Nankin', a term which equated with blue and white, then one whole class of Mason's porcelain was decorated in underglaze blue after the Chinese originals. The enamelled wares he perhaps sought to link with Sèvres porcelain! By far the most popular of Mason's 'British Nankin' was his version

Plate 40. A Miles Mason oval teapot bearing the Staffordshire version of this popular underglaze-blue print. Impressed mark 'M. MASON'. c.1805. 10½ins. long. Miss J. Magness Collection

Plate 41, below. A Miles Mason sugar box bearing Miles Mason's Staffordshire version of this Pagoda blue print, in this case enhanced (?) with a gilt border. Pattern number '49' added in gold. c.1805. 5¼ins. high. Godden of Worthing Ltd.

Plate 42, right. A Miles Mason creamer turned to show the reverse side of this blue-printed design. c.1805. 5ins. high. Geoffrey Godden, Chinaman

of the Pagoda pattern, or Broseley-Willow as some describe the same pattern. This design is basically the same as that discussed in the previous chapter when we were dealing with the Liverpool products, but Miles Mason's Staffordshire version shows several salient differences.

Let us first examine the teapot shown in Plate 40. This is one of the earliest forms, oval with slight moulded fluting, and is a convenient starting point as the foot rim is clearly impressed-marked 'M. MASON'. On the larger pieces such as teapots the zigzag wall is lower and longer than the Liverpool version and has three square windows in it. The doorway does not show any shading, there is no third figure approaching the steps and the spire at the top of the pagoda is shorter

58

and fatter than that on the Liverpool version. The two figures crossing the bridge are more stooped and the bridge itself is more angular and has a line of piercing. You will see several other differences if you compare the teapot shown in Plate 40 with the detail shown in Plate 12.

This teaset does not bear a pattern number but the covered sugar bowl shown in Plate 41 is of the same type — notice the characteristic knob form as well as the same print, and bears the pattern number '49' in gold which refers to the added gilt border and not to the basic print, although the number serves to show the relatively early period of this example.

In Plate 42 the creamer matching this teapot form and the covered sugar shows the reverse side and illustrates the angular form of the bridge and the short rather stooping figures. The buildings on the island differ materially from those on the Liverpool examples. This jug form is a very typical Miles Mason shape but it follows extremely closely the earlier Liverpool example and also the shape made by the unknown manufacturer of the teaset shown in Plate 22.

Other Miles Mason forms matching these blue-printed pieces are shown in Colour Plate 2.

The teapot shown in Plate 43 bears the same Miles Mason version of the Pagoda pattern. It also bears the impressed mark 'M. MASON' on the foot rim but no pattern number. The basic oval fluted body shape is the same as that shown earlier but we now find a slightly curved spout and a new handle form with a forward-facing turned-up thumb rest. The knob form is also different, being of a rather thin oval form with the usual nipple.

The part teaset featured in Plate 44 enables us to see together the basic shapes of such a set and also a different teapot form. In all respects except the handle this is the same as that shown in Plate 43 but the handle has an added member from the thumb rest to the cover which it overlaps slightly to hold the cover in place when the pot is tipped.

Plate 43. A Miles Mason oval teapot bearing the Pagoda print of different form to the pot shown in Plate 40. Impressed mark 'M. MASON'. c.1805. 10¼ ins. long. E.H. Chandler Collection

The creamer form is slightly amended and shows a different handle to that shown in Plate 42. I regard this shape as the later variation and the handle with its curling-back thumb rest is a standard Miles Mason shape. The handle of the coffee cup, too, is very characteristic with its rather fat projection at the top — this is sometimes cited as a clear indication of a Mason origin although other firms also used this feature. Note that at this period, before 1805, the coffee cup still has a shaped body — it is a cup not a straight-sided coffee can.

The group in Plate 44 also enables me to make an important point regarding the Pagoda print. On page 36 I listed the Miles Mason features which relate to the larger pieces such as the teapot, its stand and the plates, and whilst most features are constant over all the components in a teaset, the number of windows in the wall does vary. The smaller articles, the saucer, the cup, the teabowl and the creamer bear compressed designs showing two windows in the wall, not three.

This Miles Mason version of the very popular Pagoda pattern enables us to identify and so follow a succession of teaware forms, although it must be stated that some Miles Mason shapes do not appear to have been decorated with the less expensive blue prints.

The part set featured in Plate 45 interestingly includes the old fashion Chinese-type handleless teabowl and the shaped coffee cup

Plate 44. Representative pieces from a Miles Mason teaservice showing standard shapes of the 1803-5 period, all bearing the popular Pagoda pattern printed in underglaze blue. Teapot 10¼ ins. long. Godden of Worthing Ltd.

Plate 45. A Miles Mason sugar box, teapot stand and trio of coffee cup, tea bowl and saucer bearing the Pagoda print with the gilt border design no.48. Sugar impressed marked 'M. MASON' and gilt 'N.48'. c.1806-07. Sugar 5¾ ins. long. Geoffrey Godden, Chinaman

rather than a can. The new shaped pillow-like covered sugar bowl bears the impressed mark 'M. MASON' and the pattern number 48 on account of the added gilt border. This sugar bowl retains the earlier shallow vertical body fluting and the shallow oval knob seen on the teapots shown in Plates 43 and 44.

The large size oval teapot shown in Plate 46 is also impressed marked 'M. MASON'. Here we have a completely new form but one in general use at all English factories in the approximate period 1805-10. Apart from the print, the Mason characteristics are in the knob form, now of a different domed profile, the low position of the handle joint and the short link piece (taken from the insulating member found on silver pots). The shape of the oval teapot stand is highly characteristic.

Shapes made *en suite* with this teapot form are shown in Plate 50, where it can be seen that the teacups have handles and the coffee cups are now straight-sided cans.

Plate 46. A Miles Mason oval teapot of a basic form popular with most English manufacturers of the 1808-12 period. Note the Mason version of the Pagoda print and the shape of the stand. Impressed marked 'M. MASON'. c.1808-12. 10½ ins. long. Geoffrey Godden, Chinaman

Plate 47. A Miles Mason teapot with matching creamer and teacup and saucer, all decorated with Miles Mason's Pagoda pattern. Blue-printed, Chinese-styled seal mark. c.1810-12. Mason's Ironstone Collection

Plate 48. A fine Miles Mason teapot and stand with the Pagoda pattern with gilt border of pattern 1125. Blue-printed, Chinese-styled seal mark. Pattern number 1125 in gold. c.1810-12. 11ins. long. Mr. and Mrs. A.E. Grove Collection

A slightly later teapot form of about 1810-12 is shown in Plate 47 with the accompanying creamer and cup and saucer shape. These forms are quite rare. These pieces bear a blue-printed Chinese-type square seal mark, see page 198.

The same form of teapot is shown in greater detail in Plate 48 where it rests on its slightly moulded stand. This piece bears the printed seal mark and the pattern number '1125' relating again to the gilt border. It is interesting to see this same print bearing pattern numbers as far apart as 48 and 1125 applied to different shapes and enhanced (?) with different gilt borders. A fact which reflects the changing fashion for tea-wares. Some of these added gilt borders are extremely overbearing, the gilding on pattern 266 covers almost half the standard blue print.

A trio of coffee can, teacup and saucer from the teaset matching this 1125 patterned teapot and stand is shown in Plate 49. The standard Miles Mason coffee can which was probably introduced some ten years earlier is still in use but the cup handle is a new and most unusual one.

Plate 49. A Miles Mason trio bearing the blue-printed Pagoda pattern with added gilt border. Note the new teacup handle. Blue-printed, Chinese-styled seal mark. c.1810-12. Mr. and Mrs. A.E. Grove Collection

I now turn to consider another Miles Mason blue-printed design, still in the Chinese manner although the period is now about 1810 or slightly later. The teapot and stand shapes have already been featured in Plate 46 but the accompanying forms are shown in Plate 50. The covered sugar shape is rather unusual and perhaps a little later in its period of introduction than the other pieces (note the heavier knob). Unfortunately this set does not bear a pattern number since there is no added gilding, but there can be no doubt about its source as these pieces bear the square Chinese-type seal marks with the name 'Miles' above and 'Mason' below the seal, see page 198.

However, we have to be rather more careful about the print for, as with the Pagoda design, this is not confined to Miles Mason's factory; at least one other manufacturer made a version which at first sight is similar to this Mason print, Plate 50a. This other version has been attributed to the New Hall factory though this is by no means certain.

I now turn to the enamelled tewares, that is wares decorated in colours over the glaze. Whilst it is not possible to identify the first design in Miles Mason's pattern book I can show you examples of his

Plate 50. *Representative pieces from a marked Miles Mason blue-printed teaservice of the so-called Veranda pattern showing typical shapes. Seal mark with 'Miles' above and 'Mason' below. c.1810. Teapot 11ins. long.* Godden of Worthing Ltd.

Plate 50a. *A saucer bearing a slightly different version of Miles Mason's Veranda pattern but this is not a Mason example. c.1810-15.* Godden of Worthing Ltd.

patterns 2 and 3 (Plates 51, 52, 54 and 55). These, as you may expect, are simple floral designs in the taste of the late eighteenth century Chinese export market porcelains.

Pattern 2 is recorded on two shapes, the earliest probably being the teapot in the Royal Ontario Museum in Toronto. This has a swan knob and in basic shape is as my Plate 52.

My own example of pattern number 2 is on a slightly later Mason's teapot shape (Plate 51). A basic form which proved very popular in its various versions, i.e. with a plain unfaceted body.

Miles Mason's pattern number 3 is here represented by the early teapot seen in Plate 52.

The reader is warned that some other manufacturers made swan knobs — this is not a sure sign of a Mason origin. The teapot shown in Plate 53 is not, for example, a Miles Mason specimen; it bears the pattern number 37, not 3; the handle and spout are of incorrect shapes and the body is too soft and the glaze is slightly crazed. The Mason handle form is a useful one to note but some teapots made by Machin & Co., of Burslem, have a rather similar curled-over handle form as do some earthenware teapots.

The point to note regarding this teapot is the pattern when associated with the pattern number 3. It follows, therefore, that plain forms such as the plate and teabowl and saucer shown in Plate 54,

Plate 51, above left. An attractive early Mason teapot bearing a simple enamelled floral design in the style of the earlier Chinese porcelain imports. Painted pattern number 'No. 2'. c.1805. 10½ ins. long. Geoffrey Godden, Chinaman

Plate 52, above. A rare early Miles Mason teapot of pattern number 3, again in the style of the earlier Chinese imports. c.1804-05. 10¾ ins. long. Miss M. Martin Collection

Plate 53, left. A non-Miles Mason teapot of similar form to the Mason example shown in Plate 52. Pattern number 37. c.1800-05. 6¼ ins. high. Geoffrey Godden, Chinaman

Plate 54. A Miles Mason plate of pattern 3 and a teabowl and saucer. The plate impressed marked 'M. MASON' with painted pattern number. c.1804-05. Diameter 7⅞ ins. Victoria and Albert Museum (Crown Copyright)

Plate 55, below. A typical Miles Mason sugar box of pattern 3. Painted pattern number '3'. c.1804-05. 4½ ins. long. Geoffrey Godden, Chinaman

which have no characteristic shape or identifiable feature, will be Miles Mason if they also bear the pattern number 3 with this design. As an added cross-check the plate is in fact impressed marked 'M. Mason'. From this pattern and its number we can also correctly identify the covered sugar box shown in Plate 55 which is of a more conventional form than the swan-knobbed teapot.

Another simple floral pattern in the style of the earlier Chinese export market porcelains is Miles Mason's design 22 seen here in Plates 56 and 57. The teapot has the same knob we saw in Plate 40 and which we will see again in Plates 67 and 68, but this example bears a rather rare simple handle without a thumb grip. The oval sugar box shown in Plate 57 bears the same design and is inscribed 'N.22'. This shape, although it differs in some respects, is related to those shown in Plates 92 and 95.

Another simple floral design is shown in Plate 58. This design may well be taken for New Hall and indeed that factory and several of its competitors issued tewares painted with this design. However, on the evidence of this coffee can, and in particular its characteristic knob at the top of the handle, this version appears to be a Miles Mason version of about 1805. Unfortunately this trio does not bear a pattern number. A point to note is that the painting is carried out more carefully than one would expect with New Hall examples. The New Hall pattern number for this design is 241.

My next illustration, Plate 59, shows a rather unusual form of oval Miles Mason sugar box, a plain, unfluted version of that shown in Plate 45. This example bears the impressed mark 'M. MASON', and the gilt pattern number, although rather rubbed, appears to read 'N 217'. The wide border design is richly gilt. A sugar box of similar form is shown in Plate 90 with rare gold and silver decoration.

The teapot shown in Plate 60 has the same characteristic handle as that shown in Plate 44 but has a straight spout. It is shown here with a standard coffee can and 'Bute' shape cup. This pattern is number 161.

Plate 56. A Miles Mason teapot with typical knob form, painted with Mason's pattern 22. c.1805. 10ins. long. Mr. and Mrs. P. Miller Collection

Plate 57. An oval Miles Mason sugar box of a rather unusual form painted in the style of the Chinese export market porcelain with pattern 22. Painted pattern number 'N.22'. c.1807-10. 6¾ins. long. Mr. and Mrs. P. Miller Collection

Plate 58. A trio of fluted saucer, teabowl and coffee can — with typical Mason knob to the handle. Unmarked. c.1805-10. Diameter of saucer 5½ ins. C.H. May Collection

The same shape is seen again in Plate 61 bearing a standard Miles Mason print which I term the 'Shepherd'; this design does not normally bear a pattern number but Mr. Haggar states that it is pattern 74. This basic shape of teaware was also issued with groups of vertical fluting.

The sugar box shape to accompany this oval, straight-sided teapot is shown in Plate 62, where the various panels bear Miles Mason's 'Four Seasons' prints. The jug form is shown in Plates 63 and 64, one showing Spring the other the Mason version of Moses in the bulrushes. Note the two figures and the baby in the rushes and compare with the

Plate 59, above. An oval Mason sugar box with a wide gilt border, pattern 217. Impressed mark 'M. MASON'. c.1805-10. 6¼ ins. long. C.H. May Collection

Plate 60. Representative pieces from a teaset of pattern 161. The teapot and cup handles with characteristic handle form. c.1805-08. Teapot 10ins. long. Godden of Worthing Ltd.

Plate 61. A very typical Miles Mason porcelain teapot with characteristic handle and printed design. Unmarked. c.1805-08. 10ins. long. Godden of Worthing Ltd.

Plate 62. A decorative Mason porcelain oval sugar box with typical prints depicting the seasons. Subjects found on marked examples. Unmarked. c.1805-10. 4¾ ins. high. Geoffrey Godden, Chinaman

Plate 63. An impressed marked 'M. MASON' creamer bearing the Spring print from the set of seasons, see Plate 62. c.1805-08. 4½ ins. high. Sothebys

Plate 64. An impressed marked 'M. MASON' creamer bearing the Mason bat-printed version of Moses in the bulrushes. Compare with Plate 77. c.1805-08. 4½ ins. high. E.H. Chandler Collection

Spode version illustrated in Plate 77. This and other bat prints were sometimes painted over to give richer effects but such tinted-in examples are rare.

Another teapot form which follows the oval straight-sided style, is illustrated here in Plate 65. The particular variation is very rare, note the high curved shoulder to the pot, the handle form and especially the knob with its four upward turned corners. This example bears Miles Mason's Shepherd print which makes up for the lack of a name mark. Note that with this shape the fluting does not reach up to the top of the main body and ends some two thirds of the way up the spout.

Colour Plate 3. A rare Mason porcelain teapot form of the 1812-15 period. This basic shape with variations occurs decorated with several different styles of decoration. Unmarked. 10½ins. long. R.G. Austin, Esq.

The more usual form of this teapot is shown in Plate 66 — note the same knob and spout — but now a new, simplified handle has been added and the shoulder does not rise as high as on the earlier version. The stands to these pots are a fluted oval, without the rather later end handles as seen in Plates 87 and 88.

I now discuss other enamelled shapes which link with Pagoda printed teawares (see Plates 40-42). This Chinese mandarin-type design consists of a printed outline which is painted in by semi-skilled and inexpensive labour. Consequently it was popular with the management as well as with the buying public who received colourful mock-Chinese porcelains at relatively low cost. Representative pieces from such a teaset are shown in Colour Plate 2, which illustrates both sides of this stock design and the various shapes of the period c.1802-5.

A teapot and covered sugar bowl are shown in more detail in Plates 67 and 68. Note the basic shapes and in particular the knob form.

Plate 65. A Miles Mason porcelain teapot with rare handle form but bearing the helpful Shepherd print. Note also the knob form. c.1805-08. City Museum and Art Gallery, Stoke-on-Trent

Plate 66. A variation of the teapot form shown in Plate 65, the simple and tasteful design in green and gold. Unmarked. c.1805-08. 10¼ ins. long. Godden of Worthing Ltd.

Plate 67. A Miles Mason teapot of a standard form with indented fluting showing in detail the Boy in the Door outline print coloured in by hand. See also Colour Plate 2. c.1804-08. 6ins. high. Mason's Ironstone Collection

Plate 68, above. A typical Miles Mason sugar box bearing the Boy in the Door design. See Colour Plate 2. c.1804-08. Sothebys

Plate 69. A very rare Miles Mason tea canister bearing the Boy in the Door design. Unmarked. c.1804-05. 5¼ins. high. Miss M. Martin Collection

These two illustrations also serve to make the point that several different engraved copper plates were used for the various parts of a teaset, according to the size of the piece, and that some differences of detail can occur — both in the basic printed outline, in the way that the print is coloured in, and in the treatment of the added background and foreground. The reader will find for himself many differences in the design as shown on these two undoubted Mason pieces.

This design which may be called 'Mandarin' or 'Boy in the Door' does not bear a pattern number on Mason examples; perhaps it was the missing first design? Its popularity enables us to identify today rare Mason shapes such as the tea canister shown in Plate 69, or articles such as punch bowls (Plate 133) where the only identifying feature is the added print. However, caution is required as several other firms produced near versions of this design — some of which are entirely hand-painted without any printed outline. Remember also that at the period when this design was in fashion, up to about 1808, the Miles Mason porcelain is of the hybrid hard paste type and that this Mason pattern does not bear a pattern number.

The next series of teaware forms to be discussed seem to have been very popular for overglaze designs but not for underglaze blue patterns. The basic shape is a narrow oval boat shape with a peculiar three-nipple knob. This shape is well shown in Plates 70, 73, 74, 78 and 79. The example shown in Plate 70 is particularly attractive and of superb quality. The pattern number is 83 and in this illustration the shape of the pouring guard can be seen.

71

Plate 72. The base of the creamer shown in Plate 71 illustrating the standard impressed name mark on the foot and the painted pattern number, in this case prefixed with the initial 'N'. Sothebys

Plate 70. A superbly decorated Miles Mason porcelain teapot of pattern 83. Note the characteristic knob form. c.1805-08. 10½ ins. long. Godden of Worthing Ltd.

Plate 71 shows the next pattern, number 84 in the factory pattern book. This plate also illustrates the shapes which normally accompanied the teapot shape in Plate 70. The coffee can handle is interesting in that the thumb rest faces backwards and does not match the handle of the standard Bute shape cup.

The base of the jug to this part teaset is shown in Plate 72, and illustrates a typical impressed name mark and its normal placing on the foot. It also shows the painted pattern number, in this case prefixed 'N', but this feature is not constant.

Plate 71. Representative pieces of superb Miles Mason tewares of pattern 84, a variation on pattern 83 shown in Plate 70. This set shows shapes to match the teapot shape shown in Plate 70. c.1805-08. Sothebys

Another boat shape teapot is shown in Plate 73 bearing the Shepherd print. This is a bat-print, the engraving being accomplished with dots of various sizes or depths rather than with straight lines. The motifs were transferred from the flat copper plate to the curved porcelains by means of a pliable glue-like 'bat' or slab. It seems that the bat transferred to the porcelain only an oil on to which the colour was dusted. I would draw your attention to the unnatural looking trees favoured by Mason's engraver, particularly those on the right which look rather like two haystacks one on top of the other, and the three-tier effort in the centre.

Another characteristic Miles Mason bat-printed design is shown in Plate 74, which depicts Moses in the bulrushes whilst unrelated secondary prints appear on the covers. Other Mason bat prints feature landscapes, various classical and other figure designs and tasteful shell groupings.

Plate 75. Representative pieces from a Miles Mason teaset printed with various scenes in a new etched technique, see Plates 76, 104 and 107. Teapot impressed marked 'M. MASON'. c.1805-08. Teapot 10½ ins. long. Godden of Worthing Ltd.

Plate 76. A detail of the printed panel on the teapot shown in Plate 75. Note the fine 'grain' and the absence of dots or engraved lines. Panel 4½ ins. long. Godden of Worthing Ltd.

At this stage I must cast personal doubts on the origin of the gold-printed bowl shown as Plate 66 in Reginald Haggar and Elizabeth Adams' book *Mason Porcelain and Ironstone*. To me this is a Spode example, in that it is typical of Spode's essays in this gold printing on a blue ground, a technique patented by Peter Warburton, one of the New Hall partners in 1810. At Spode these gold prints are normally in the pattern number range 1690-1700 and teawares normally have the same border as the unmarked example shown by Haggar and Adams as a Miles Mason example. Plate 77 shows the normal non-gold printed Spode example of the bowl which bears the correct Spode pattern number 557; this bowl serves to illustrate the basic differences between the Spode and the Mason version of the Moses in the bulrushes subject (compare with Plates 64 and 74).

A totally different type of print is seen on the part teaset shown in Plate 75 and in the detail of the teapot panel, Plate 76. This new style has an extremely fine grain and most delicate shading. I believe this engraving technique to be aquatint and it seems unique to Miles Mason's porcelains of approximately the period 1805-10. Once seen, it is easy to recognise the different, superior style, though specimens are

Plate 77. A Spode bone china waste bowl showing the non-Mason version of the Moses in the bulrushes print. Part of a Spode teaset of pattern 557 which embraces many different bat-printed designs. c.1805-10. Geoffrey Godden, Chinaman

very scarce. A range of these designs is seen on this teaset and on the dessert service shown in Plate 104.

Whilst discussing the narrow boat-shaped teapot shape, I must show a very colourful example decorated in yellow, orange and gold. I owned this pot for fully five years before, while washing it one day, I found the impressed mark on the outside of the foot — it can be seen in Plates 78 and 78a, under the gilt line edge in the centre of the base. Perhaps some new employee misunderstood the instructions to apply the stamp on the foot, but on the exterior it certainly makes a good publicity point.

Plate 78. A very finely decorated Miles Mason teapot in yellow, orange and gold with the impressed name mark on the outside of the foot. c.1805-08. 10½ ins. long. Geoffrey Godden, Chinaman

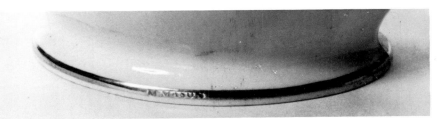

Plate 78a. Detail of the impressed name mark on the teapot, see Plate 78.

Plate 79. Representative pieces from a fluted tea-set of the basic form shown in Plates 70-78. Note the new coffee can handle and the creamer handle. c.1805-08. Teapot 10½ ins. long. Godden of Worthing Ltd.

Plate 80. A sugar box as Plate 79 but with a new 'spire' knob form, and creamer. Painted mark of the London retailer 'Hewson, Aldgate'. c.1805-08. Creamer 4¼ ins. high. Godden of Worthing Ltd.

Plate 81. A rare Miles Mason sugar box, as Plate 80 but with a version of the Worcester Dragon pattern. c.1805-08. 5½ ins. high. Geoffrey Godden, Chinaman

The basic type of teasets just discussed and illustrated in Plates 70-78, have plain, unfluted bodies but the same shapes also occur, though rarely, in a fluted form. Representative shapes are shown in Plate 79. The design is an inexpensive but tasteful, simple gilt pattern and is unnumbered on these specimens.

The new shape of jug handle should be noted and compared with those in Plates 71, 74 and 75. The handle of the coffee can should also be remembered since it is not the standard form.

The white and gold creamer shown in Plate 79 links with that illustrated in Plate 80, with a sugar bowl of a new and rare form. The spire-like knob is the feature to note here. On turning up the cover one finds the name of the London retailer, or Chinaman, 'Hewson, Aldgate', one who presumably bought and sold Mason's porcelains although he certainly stocked other makes as well. The teapot which would have been supplied with this teaset has the same spire knob and an enlarged version of the jug handle, but these forms are rare.

A sugar bowl of the same shape is shown in Plate 81, with Mason's version of the popular Dragon pattern — better known on Worcester porcelains. Unfortunately this piece does not bear a pattern number or a name mark, but the knob form is enough to identify its true source.

A very rare teapot form links with the spire-type knob shown in Plates 80 and 81. This new version illustrated in Plate 82 has the same handle seen in Plates 78 and 79, but the main body now follows closely the shape of the standard sugar box seen in Plates 80 and 81 except that the cover is low and slightly recessed into the top. This example, the only one known to the author, is unmarked but the spire knob enables a good identification to be made.

Plate 82. A very rare Miles Mason teapot form following in general shape the sugar boxes shown in Plates 80 and 81. The decoration is in red and gold. Unmarked. c.1805-08. 10½ ins. long. C.H. May Collection

Before proceeding too far with the known Miles Mason teaware forms I should illustrate here a recent discovery of some seemingly trial or half-finished cups, coffee cans and saucers decorated only with various blue borders, see Plate 83. This selection of pieces includes a coffee can matching those in Plates 71 and 75, and a can matching the one shown in Plate 79.

77

However, with these standard pieces were two coffee cups and a small bowl with spiral fluting, see Plate 84. To date, these 'shanked' shapes appear to be unknown on finished Miles Mason porcelains, but on the evidence of these unfinished pieces at least one form of spiral-fluted teaware should exist with a matching teapot and all the other pieces. On form alone these spiral fluted teawares should be quite early, say about 1805 and, as the reader may recall, the pre-1800 Wolfe-Mason partnership at Liverpool produced (as yet unidentified) spiral fluted teawares as is evidenced by the unglazed site waster shown in Plate 37.

These unfinished teawares are all of a very soft body — perhaps a trial batch — differing in appearance and feel from the normal early Mason greyish hybrid hard-paste porcelain and the later bone china. Even though several of the pieces are discoloured and the saucers show quite blatant firing cracks, the range of cup shapes is illuminating.

We now progress to a new teapot form, one with a large capacity. This is a graceful, if rather plump, boat-shape — a basic form made by most English porcelain manufacturers of the 1810-15 period with, of course, small differences of shape. It is known as 'new oval'. The Miles Mason version, which shows pattern number 487, is seen in Plate 85. Some pieces of this service were impressed marked 'M. MASON', although proof of the origin of this shape is given in the blue-printed Pagoda patterned teawares (see Plate 46). A handled teapot stand to this shape is seen again in Plate 87 where pattern 240 is illustrated, and another in Plate 88 where pattern 540 is shown.

A matching trio of teacup, coffee can and saucer is shown in Plate 86. The overall effect of this tea service is quite startling and rivals any English porcelain of the period.

Plate 83. A trial batch of Miles Mason cups and saucers bearing only dark blue borders but illustrating standard as well as new shapes — see Plate 84. c.1805-08. **Godden Reference Collection**

Plate 84. The spiral-fluted or 'shanked' coffee cup and small bowl from the trial unfinished batch shown in Plate 83. These spiral-fluted forms are as yet unrecognised in completed designs. c.1805. Godden Reference Collection

Plate 85. A fine Miles Mason teapot and stand and creamer of pattern 487 decorated with bat-printed figure subjects within orange and gold borders. The plates to this set are impressed marked 'M. MASON'. c.1810. Teapot 10½ ins. long. Sothebys

Plate 86. A trio of Miles Mason's pattern 487 matching the teapot shown in Plate 85 bearing bat-printed classical figure motifs within orange and gold borders. c.1810. Geoffrey Godden, Chinaman

How one firm's patterns sometimes came to be copied and added to a new firm's pattern book is illustrated by the group of teawares shown in Plate 89. Here, the teapot is a Miles Mason replacement to an earlier service made by an as yet unnamed manufacturer. The pattern number of the original is 25 and, whilst these wares display some Mason features, the class has been proved by pattern numbers not to be Mason. Yet Mason made, probably by special request, this replacement teapot using his own shape of teapot, and the horizontal ribbing sometimes found on this shape is clearly seen.

The covered sugar box shown in Plate 90 represents an unusual form which is slightly earlier than the teapot shape here under discussion. The added pattern too is unusual being in silver (or platinum) and gold. The companion teapot stand is impressed marked 'M. MASON' and bears the pattern number 43.

Plate 91 shows a similar covered sugar box but with graceful spiral fluting (shanked) which would, of course, be reflected in all pieces in the teaset. This simple design is pattern number 325. The spiral fluted cup and bowl shown in Plate 84 appear to be of an earlier date.

Plate 87. An impressed marked 'M. MASON' teapot stand of pattern 240 bearing a bat-printed landscape design in the manner of Spode's pattern 557. c.1808-10. Geoffrey Godden, Chinaman

Plate 88. An elegant impressed marked 'M. MASON' teapot stand of typical form. Painted pattern number 540. c.1810. 8 by 5½ ins. Godden of Worthing Ltd.

Plate 89. A Miles Mason replacement teapot painted to match an earlier teaset of unknown make. Replacement of items is one reason why unrecorded patterns appear on any given make of porcelain. c.1810. 10½ ins. long. Godden Reference Collection

Plate 90. An impressed marked 'M. MASON' sugar box of pattern 43 decorated with a rare combination of gold and silver (platinum). c.1805. 5ins. high. A.S. West Collection

Plate 91. A simple but attractive spiral-fluted Mason's sugar box painted with floral sprays. Impressed marked 'M. MASON'. Pattern number 325. c.1810. 6ins. long. Geoffrey Godden, Chinaman

Some tea services with a boat-shaped teapot as shown in Plates 46 and 85, have a covered sugar box of the form shown in Plate 92 with the shepherd's-crook handle. The coffee can is of the standard shape. The gilt pattern on a dark-blue ground is pattern number 473.

The accompanying cream or milk jug is a simple attractive shape as seen in Plate 93, but in this case with rather rare vertical fluting. Most specimens have a plain body.

We now turn to a low, wide teapot shape, with a rather high 'prow' rising above the height of the spout. This form is seen in Plates 94-96. Firstly, in Plate 94, we have a hand-painted leaf border, pattern number 91. The other part service (Plate 95) shows various printed designs within rather wide gilt borders, pattern number 351. This illustration shows the standard shapes associated with this teapot form. It can usefully be mentioned that several pieces in this service show staining in the body, a not uncommon fault found with some bone china. This can be seen in the detail of the teapot (Plate 96), particularly on the shoulder by the handle. This staining, which does not occur with the earlier hybrid hard-paste porcelain, serves to make the

Plate 92. A blue and gold Miles Mason sugar box (and coffee can) of pattern 473, showing a rare handle form. c.1810. 7½ins. long. Godden of Worthing Ltd.

Plate 93. An attractively simple gilt Miles Mason creamer of standard form. Unmarked. c.1810. 4½ins. high. Miss J. Magness Collection

Plate 94. *Representative pieces from a Miles Mason teaservice of pattern 91. The plate is impressed marked 'M. MASON'. c.1810. Teapot 9½ ins. long.* Godden of Worthing Ltd.

point that the basic body changed to a softer bone china sometime in the 1807-10 period.

A very recently discovered trio, Plate 96a, which bears the figure subject prints found on this teaset and also displays the typical Miles Mason handles, is most interesting in that the wide top border is in silver or rather platinum lustre rather than gold. In the past there has been great discussion over the problem of whether Miles Mason produced silver-lustre decoration and this trio seems to settle the point.

Plate 95. *Representative pieces from a Miles Mason teaservice of pattern 351, decorated with various bat-printed figure subjects. Teapot impressed marked 'M. MASON'. c.1810-12. 9½ ins. long.* Geoffrey Godden, Chinaman

Plate 96. The impressed marked 'M. MASON' teapot from the service shown in Plate 95. Pattern 351. c.1810-12. Geoffrey Godden, Chinaman

Plate 96a. A rare trio bearing figure subject prints linking with the teaset shown in Plate 95 but with silver or platinum-lustre borders. c.1810-12. Geoffrey Godden, Chinaman

Plate 97. A rare Miles Mason coffee pot of pattern 422. The handle matches that of the teapot shown in Plate 96. c.1810-12. 8ins. high. Dr. and Mrs. G. Barnes

The coffee pot seen in Plate 97 is a very rare and graceful article. All nineteenth century coffee pots are rare and the Mason ones of this shape particularly so. These items were not included in the normal tea-set although all full sets included coffee cups or the cylindrical coffee cans as a matter of course. Perhaps it was assumed that the purchaser owned a silver or plated coffee pot. This example would be of the form associated with the teapot shape shown in Plate 96; note the knob and handle form and the manner in which the top junction of the handle divides, the front forming a retainer to hold the cover in place when the pot is tilted. The pattern number is 422.

An earlier, rarer and unsatisfactory Mason coffee pot form is recorded with a handle like that shown in Plate 134.

The curious moulded teapot shown in Plate 98 is a puzzle. I do not know of any name-marked examples but on balance it appears very likely that this, and the slight variations which occur, are of Mason's

Plate 98. A rare teapot form of the 1812-15 period, linking in general form with examples shown in Colour Plate 3 and in Plates 99 and 101. 10¼ ins. long.
Geoffrey Godden, Chinaman

Plate 99. A Mason teapot of slightly different form to that shown in Plate 98; note the knob and the leaf moulding. Richly gilt ground. Pattern number 873. c.1810-15. 10½ ins. long.
Sotheby's

Plate 100. A Mason's Patent Ironstone china cup having the same handle form and relief-moulded leaf border as the unmarked porcelains associated with the pieces shown in Plates 99 and 101. c.1813-15. R.G. Austin Collection

Plate 101. A Mason porcelain waste bowl of the basic relief-moulded leaf design shown in Plate 99. Pattern 873. c.1812-15. Diameter 6½ ins.
Geoffrey Godden, Chinaman

make of the period 1812-15, that is about the time of Miles Mason's retirement and the succession of his sons. Slight body staining occurs on this example which does not have a pattern number.

The related teapot shown in Plate 99 has a different knob to the cover, and the leaf pattern relief moulding on the body differs materially from the floral moulding on the previous pot. The ground around the leaf moulding is gilt and the pattern number of 873 fits in reasonably with the Mason sequence, although this number is some 250 below that on the blue-printed Pagoda patterned teapot shown in Plate 48. Other pattern numbers on these shapes are higher — I have seen 1134 and numbers above 2000 have been reported. A curious feature occurs under this pot where it has been painted over and a Chinese-style leaf motif scratched through the enamel. Other teawares follow this basic relief-moulded leaf border motif and are found decorated in various styles, sometimes with a pale blue ground. The same basic moulding and cup handle form occurs on Ironstone wares, see Plate 100. Dessert services match these teasets in general style, see Plate 121.

Plate 102. A rare impressed marked 'M. MASON' porcelain caudle or chocolate cup, cover and stand. c.1808-10. W. Pick Collection

Plate 103. A very rare Miles Mason covered bowl bearing printed designs which also occur on marked examples. c.1808-10. 4⅛ ins. high. Miss M. Martin Collection

I now illustrate two articles which can reasonably be considered under the teaware heading. Firstly, in Plate 102, a very rare covered cup and stand which is helpfully impressed-marked 'M. MASON', although it is difficult to say exactly to what use this cup was put, perhaps it was for chocolate? There is also the possibility that it was a caudle cup and a Mason letter of 27th February, 1810 quotes a price of 'about 5s.' for supplying such an item to Wedgwood.

Secondly, in Plate 103, I illustrate a very rare covered bowl, probably for broth or some like brew and originally this form would have boasted a stand. It is unmarked but the music subject prints are known on impressed-marked 'M. MASON' porcelains or associated with known Miles Mason prints.

Before leaving the subject of teawares I must again point out that comparatively few pieces bear an impressed name mark; the post-1808 pieces in particular are seldom marked and very many pieces do not bear a pattern number. I have had complete sets without any vestige of a mark. Our identification rests in most cases on a knowledge of the shape or the printed pattern and in these fields the preceding illustrations should provide a good guide.

DESSERT SERVICES

Miles Mason's dessert wares are all quite rare, especially examples bearing the standard blue-printed Pagoda pattern which proved so popular on teawares.

It is difficult to date the dessert wares but I regard the hybrid hard-paste ones as being earlier than the bone china examples, and some printed designs link with those on teawares, a fact which allows some degree of dating. Unfortunately the earlier dessert services do not seem to bear pattern numbers.

Let us first discuss the hybrid hard-paste service shown in Plate 104

Plate 104. Representative pieces from a Miles Mason dessert service decorated with various printed scenes. c.1805. Oval footed dish 12½ins. long. Godden of Worthing Ltd.

Plate 105. A comparison photograph showing the slightly different elevations of Coalport (right) and Miles Mason (left) oval centre pieces. 12½ins. long. Godden of Worthing Ltd.

Plate 106. A comparison photograph showing Coalport (left) and Miles Mason (right) dessert service tureens and covers. Note especially the knob forms. 7ins. long. Godden of Worthing Ltd.

Plate 107. Panel on a dessert dish from the service shown in Plate 104, showing the aquatint style of etching without the dots or lines of more conventional ceramic engraving. c.1805. 8¼ ins. Godden Reference Collection

which I would date to about 1805. This dessert set, which is now in the Haggar collection, came from a good source and I know it well. The plates were impressed-marked 'M. MASON' but no pattern number was added. The group photograph of the main pieces from this dessert service serves to show the basic shapes of the period, but unfortunately is not particularly helpful since other factories, notably the two at Coalport, produced dessert wares of almost identical form and a very close comparison must therefore be made. Similar group photographs of Coalport dessert wares are shown in my book *Coalport and Coalbrookdale Porcelains* (Herbert Jenkins, London, 1970, Plates 24-27). The main difference is that the Coalport plates normally have six slight indentations around the rim. The Mason oval dishes are rather longer than the Coalport ones, but in regard to the oval centre pieces and the small tureens the differences are very slight — as can be seen from the comparison poses shown in Plates 105 and 106.

Plate 108. An impressed marked 'M. MASON' handled dish bearing the same painted border as the service shown in Plate 104 and a standard Mason scenic print. c.1805. 7¾ by 8ins. Mason's Ironstone Collection

Plate 109. An impressed marked 'M. MASON' dessert dish of a standard form bearing a standard printed landscape design within a typical hand-painted border. c.1805. 10¾ by 7¼ ins. Victoria and Albert Museum (Crown Copyright)

Colour Plate 4. A very finely decorated, impressed marked 'M. MASON' vase of typical form. Note the mask-head handles. c.1810. 6¼ ins. high.
Geoffrey Godden, Chinaman

Plate 110. Two Miles Mason porcelain dessert dishes of a standard shape hand-painted with dog subjects in monochrome. c.1805. 10¾ by 7¼ ins. Godden of Worthing Ltd.

Plate 111. An impressed marked 'M. MASON' porcelain dessert dish hand-painted in sepia within gilt edges. c.1805. 10¾ ins. City Museum and Art Gallery, Stoke-on-Trent

Plate 112, below. An impressed marked 'M. MASON' porcelain dessert centre piece decorated with the Pagoda or Broseley-Willow print in underglaze blue. c.1808. 12½ ins. long. C.H. May Collection

I have shown separately one of the square dishes from this service, Plate 107, from which it is possible to see that the printing is of the aquatint type, linking with the teawares shown in Plates 75 and 76.

The strange border design to this service is one unique to Mason's porcelains of this 1805 period and it serves to link with other dessert wares bearing other printed centres, see Plates 108 and 109. The handled dish is of another form used by most porcelain manufacturers of the period and here the border and print are the key identifying features, not the shape. A standard shape oval dessert dish is shown in Plate 109 illustrating another Mason print.

The same standard oval shape is shown again, in Plate 110, on two dishes charmingly hand-painted with dog-subjects; these, too, are in the hard early body. This service was variously painted with other animal studies.

Plate 113. A finely decorated Miles Mason centre dish from a dessert service of pattern 100. c.1808. 12¾ ins. long. Godden of Worthing Ltd.

Plate 114. An impressed marked 'M. MASON' dessert service dish of pattern 100 displaying very fine decoration and gilding. c.1808. 7¾ ins. Godden of Worthing Ltd.

Plate 115. An impressed marked 'M. MASON' dessert plate of pattern 100. c.1808. Diameter 8½ ins. Godden of Worthing Ltd.

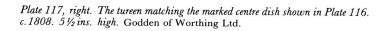

Plate 116, above. An impressed marked 'M. MASON' yellow, red and gold centre piece from a finely decorated dessert service of pattern 131. c.1808. 13¼ ins. long. Godden of Worthing Ltd.

Plate 117, right. The tureen matching the marked centre dish shown in Plate 116. c.1808. 5½ ins. high. Godden of Worthing Ltd.

An early square-shaped dish, Plate 111, has a central panel hand-painted in sepia monochrome. The outer edge of the central framework is rather badly drawn, a fault which occurs on other pieces.

The dessert wares now discussed are of the later bone china body, having a softer body and glaze than the earlier pieces, Plates 104-111. The body is also rather prone to discoloration.

Firstly, in Plate 112, I show a centre piece of typical oval form bearing the Pagoda or Broseley-Willow print in underglaze blue. This example is impressed marked 'M. MASON'. Undoubtedly many complete dessert services were made and decorated with this print, which proved so popular on teawares.

The oval centre piece shown in Plate 113 is much higher than an earlier example (Plate 105) and is of pattern 100. The impressed-marked handled dish (Plate 114) and the plate (Plate 115) from the same service show well the fine quality of the gilding on this part service. The handle on the dish is a simplified version of the relief-moulded handle shown in Plate 108.

The impressed-marked plate in Plate 115 serves to make the point that dessert plates are of relatively small size with a diameter of about 8½ ins., against some 10ins. for a meat or soup plate from a dinner service.

The next illustration, Plate 116, shows an impressed-marked 'M. MASON' centre piece from a dessert service of pattern 131, richly decorated in yellow, red and gold, while Plate 117 illustrates the matching covered tureen from the set. This form is a particularly rare shape — large lion-head handles with open mouths. The lion knob is very finely modelled. The same shape of tureen is seen in Plate 118 and that example bears the pattern number 102. The same lion finial appears on the Mason's Ironstone bulb pot shown in Plate 206.

The open-mouthed, lion-head handles link with an oval dish of pattern 108 in the Mason Works Collection, an item which would seem to be from a dinner service rather than a dessert set.

Plate 118. A richly decorated dessert tureen of pattern 102. The finely moulded lion knob also occurs on Mason's Ironstone wares. c.1808. 6¾ ins. long. Geoffrey Godden, Chinaman

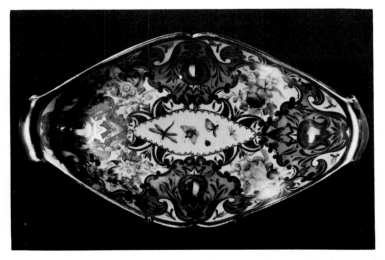

Plate 119. A superbly decorated Miles Mason dessert dish of pattern 130 Orange and gold ground with panels of flowers. Impressed-marked 'M. MASON'. c.1810. 12 by 7ins. W. Davidson Collection

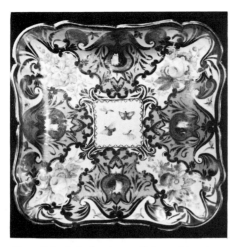

Plate 120. A further dessert dish matching that shown in Plate 119. Pattern 130. Impressed name mark. c.1810. 8½ins. W. Davidson Collection

Plate 121. A two-handled porcelain dessert dish with relief-moulded leaf border matching teawares of the class of the teapot shown in Colour Plate 3. Unmarked. c.1813. 9¼ by 8¼ ins. Geoffrey Godden, Chinaman

Plate 122. Representative pieces from a Mason's Ironstone post-1813 dessert service showing basic shapes found also in the porcelain body. c.1813-18. Godden of Worthing Ltd.

The two dessert dishes illustrated in Plates 119 and 120 are impressed marked 'M. MASON' and bear the pattern number 130. The shapes are slightly different to those already illustrated and the decoration is particularly fine, the border being in orange and gold. The approximate period would be 1810.

The two-handled dessert dish illustrated in Plate 121 relates in its relief-moulded leaf border with the rather problematical teawares shown in Colour Plate 3 and Plate 101. Even the painted centre links with some of these teawares and both must originate from the same source. Alas, there is no name mark or pattern number to prove its origin. This piece is rather thickly potted and the translucency is poor.

At this stage there is a gap in our knowledge of Miles Mason dessert wares, indeed the next known shapes may have been produced by the sons after Miles Mason's retirement in about 1813. The next shape to be considered certainly links with the post-1813 Ironstone wares.

I show in Plate 122 representative pieces from an Ironstone dessert service, some pieces of which bear a moulded Royal Arms type mark incorporating the words 'Patent Ironstone China', and whilst the name Mason does not appear, they alone could rightly use the description 'Patent Ironstone'. Note particularly the intricately-moulded plate form, at the top of this group.

Plate 123. Representative pieces from a porcelain dessert service matching in general form the marked 'Patent' Ironstone set shown in Plate 122, except that the centre piece is much more ornate. Unmarked. c.1813-18. Christie's

93

Plate 124. *A porcelain tureen and cover from a dessert service showing the well-modelled cow finial and handle. Unmarked. c.1813-18.* Geoffrey Godden, Chinaman

Plate 125. *A porcelain plate matching in shape and moulding the 'Patent' Ironstone example shown in Plate 122. Unmarked. c.1813-18. Diameter 8¼ ins.* Geoffrey Godden, Chinaman

My next illustration, Plate 123, shows representative pieces from a fine quality, thinly potted porcelain dessert service of the same basic moulding, although in this particular service the centre piece is rather larger and more elaborate than the Ironstone example which would have been less expensive.

In Plate 124 I show a porcelain dessert tureen from such a set to illustrate the elaborate moulding. This set is painted with birds, named on the bases or reverse sides.

Plate 125 shows a porcelain plate displaying the same ornate and characteristic moulding. A companion dish is shown in Plate 126.

Plate 126. *A porcelain dessert dish from the same service as the plate shown in Plate 125. Unmarked. c.1813-18. 10½ by 7¼ ins.* Geoffrey Godden, Chinaman

These specimens are completely unmarked and are of a very white porcelain, rather more compact in appearance than the earlier impressed marked 'M. MASON' porcelains displayed in Plates 114-120. In reality the only link with Mason rests on the moulded design which appears on 'Patent Ironstone China' marked dessert wares (Plate 122).

These two pieces (Plates 125 and 126) are rather attractively painted with landscapes and figures, perhaps by Samuel Bourne (see page 192), but other sets of this type are painted with named birds and with animal subjects or with flowers. In some instances parts of the relief mouldings are picked out in gold giving a very rich, if fussy effect (Plate 123).

DINNER SERVICES

Marked 'M. Mason' porcelain dinner wares are extremely rare although, of course, the post-1813 Ironstone examples are (or were until recently) quite common.

A likely reason for this is that the earthenware examples were so cheap that they captured the market for the less expensive sets and the established factories such as Spode, or those at Derby, Worcester or Coalport already had the market for the more expensive porcelain services. This is not to say Miles Mason did not make dinner services, he almost certainly did. I have for years been expecting to find a service bearing the Mason version of the blue-printed Pagoda pattern (see page 58) but without success. However, an odd plate in the Victoria and Albert Museum (similar to Plate 127) proves such sets were made and that at least the plate shapes follow that used by the Chinese potters late in the eighteenth century. This porcelain example bears the standard impressed mark 'M. MASON', but other examples were made at a later period with Chinese-type, blue seal marks, with or without the name 'MILES' above and 'MASON' below the seal mark;

Plate 127. An impressed marked 'M. MASON' dinner plate bearing the popular Pagoda or Broseley-Willow design. This is a good close copy of a Chinese original. c.1805-10. Diameter 9⅛ ins. Dr. A. Gregory Collection

Plate 128. A very rare impressed marked 'M. MASON' porcelain sauce boat bearing the Pagoda print. Part of the thumb rest on the handle is missing. c.1805-10. 7½ ins. long. C.H. May Collection

Plate 129. An English porcelain copy of a Chinese export market dinner plate, perhaps of Mason manufacture. Unmarked. c.1804. Diameter 8½ ins. Mr. and Mrs. B. Halls

Plate 130. An English porcelain soup plate almost certainly made as a replacement to a Chinese export market service. Unmarked. c.1804. Diameter 8¾ ins. Godden of Worthing Ltd.

such pieces bear a very slightly different version of the standard Pagoda print to that on the earlier impressed-marked example. For instance the figure approaching the steps is no longer silhouetted in an unshaded area.

The sauce boat shown in Plate 128 was almost certainly sold as part of a large dinner service, at least the Chinese sets which Miles Mason was striving to emulate had some sauce boats and stands. This example is impressed-marked 'M. MASON' and probably dates between 1805 and 1810 and is contemporary with the dinner plate shown in Plate 127.

You will recall that in Miles Mason's 1804 advertisement he proposed ''to renew or match the impaired or broken services of the nobility and gentry...'' — which in most cases would have been eighteenth century Chinese services. The admittedly unmarked dinner plates shown in Plates 129 and 130 could be of this type although Mason would not have been the only manufacturer to have supplied such replacement pieces, or extra articles, to an existing dinner service.

Whichever English porcelain manufacturer made the plate shown in Plate 131, he certainly went to great trouble to please his customer. The plate exactly matches a Chinese original made in about 1780 for Sir James Ibbetson of Denton Park, a service recorded in David S. Howard's standard work *Chinese Armorial Porcelain* (Faber, London, 1974). In the case of this replacement, however, the manufacturer had to have a special copper plate engraved for the intricate but typical Chinese underglaze blue border and a separate one for the inner border; these were applied separately as is evident by the join marks which are in different positions. The outline of the armorial shield and crest is also printed and an engraved copper plate was therefore needed.

Plate 131. An English porcelain dinner plate, a later replacement made to a Chinese service of the 1780s, perhaps by Miles Mason. Unmarked. c.1804-05. Diameter 9½ ins. E.H. Chandler Collection

These last three specimens were in the nature of one-off replacements, but the two plates shown in Plate 132 are of a stock Miles Mason design, (see Plates 67-69 and Colour Plate 2). The reversed example enables the reader to see the impressed name mark, as well as the Chinese type of foot and the glaze free line turned away just outside the edge. Unfortunately the small size of both these plates, which have diameters of only 7¾ ins., makes it difficult to say whether these are the small pudding or cheese plates from a dinner service or plates from a dessert service, but such early examples of the approximate 1805 period are extremely rare.

Plate 132. Two impressed marked 'M. MASON' porcelain plates bearing standard Boy in the Door printed outline design. One plate turned to show mark and the Chinese-style foot. c.1805. Diameter 7¾ ins. Godden of Worthing Ltd.

Miles Mason dinner services certainly were made and the various component parts such as tureens should exist. In August 1946 the following service was sold in London:

> A Staffordshire dinner service, by M. Mason, painted with foliage and tendrils in blue and gold on a white ground comprising: a soup tureen, cover and stand, two vegetable dishes and covers, an entrée dish, cover and liner, sixteen meat dishes in sizes, two strainers, a large deep dish, two sauce tureens, covers and stands, a salad bowl, eighteen soup plates, thirty six meat plates, six pudding plates, twelve cheese plates, impressed mark 'M. MASON'.

Such a large dinner service if bearing the impressed name mark 'M. MASON' would have been of porcelain, not of the later Ironstone. The writer would dearly love to hear of the whereabouts of this service today or indeed of any other Miles Mason porcelain dinner wares.

An oval deep dish just over 12ins. long is in the Mason Works Collection; this piece, with lion-head handles similar to those on the small tureens shown in Plates 117 and 118, could well be the base of a vegetable dish or entrée dish from a Mason porcelain service such as that listed above.

Plate 133, above. A Miles Mason porcelain punch bowl bearing the popular Boy in the Door design, with a hand-painted interior very much in the style of the earlier Chinese imports. Unmarked. c.1805-10. Diameter 8¾ ins. E.H. Chandler Collection

Plate 134, right. A rare Miles Mason porcelain jug bearing prints found on marked porcelains. c.1808-10. Miss M. Martin

PUNCH BOWLS

One of the most popular lines in eighteenth century Chinese export market porcelains was decorative punch bowls, and so it is probably not surprising that Miles Mason should have emulated these in his Staffordshire porcelain.

The example in Plate 133 bears on the outside the standard early Mason Mandarin or Boy in the Door design in printed outline, matching teawares such as those shown in Plates 67-69 and Colour Plate 2. These bowls were made in various sizes, one in the Mason's Works Collection has a diameter of 11ins. In some cases apparently the management did not have the correct size of print for the inner border which would then have to be entirely hand-painted as is the case with this punch bowl. The Chinese figure subject inside the bowl is also entirely hand-painted.

Most, if not all, of these early Miles Mason punch bowls were unmarked and, since such a hand-thrown object does not have any distinguishing feature, as a handle or knob, they can therefore only be identified if they bear a known Mason design.

Small bowls with a diameter of under 6ins. would be the waste, or slop, bowl from a teaservice.

JUGS

Miles Mason must also have produced a range of jugs, several of which were undoubtedly embellished with the Boy in the Door pattern, or with the blue Pagoda print.

The superb example in Plate 134 is unmarked but it can be identified by the Mason version of the Moses print which it bears. Many other examples must await discovery.

Mugs too must surely have been made and some should bear standard designs which will assist the reader to identify the Mason examples.

Plate 135. A segment dish from a supper set (the cover is missing). Impressed marked 'M. MASON'. c.1808-10. 10¼ by 7¼ ins. C.H. May Collection

SUPPER SETS

Miles Mason also made supper sets on the evidence of the impressed marked dish shown in Plate 135. These supper sets comprised four such segment dishes (with covers) which, when fitted together, formed a round or oval assembly in a mahogany tray. At the centre stood a covered centre bowl and perhaps, in the case of the example illustrated, condiment trays fitted in the four spaces which would have been formed by the concave sections at the sides of the dishes.

These supper sets were also made in the Ironstone china body and examples are listed in the 1822 Sale Catalogues, see Chapter Five.

Plate 136. Two from a set of three Miles Mason vases of typical form — see also Colour Plate 4, page 88. The hand-painted scenes run continuously around the vases. The larger example only is impressed marked 'M. MASON'. c.1810. 8 and 6¼ ins. high. Godden of Worthing Ltd.

VASES

Miles Mason certainly made an imposing array of porcelain vases, sometimes in sets of three. These vases are sometimes impressed-marked 'M. MASON', but even if they do not bear this feature examples should be identified with little difficulty as the shapes in all cases seem characteristically unique to this one manufacturer. The handles appear rather too heavy or large for the object, and the masks on the items shown in Colour Plate 4 and in Plates 136 and 137 should be especially noted.

The Mason vases shown in Plates 136-140 are probably of the 1805-13 period, and these illustrations give a good idea of the standard forms of decoration.

Plate 137. A rare form of Miles Mason vase (now without its finial) with richly gilt ornamentation. Impressed marked 'M. MASON'. c.1810. 7ins. high. Phillips

Plate 138. An unusual Miles Mason vase form with rather top-heavy cover but very finely decorated. Impressed marked 'M. MASON'. c.1810. 7ins. high. Beaverbrook Art Gallery, Canada

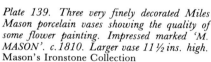

Plate 139. Three very finely decorated Miles Mason porcelain vases showing the quality of some flower painting. Impressed marked 'M. MASON'. c.1810. Larger vase 11½ ins. high. Mason's Ironstone Collection

Plate 140. An impressed marked 'M. MASON' porcelain vase of the same quality and form as Plate 139 but of smaller size. c.1810. 9½ ins. high. Mr. and Mrs. Roy Taylor Collection

Plate 141. A very rare bulb (or bough) pot and cover bearing bat-printed figure subjects. A basic shape which may be of Mason origin. Unmarked. c.1808-10. 10¾ ins. high. Christie's

OTHER OBJECTS

It is likely that Miles Mason made many other forms of porcelain articles which have not as yet been identified or reported. Apart from plainly marked examples, possible means of identification are the known Mason prints used, particularly the Mandarin or Boy in the Door design (Plates 67-69, 132, 133 and Colour Plate 2), or some of the bat prints which are found on teawares or dessert services and which have been illustrated under those headings.

I have recently seen photographs of two impressed-marked 'M. MASON' porcelain spill vases, of which the basic cylindrical shape is unusual in that a narrow collar appears at about the half way mark.

The bulb pot shown in Plate 141 may well represent a Miles Mason shape for a similar example, with a different finial, is known with the Boy in the Door design which I have just cited as a means of identifying unmarked Miles Mason forms. The example illustrated in Plate 141 however bears bat-printed figure designs not as yet known on marked Mason objects.

Mr. Reginald Haggar has illustrated in the Journal of the *Northern Ceramic Society* (vol.3, 1978/9, plate 6), a further D-shaped bulb pot as 'attributed to Miles Mason'. This example was examined by me when it was sold at Christie's in June 1975, but in body, glaze and in the style of decoration I did not accept this unmarked example — with its view of the City of Edinburgh — as being of Mason's manufacture, although it is extremely likely that the factory produced some of these then fashionable objects.

Other popular items of the period include baskets, cachepots or jardinières, candlesticks, ice pails, ink pots, ink stands, pen trays, and the like. Keep a weather-eye open!

Chapter Four

The Introduction of Ironstone-type Earthenwares

THE IRONSTONE-TYPE earthenwares came very close to emulating the earlier rather heavily potted Chinese porcelain dinner wares, one type of Chinese ware was even described as 'Nankin Stone China' in the eighteenth century, and it is appropriate that the introduction of this body should be linked with the son of our former London dealer in Chinese porcelains. Later, as the new ceramic was taken up by nearly every English potter these gay, durable and reasonably priced wares furnished the world.

Miles Mason's third son, Charles James Mason, took out his famous patent for 'Ironstone China' in 1813 (see page 104). He was, however, by no means the first to introduce a durable earthenware body able to compete in price, as well as in quality, with the imported and highly fashionable Chinese ware.

The first of these special bodies often bears the mark 'Turner's Patent'. This compact body was patented in the names of William and John Turner in January 1800. Part of the specification reads:

> A new method or methods of manufacturing porcelain and earthenware, by the introduction of a material not heretofore used in the manufacturing of those articles. The material is known in Staffordshire by the names 'Tabberner's Mine Rock'; 'Little Mine Rock'; 'Mine Rock' or 'New Rock'. It is generally used as follows — ground, washed and dried, mixed with certain proportions of growan or Cornish stone, previously calcined, levigated and dried, a small quantity of flint similarly prepared is also added, but in different proportions according to the nature of the ware...

Ware made under this patent bears the written mark 'Turner's Patent' and normally displays decoration in Chinese taste, although some rare and fine specimens depict English views (see Plates 350 and 351). Dessert services were a feature, but all examples are comparatively rare, partly because the Turner brothers became bankrupt in July 1806. S. Shaw, writing in 1829 (*History of the Staffordshire Potteries*), suggests that the rights were sold to Josiah Spode, probably some months before the bankruptcy was announced.

Spode, of Stoke-on-Trent, certainly produced a similar heavy durable earthenware body, but the date of its introduction is in doubt. Leonard Whiter, in his excellent book on Spode ware, suggests that the Spode stone china body was not introduced until 1813 or 1814, to compete with the newly patented Mason Ironstone china. Spode called his ware 'Stone China' to emphasise its strength; a later variation was known as 'New Stone'. The Spode ware is of the finest quality, neatly potted, thinly turned and, in general, well produced. Again, the painted or printed designs show strong Chinese influence, occasioned by the popular Chinese export porcelain they were imitating. Fine large dinner and dessert services were made, as well as a host of other articles (see Plates 339-346). Further information on the Spode products is given in Chapter Seven.

Plate 142. Representative pieces from an early Mason's Patent Ironstone China dessert service of the 1813-18 period showing typical forms. Impressed name mark. Centre piece 14¼ ins. long. Godden of Worthing Ltd.

Davenport, of Longport in Staffordshire, produced 'Stone China' early in the nineteenth century which often rivals the Spode examples in quality and design. Both Spode and Davenport included their names in their 'Stone China' marks. Typical marked examples are illustrated in Plates 309-312. But other firms produced comparable decorative Japan-style designs on 'Stone China', 'Semi Porcelain', 'Opaque China' and similarly titled bodies, without including their own names.

The identity of many of these makers will probably never be known, but one of the leading manufacturers was undoubtedly Hicks & Meigh of Shelton, in the Staffordshire Potteries. Their working period was from 1806-22, when they were succeeded by Hicks, Meigh & Johnson, 1822-35. Blue-printed marks, incorporating the words 'Stone China' with the Royal Arms or a crown, were extensively used, and fine dinner and other services were produced.

The marks and basic details of many Stone China and Ironstone-type pottery manufacturers are given in Chapter Seven.

The popularity of this durable, gaily decorated, Stone China-type ware cannot be denied. While the 'landed gentry' probably preferred the more expensive porcelain services, there was a vast middle-class market for the less expensive but more utilitarian Stone China ware.

It was this market which Charles James Mason sought to expand and satisfy when he introduced his 'Patent Ironstone China' in 1813.

The choice of name was a masterly stroke that did much to popularise his new ware and outsell his existing rivals. Each word has meaning: 'Patent' suggesting a new, unique discovery; 'Ironstone' suggesting great strength and durability; 'China' suggesting a delicate ware capable of gracing any table or home and, although this 'Ironstone China' is normally regarded as earthenware today, some thinly potted pieces do in fact show a slight translucency. The lasting qualities of 'Ironstone China' are attested to by the fact that it would be difficult to find an adult in the civilised world who has not heard the term 'Ironstone', first put into the ceramic vocabulary by Charles James Mason in July 1813. The abstract of the patent reads:

> A process for the improvement of the manufacture of English porcelain, this consists of using the scoria or slag of Ironstone pounded and ground in water with certain proportions, with flint, Cornwall stone and clay, and blue oxide of cobalt.

The details are given more fully in the full patent specification, after the usual written preliminaries:

> . . . The Ironstone which contains a proportion ot argil and silex is first roasted in a common biscuit kiln to facilitate its trituration, and to expel sulphur and other volatile ingredients which it may contain. A large earthen crucible is constructed after the exact model of an iron forge, a part of the bottom of which is filled with charcoal or coaks [sic]; these, having been previously strewed with ore and about one third part of lime, are raised to an intense heat by a strong blast of air introduced under the coaks at the bottom.
>
> By this heat ore is fused, and the fluid iron drops through the fuel to the bottom, then follows the scoria, which floats upon the top of the fluid iron. This latter scoria, or as the workmen call it slag, is the material used in the manufacture of china, and is much impregnated with iron, and of a compact and dense structure. The slag is next let off by a hole through the forge into a clean earthen vessel, where it cools. . . The scoria is next pounded into small pieces and ground in water to the consistence of a fine paste at the flint mills of the country. This paste is next evaporated to dryness on a slip kiln well known amongst potters. Thus evaporated to dryness, it is used with the other ingredients to the following proportions, viz.:

	Cwts.	Qr.	Lbs.
Prepared Iron Stone	3	-	-
Ground Flint	4	-	-
Ground Cornwall Stone	4	-	-
Cornwall Clay	4	-	-
Blue Oxide of Cobalt	-	-	1

> These, having been mixed together with water by the slip maker, are again evaporated in the slip kiln to the proper consistency for use. . .

Several authorities have stated that the materials mentioned in the patent would not, on their own, make a workable ceramic body, and that the patent specification was a misleading front. Be this as it may, from 1813 the brothers George and Charles James Mason produced a durable, heavy earthenware bearing the trade name 'Patent Ironstone China', with or without the Mason name preceding the new descriptive title.

In view of the controversy over the workable qualities of Mason's patent specification, I asked the Director of the Ceramic Testing Laboratory at the North Staffordshire College of Technology at Stoke to analyse an early impressed marked 'Mason's Patent Ironstone China' plate. The result was:

	%
Silica (SiO_2)	76.00
Alumina (Al_2O_3)	18.87
Potash (K_2O)	1.77
Lime (CaO)	1.31
Soda (Na_2O)	.75
Ferric Oxide (Fe_2O_3)	.41
Titanic Oxide (TiO_2)	.40
Magnesia (MgO)	.25
Loss (Calcined at 950°C)	.44

As a comparison, I also sent a marked example of Ridgway's 'Stone China' of about 1820. The resulting analysis read:

	%
Silica (SiO_2)	72.71
Alumina (Al_2O_3)	21.48
Potash (K_2O)	2.02
Lime (CaO)	1.15
Soda (Na_2O)	1.08
Ferric Oxide (Fe_2O_3)	.43
Titanic Oxide (TiO_2)	.40
Magnesia (MgO)	.20
Loss (Calcined at 950°C)	.35

The Director of the Ceramic Testing Laboratory (Dr. W.L. German, D.Sc., M.Sc., Ph.D., F.R.I.C., F.I.Ceram.) comments that the small amount of iron (ferric oxide (Fe_2O_3)) found in the marked Mason sample indicated that the body was not prepared in accordance with the published patent specification.

The patent of 1813 was granted for an initial period of fourteen years, taking the coverage up to 1827. It was not then renewed, probably as very similar bodies were in general use. William Evans, in his *Art and History of the Pottery Business* (1846) published several recipes for Ironstone bodies.

One of these was:

350lbs. Cornwall stone.	300lbs. Cornwall clay.
160lbs. Blue clay.	60lbs. Flints, 14oz. Blue calx.
Fritt for Ironstone body:	
90lbs. Cornwall stone.	20lbs. Salts of soda.
Glaze:	
33lbs. of above fritt.	33lbs. Cornwall stone, 35lbs. whiting, 80lbs. white lead.

Here there is no mention of Ironstone, but in another part of the book Evans states: ''The Ironstone china is formed by introducing ground clay from the smelting furnace in the proportion of 28 (parts) for 72 (parts) of No.3 or 8 (other recipes listed) carefully blunging (mixing) the fluids together.''

Whilst writing of Ironstone it is interesting to note that the term had at least one other meaning. Under the date Saturday 14th May, 1796 the knowledgeable Charles Hatchett, noted in his diary:

To the east of the Town are some rocks on the shore which on their upper strata consist of a schorl intimately mixed with quartz forming what in Cornwall is called Iron Stone...

Mason's new Patent Ironstone body quickly became very popular (perhaps because of its claimed cheapness rather than for its durability), as is shown by a letter preserved in the Wedgwood archives. The note is dated 19th March, 1814, and is additionally interesting because it shows that Spode 'Stone China' was also popular and was linked with the new Mason Patent Ironstone china:

> Every one enquires for the Stone china, made by Spode and Mason and it has a very great run. I presume you know what it is — it is a thick coarse china body, not transparent, with china patterns...

The original makers of Mason's Patent Ironstone China were the brothers Charles James Mason and George Miles Mason. Charles, the youngest son of Miles and Ruth Mason (see page 17) was born in London on 14th July, 1791. Little is known of his early life; but he must have assisted his father and elder brother in the potting business, for when only twenty-one he took out the all-important patent for 'Ironstone China'. It is open to some doubt whether he alone invented the body. It is more probable that it was the result of experiments carried out by Miles Mason and his sons over several years. Nevertheless, the patent was in Charles James Mason's name. A month before the patent, Miles Mason had formally transferred the business to his two sons, George Miles and Charles James, who traded as G. & C. Mason.

George Mason, Miles' second son, was born on 9th May, 1789. Besides being an Oxford graduate, and a man of cultivated taste, he was to be a prominent figure at Stoke, being responsible in part for establishing both a mail coach through the Potteries as well as a police force, and introducing several other improvements — listed by Reginald G. Haggar in his excellent book *The Masons of Lane Delph*.

From 1813-26, George and Charles traded in partnership — George looking after the administrative side of the large, thriving concern. After retiring from active participation, George remained in the district and may even have retained a financial stake in the pottery, for Charles James Mason's bankruptcy in February 1848 seems to have affected George's resources — a fact that would, however, be explained if George had stood security for his brother on the factory premises or on any loans. George Miles Mason died on 31st August, 1859.

Apart from Miles Mason's two sons, Charles James Mason and George Miles Mason, who succeeded their father and won fame with their newly invented 'Patent Ironstone China', there was a third son — the eldest — named William. Little is known about William, but at one period he had his own factory and a retail shop in Manchester. He was born on 27th January, 1785. On coming of age, in 1806, he seems to have joined his father, which accounts for the style M. Mason & Son, although the impressed mark remained M. Mason up to 1813. As previously stated, William Mason's name is given in rate records as the tenant of Bagnall's Minerva Works at Fenton from 1812-16. The following document offers proof that Miles Mason and William were in partnership by March 1811, and evidence that Miles Mason was the dominant partner, even though the wording "the manufactory of Mr. William Mason" is used:

In consequence of an advertisement having appeared in the last *Staffordshire Advertiser* given in that of 9th, 16th and 23rd March noticing that Thomas Appleton had procured a parcel of moulds in an improper manner from the manufactory of Mr. Josiah Spode of Stoke, pottery, and that he carried the same to the manufactory of Mr. William Mason of Lane Delph —

We, the undersigned, Miles Mason and William Mason, partners and manufacturers of chinaware do hereby declare that so far from our soliciting or obtaining in a clandestine manner from the said Mr. Spode, his patterns moulds or shapes, or those of any other persons, we should not deem ourselves worthy of the patronage of the public, if our chinaware and shapes were not equal or something superior to any manufactory in the British Dominions.

Witness our hands this 14th March, 1811.

Miles Mason, Wm. Mason.

The use of the word 'chinaware' is interesting, for the only marked pieces of William Mason's products are of earthenware. This notice could well relate to Miles Mason's china or porcelain, not directly to his son's earthenware.

The reason for the insertion of this notice is evident; but the Masons turned the affair into an opportunity to advertise their own products. The same incident reveals the name of one of Mason's workmen, for the following statement was also published, together with one from Thomas Appleton, who was the person accused of stealing the moulds:

...and I the undersigned Daniel Goostry, a workman of the said Messrs. Masons, do here by certify, that when Mr. Wm. Mason observed that I was going to make use of the moulds alluded to, he requested that they might not be used in his Manufactory.

David Goostry.

On Miles Mason's death, in 1822, William Mason took a pottery belonging to John Smith (and formerly worked by James Hancock) at Fenton Culvert. His name is given in rate records of 1823, but the record dated 29th May, 1824 is marked "Wm. Mason to Thomas Roden & Co", indicating that William Mason had lately given up the works.

William Mason's short-lived factory at Fenton Culvert seems to have produced earthenware, but only a very few marked specimens are at present known; all are printed in underglaze blue. One of these is a fine platter, 20ins. long, from a dinner service decorated with an underglaze blue landscape within an ornate wide floral and scenic panelled border. This specimen from the late Alfred Meigh's collection is reproduced in Plate 389 of my *Illustrated Encyclopaedia of British Pottery and Porcelain*. Other examples are shown in Reginald Haggar's and Elizabeth Adams' book.

William Mason also had a retail establishment at Smithy Door, Manchester, where Wedgwood supplied creamware to him in January 1815, the order for which is still preserved. Later in 1815, he was unable to pay Wedgwood, and his father, Miles, came to his aid, but in November 1828 three meetings were held for the 'Creditors of William Mason of Lane Delph' after which he moved to London where he acted as an auctioneer.

The duration of his father's porcelain manufacture in Staffordshire falls within the period c.1802 to c.1813. This period could have been extended into the 1820s, as Charles and George continued the works using the original title Miles Mason (& Sons). But it is likely that the manufacture of porcelain and earthenware (sometimes marketed under the name 'semi-china') was carried on in a very reduced scale after 1813, when the patent for the newly introduced 'Ironstone China' was taken out (see page 104). The success of this durable and relatively inexpensive body, over which they had sole patent rights, would quickly have taken over the productive capacity of the factory and caused the manufacture of competitive porcelain to be all but abandoned.

Miles Mason seems to have retired from active participation in the manufacturing of ceramics in 1813, leaving the business to his sons, who henceforth concentrated on the production of the new durable Ironstone body. Miles Mason died on 26th April, 1822.

Whereas sale catalogues of household goods sold in the pre-1810 era include a good proportion of Chinese export porcelain, especially in dinner services, by the late 1820s Ironstone ware had taken its place. In a sale held in January 1827, Christie's sold:

> A dinner service of blue and white Iron-stone china, with gilt edges, consisting of two soup tureens, covers and dishes, six sauce ditto and stands, four vegetable dishes and covers, a salad bowl, nineteen dishes in sizes, two fish plates, 60 table plates, 18 soup and 48 pie plates. [Sold for £12 12s.]

> A dessert service of Iron-stone china, in imitation of Oriental burnt-in, consisting of centre piece, two cream bowls and stands, 12 dishes and 24 plates. [Sold for £2 12s. 6d.]

Perhaps such a service was similar to the samples shown in Colour Plate 5.

In May 1827, the contents of Clarence Lodge, Roehampton, were sold and contained:

> A dinner service of Iron-stone china, in imitation of Japan, consisting of 2 tureens, covers and stands, 2 vegetable dishes, 7 corner dishes, 6 covers, 3 sauce tureens and stands, 22 dishes in sizes, 49 table plates, 19 soup, 18 pie and 11 cheese plates. Some pieces imperfect. [Sold for £15 5s.]

This secondhand dinner service may well have been similar in design to the articles shown in Plate 143. Note from this listing that four sizes of plates were included, meat plates, soup, pie or pudding and cheese plates.

> A pair of handsome octagonal Iron-stone jars, in imitation of Oriental burnt in. [Sold for £5. 5s.]

> A pair of smaller ditto. [Sold for £3.]

> A vase of Iron-stone china with rams heads and the companion, broken and 2 ditto bowls. [Sold for £3. 3s.]

> A pair of very handsome bottles of Iron-stone china, pencilled with gold upon mazarine blue ground, and painted with landscapes and bouquets in compartments. [Sold for £3. 10s.]

On George Miles Mason's retirement from the partnership of G. & C. Mason in 1826, Charles James Mason traded as Charles J. Mason & Co. (the & Co. perhaps relating to Samuel Bayliss Faraday, who died in 1844, as some rate records and Pigot's Directory of 1841 refer to Mason & Faraday). Charles James Mason was an enlightened master potter in days when little light was evident. He was a supporter

Colour Plate 5. *Representative pieces of an impressed marked 'Mason's Patent Ironstone China' dessert service, painted with a typical 'Old Japan' pattern. c.1815-20. Centre piece 14 ¼ ins. long.* Godden of Worthing Ltd.

Colour Plate 6. *A good quality and attractive marked 'Mason's Patent Ironstone China' vase in the Chinese style. With special 1851 Exhibition printed mark — this is perhaps one of the 'Jars with raised enamel Mandarin figures and sea-dragon handles' (see page 116). 1851. 17 ½ ins. high* Godden of Worthing Ltd.

of the new unions struggling to establish themselves against strong opposition from most pottery owners, and he saw the desirability of improving working conditions and having happy, contented workmen earning a fair wage.

Since writing the above paragraph for the first edition of this book I have been made aware of the fact that Charles Mason awoke wrath in the workers for his efforts to introduce machinery into his works. The following contemporary quotations are taken from a paper by Andrew Lamb, B.A., M.A., published in the *Journal of Ceramic History* (No.9, Stoke-on-Trent Museums, 1977). The first quotation is taken from the *Potter's Examiner and Workmen's Advocate* and obviously reflects the workmen's own point of view:

> The curse is stealing in amongst us...Mr. C.J. Mason of Fenton, is now in possession of machines for the making of flat-ware...Master potters are only waiting for one successful experiment, and the mischief is accomplished...your doom will then be sealed...[2nd November, 1844].

The union called a public meeting for 12th November, 1844, the

Plate 143. Representative pieces of a Mason's Patent Ironstone China dinner service showing typical Oriental tureen forms (see Plates 1 and 3) and a Chinese styled design — the Table and Flower-pot pattern (see page 108). c.1813-20. Godden of Worthing Ltd.

hand-bill notice of which read in part:

> Men of the potteries, a crisis has arrived...Mr. C.J. Mason of Fenton, is now in the possession of machinery for the making of all kinds of Flat Ware, which may be worked either by steam or hand power and the principles of which may be extended to the other branches. Arise and prepare for the worst...

The Union was pressed to raise funds to enable Mason's workforce to be withdrawn and paid by the Union's funds but in the event by the middle of December 1844 Mason withdrew the new machinery — which apparently was prone to producing faulty articles, and the advance of the pottery industry was stilled, at least for the time being. One will see, however, from the quotation below that the Mason factory boasted a steam engine before 1829 and this presumably assisted the workers in some of their labours.

Mason's Ironstone China was first produced at Miles Mason's former porcelain factory known as the Minerva Works at Lane Delph, Fenton on 13th June, 1813, that is, just before the Patent for the New Ironstone China was published — the brothers William, Charles James and George Miles Mason bought the Fenton Stone Works at Lane Delph, Fenton from Sampson Bagnall. This factory had earlier been let to Josiah Spode under a lease dated July 1805. The Fenton premises were depicted on several printed marks (see page 202) and are described in two contemporary accounts:

> The manufactory of Messrs. G. & C. Mason, for Patent Iron Stone China, is commodious. Here is a steam engine of some peculiarity in its construction by Holford of Hanley...The front warehouse is four stories high, is fire proof, and has the most beautiful facade of any in the district. [S. Shaw, *History of the Staffordshire Potteries,* 1829.]

and:

> The works of Charles James Mason & Co., standing obliquely to the turnpike road, and on the line of the Canal Company's Railway, present an extensive front of four stories in height, inscribed in large letters 'Patent Ironstone China Manufactory'... A Steam engine is employed here in aid of manual labour, and for the other uses of the trade. [John Ward, *History of the Borough of Stoke-upon-Trent,* 1844.]

The elevation is also depicted in the trade card reproduced here.

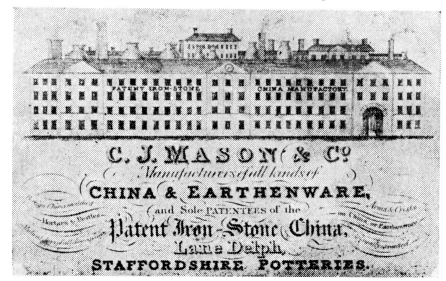

These 'Fenton Stone Works' were retained until Mason's bankruptcy in 1848, when they were taken by Samuel Boyle (1849-52) and then by E. Challinor & Co., whose successors worked them until c.1896. For many years, however, the Masons also managed Sampson Bagnall's works in Lane Delph, Fenton, just below the Minerva Works. From 1811-22, these premises were in the name of William Mason but were probably worked by his brothers, as William was then dealing in pottery at Manchester. From 1822-25, the rate records show the executors of Miles Mason as tenants. The works were then purchased by George and Charles Mason; but in the March 1827 rate records they are shown as 'void' or empty. Since the changes in the various Mason premises are rather difficult to follow they are set out at the end of this chapter.

Mr. Haggar, in his book *The Masons of Lane Delph,* tends to praise Mason's 'commercial genius' in organising auction sales of his ware throughout the country and, in "producing his famous Ironstone china in bulk for this special purpose and making the fullest use of advertisement and publicity in the press, he systematically exploited every auction mart in the country, netting in succession vast sums of money. The results of this brilliantly conceived organisation were stupendous."

This practice, however, is bad in the long term as the temptation is to include slightly faulty ware which floods the market, encouraging the buyers to obtain cheap examples and leave the more expensive perfect articles. The local auctions also destroy the trade of the retailers (the manufacturer's main and long-term link with the buying public), who are then less inclined to reorder from the manufacturer who has stolen their trade. In general, disposal of china by auction is a good expedient when one is closing a concern and has stock to clear. It is bad when the firm wishes to continue. The same policy was one of the reasons for the downfall of the Derby factory under Robert Bloor in the 1840s. It was, I believe, the main reason for Charles James Mason's downfall. I have, in fact, discovered a letter from an Oxford auctioneer which confirms my opinion:

St. Clements,
Oxford.

December 11th, 1826

...I have recently held a sale of china for the manufactory of Mason & Co., Lane Delph, it is of a very inferior quality and they have been attack'd by the Trade here since the sale and put to some expense in Penalties. They are about attempting another sale in Oxford, but I have declined officiating for them...

Wm. Wise

The Oxford Reference Librarian was able to find the original advertisement for this sale in Jackson's *Oxford Journal* of 25th November, 1826. The above letter from William Wise in which he stated that he had declined officiating for Mason should be borne in mind when one reads the rather fanciful descriptions of the auctions — in all probability supplied by the manufacturers themselves. Nevertheless, the range of articles offered is illuminating:

EXTENSIVE SALE OF CHINA
at WISE'S Room, in St. Clements,

In consequence of the dissolution of the Partnership of Messrs. GEORGE and CHARLES MASON, Proprietors of the extensive Works at Lane Delph, Staffordshire, Patentees of the IRON STONE CHINA, and late of No.11, Albemarle Street, London. Mr. WISE begs most earnestly to assure the Nobility and Gentry of Oxford and its environs, that he has been especially appointed to dispose of the whole of this truly elegant and useful STOCK by PUBLIC AUCTION; and that his Room will be opened for the view of part of this grand assemblage of China on Monday next, Nov. 27th, and on Tuesday the 28th. On WEDNESDAY, Nov. 29th, at Eleven o'clock, the Sale will commence, and continue at the same hour each following day of business, till the whole is disposed of. As it may be necessary to enumerate part of the Stock, W.W. begs to point out the great variety of Enamel and Gilt Table Sets, with the usual additions in fashionable Society of Yacht Club Finger Bowls; Ice Pails, Wine Coolers, Stilton Cheese Tubs, Custards and Covers, Celery Vases, Salts and Pickle Saucers; Dessert Services, Punch Bowls, Hydra Jugs, Egyptian Mugs, Broth Basins &c in corresponding patterns. Breakfast Services, with the addition of Honey Pots, Egg Pipkins, Tea and Coffee Sets &c; also a supply of Unmerappra Tea Extractors, which have entirely superseded the Rockingham Tea Pot. Complete Chamber Services with additional pieces, such as Foot Pails, Slop Jars &c. &c.

In matters of taste and ornament a selection will be seen peculiarly meriting attention. The Neapolitan Ewer rivals the best Work of Dresden manufactory [see Colour Plate 7]; Fish Pond Bowls, of extraordinary magnitude; Siamese Jardiniere and Plateaux, adopted by the Horticultural Society, for the culture of Bulbous Roots &c; a general and extensive variety of Jars, Beakers, Ornaments for the Cabinet and Mantel Piece, from French, Italian, Spanish, Chinese, Japanese, Berlin and Saxon Originals. The Blue Printed Table Services comprise a variety of this year's pattern. All other Earthenware in use will be found in the Stock.

Catalogues may be had, and the Property viewed, at the Room.

The Sale will commence each day at Eleven o'clock.

Packers from the Manufactory will attend, for the accommodation of Country Purchasers.

Other sales were held by individuals or firms closely connected with Mason. Samuel Faraday (later Charles Mason's partner) held many sales in his own name. The press advertisements for these sales are interesting:

Mr. Farady [sic], 190 Regent Street, has certainly collected the finest stock of china ever seen in this metropolis, and has caused the art of Potting to be carried to its highest pitch in the higher branches of that interesting manufacture. The set of fine jars of English make are the finest we ever saw, and are superior to foreign productions; we understand the models cost five hundred pounds... [John Bull, 23rd March, 1828.]

Other advertisements of the period include:

...splendid, extensive, and unique Stock of Porcelain and ...comprising, richly gilt table [dinner] and dessert services...a variety of earthenware table sets, gadroon and plain edges, in light and full patterns of the newest make, rivalling China in delicacy of colour and elegance of patterns... The Stock further embraces drawing room and vestibule vases, pot pouries, pastile burners, fine flower and scent jars, capacious fish globes, Italian urns, delicate diminutive specimens, etc... [The London Morning Herald, 1st April, 1828.]

Many hundred table services of modern earthenware, breakfast and tea ware, toilet and chamber sets, many hundred dozen of baking dishes, flat dishes, broth basins, soup tureens, sets of Jugs, and numerous other articles. The china is of the most elegant description, and embraces a great variety of splendid dinner services, numerous dessert services, tea, coffee, and breakfast sets of neat and elegant patterns, ornaments of every description that can be manufactured in china from the minutest article calculated to adorn pier table and cabinet, to the most noble, splendid and magnificent jars some of which are near five feet high. [*The London Morning Herald,* 21st April, 1828.]

It will be noted that these flowery advertisements mention both earthenware and porcelain (or china). The Ironstone body — an earthenware — was always described as 'china', even in the patent and in the marks.

Plate 144. An impressed marked Mason's Patent Ironstone china jug of plain 'antique' shape issued without a handle! 9¾ ins. high. Author's Collection

Many faulty specimens of Mason's Ironstone China will be found. Large tears in the body or chips (caused in the manufacture, as they are often glazed over) are relatively common and were, I believe, finished for the auction sales rather than rejected, as they should have been. The jug shown in Plate 144 represents the ultimate in this practice. The handle has completely come away from the body but the resulting scars have been glazed and painted over, resulting in a handleless jug being placed on the market.

For thirty-five years, from 1813-48, the Mason Works produced a vast quantity of Ironstone China, for the output was almost exclusively devoted to this ware. Some rare earthenware and stoneware moulded jugs (see Plates 240 and 241) etc., were made, but these represent less than one per cent of the total. It was almost inevitable that the market became saturated. The novelty had worn off. Vast amounts were on the market, and to some extent, by the late 1840s, the traditional Chinese-style designs were outmoded. It is also probable that the Ironstone proved too durable, reducing the demand for replacements or new services.

In view of this, it is not surprising that Charles James Mason was declared bankrupt in February 1848. The factories and private possessions were offered for sale by auction, the following notices appearing in *The Staffordshire Advertiser* in March 1848:

FENTON
PATENT IRONSTONE CHINA MANUFACTORY

—

MR. HIGGINBOTTOM
WILL SELL BY AUCTION
AT THE PATENT IRONSTONE CHINA MANUFACTORY
FENTON
THE ENTIRE OF THE FIXTURES, UTENSILS,
MATERIALS, STOCK, & BELONGING TO THE
ESTATE OF MR. C.J. MASON, ON MONDAY
[to] FRIDAY, APRIL 3rd, 4th, 5th, 6th & 7th, 1848.

A further premises was also offered:

FENTON MANUFACTORY,
TERRACE BUILDINGS

—

MR. HIGGINBOTTOM
WILL SELL BY AUCTION,
AT THE MANUFACTORY, TERRACE BUILDINGS,
FENTON
THE ENTIRE OF THE FIXTURES, UTENSILS,
MATERIALS, STOCK, ETC. BELONGING TO THE
ESTATE OF MR. C.J. MASON ON APRIL 10th,
11th, and 12th, 1848.

Further details of the factories' contents are given in other sale notices, headed:

The patent Ironstone Manufactory, Fenton and the Patent Ironstone China Manufactory, Terrace Buildings, also at Fenton...the entire of the Fixtures, Utensils, Moulds, Green [unfired] Biscuit [once fired but unglazed] and Glossed [glazed] Stock, Materials, etc., a complete Patent Printing Machine by Pott, with 17 Engraved Rollers, and all necessary appliances for immediate work.

Also, at the Ironstone China Manufactory, Terrace Buildings, Fenton, the whole belonging to the estate of Mr. C.J. Mason...

Apart from the factories, stock, unfinished goods, and all fittings, Charles James Mason's personal effects at Heron Cottage, Fenton, were offered by the assignee to the estate:

...The whole of the rich and modern dining room and breakfast room furniture, in rosewood, mahogany, and other woods, gilded cornices, draperies, magnificent pier glasses, elegant French clock in tortoishell [*sic*] and buhl; richly carved mahogany 4 post bedsteads, in chintz, damask, and morsen; hair mattresses, prime goose feather beds, mahogany wardrobes and chests of

drawers, splendidly bound books, superb collection of paintings by Michant, Hutenberg, Burney, Parnell, Robarts, Nasmyth, Hill, Richards, etc; scarce and rare prints, Oriental jars and vases, patent ironstone gilded china, table [dinner], dessert, toilette, and tea services, rich cut glasses, cellar of wines, chariot, britzha, phaeton, gig, pair and single harness, cutting and kibbling mill, patent hand corn mill, and all other effects in and out of doors...

Charles James Mason, however, survived the bankruptcy. Perhaps his brother George came to the rescue, for in the Great Exhibition of 1851 "Charles Mason, (of) Longton, Staffordshire — Designer, Manufacturer, and Patentee" exhibited the following "specimens of Patent ironstone china":

Garden Seats of mixed Anglo-Indian and Japanese pattern, representing an old dragon, in raised enamel on a gold ground.
[The description 'Indian' or 'Anglo-Indian' relates to Chinese based designs, the term 'Indian' being widely used in the eighteenth and nineteenth centuries for articles of Chinese origin.]

Garden seats of an Anglo-Chinese pattern, on a sea-green ground, with raised solid flowers and gilt panels.

Fish Pond bowls of Anglo-Chinese pattern; Gog and Magog, an Anglo-Indian pattern; The Water Lily, an Anglo-Japanese pattern.

Jars with raised enamel Mandarin figures and sea-dragon handles. Large jars and covers of Anglo-Indian pattern. There are also some open jars. Jars covered; dragon handles of Anglo-Indian and Anglo-Japanese patterns, with raised solid flowers, etc.

Specimens of plates in the Oriental style of pattern, on registered shapes, and Anglo-Japanese. Three jars and covers, with Anglo-Indian grounds. A Plate, a dish, a tureen, a covered dish, a tall coffee cup and saucer, and a sugar-basin,

116

made of the white patent ironstone china, as used in the hotels of the United States of America.

Jugs of old Indian, Japanese and gold patterns of the original shape; also Anglo-Indian and melon pattern; with Oriental figures and gold ornaments.

Ewer and basin, and mouth ewer and basin, with Oriental figures, and a rose border.

Jars: the old Indian crackle, with India red grounds. A breakfast cup and saucer.

A monumental tablet, made of Ironstone, and lettered under the glaze. Jugs, showing various patterns in Bandanna ware. Toilet ewers and basins. Antique jugs of Japanese pattern and gold ornaments. Red and gold paint jars. Zigzag beakers, on bronze. Table ware of a Japanese pattern in blue, red and gold.

It is not clear whether these 1851 exhibits were new productions or old ware rescued from the bankruptcy or 'bought in' at the sales. The Staffordshire rate records of 1849 list Charles Mason at Mill Street, Lane End. He is not listed in 1850, but in 1851 he appears at Daisy Bank, Lane End. Longton and Lane End are to all intents and purposes one, so the latter address agrees with that given in the catalogue of the 1851 Exhibition.

The list of objects shown at the 1851 Exhibition is interesting and indicates the types of ware made by Charles Mason in the late 1840s. The reference to registered shapes — ''Specimens of plates in the Oriental style of pattern on registered shapes'' — relates to a form registered at the Patent Office in Mason's name on 16th April, 1849, after the bankruptcy. Two plates of this form, with the printed Mason trade mark as well as the official registration mark, are reproduced in Plates 145 and 146. It is also interesting to read of the inclusion of ''white patent Ironstone China, as used in the hotels of the United

Plate 146. A Mason's Ironstone plate or dish of the same 1849 registered form as Plate 145 showing the continuation of Oriental-styled designs at this late period. c.1849-51. Diameter 10¼ ins. Geoffrey Godden, Chinaman

States of America''. On the evidence of the fine vase or jar ''with raised enamel mandarin figures and sea-dragon handles'', shown in Colour Plate 6, the Mason exhibits at the 1851 Exhibition bear the printed inscription, in script letters: 'Exhibition 1851', also the standard mark, the angular crown, which also occurs on the plate form registered in 1849 (see Plates 146 and 147); these late marks are reproduced on page 201.

The Potts 'Patent Printing Machine' with '17 engraved rollers' and 'the immense stock of copper plate engravings. . .' were offered for sale in the April 1848 auction sales. They were of vital importance, enabling other manufacturers to match Mason's services and other ware and to reproduce his most successful patterns.

The majority of these former Mason moulds, engraved copper plate designs, etc., were apparently purchased by Francis Morley of High Street, Shelton. The name MORLEY was added below Mason's former standard crown mark on ware made to Mason's designs. Francis Morley was an experienced potter, first in partnership as Ridgway, Morley, Wear & Co. (Ridgway & Morley c.1842-45). From 1845-58 he traded under his own name, '& Co.' being added on most marks to cover his partner, Samuel Asbury.

The next partnership, that between Francis Morley and Taylor Ashworth, during the 1858-62 period, is most important as it explains how the firm of G.L. Ashworth & Bros. Ltd. (recently retitled 'Mason's Ironstone China Ltd.') acquired the original Mason shapes and patterns. In 1862 Francis Morley retired, passing to Ashworth (with his father George L. Ashworth) the valuable Mason copper plates and trade marks which were used to great advantage by Ashworths over a long period from 1862 until 1968.

George L. Ashworth was trading under his own name from at least May 1862. Although he used the Mason printed trade mark on Ironstone ware, he also produced a wide range of earthenware which was plainly marked with his own name or initials — 'A. Bros' or 'G.L.A. & Bros' — or with the Ashworth name (see page 208). Some, but not all, 'Mason' printed marked Ashworth ware also bore Ashworth's name impressed.

The Ashworth reissues of Mason's original shapes and decorative patterns are often difficult to distinguish from the originals, especially now that some reissues are themselves antique. In general the body is not quite as compact or heavy as the original, although it is whiter — a floury white rather than a creamy tint. The underglaze blue parts of the design are normally lighter in tint than the dark blue original. Impressed numerals indicate a late nineteenth or twentieth century date and, in fact, they give the month number and the last two digits of the year in which the piece was manufactured, e.g. 7.06 for July 1906; but this practice has now been discontinued.

I have written of Ashworth's reissues but many of their designs were new ones, reflecting the traditional Chinese style designs without being slavish copies. Much Ashworth Ironstone is now antique in its own right and should be seriously studied by the collector. Many examples are highly decorative and of very good quality. Furthermore they can

Plate 147. A colourful Ashworth 'Ironstone China' plate of pattern 8689. Printed Royal Arms mark with impressed Ashworth name mark. c.1862-75. A.M. Cuthbert Collection

be quite inexpensive — the plate shown in Plate 147 was purchased by me in 1978 for less than a brand new Mason example would cost!

For over a hundred years, George L. Ashworth & Bros. Ltd. were selling, in both home and export markets, vast quantities of their Mason's-type ware decorated with traditional Oriental-styled patterns. The tradition continues. Mason's number one pattern, the Grass-hopper design — now called 'Regency' or 'Regency Ducks' — is still proudly displayed in most china shops and stores, and there can be few homes in the British Isles that cannot boast a specimen of 'Mason's Ironstone'. Indeed, two leading collectors of antique Mason owe their interest to the happy purchase of a modern Mason dinner service which took their fancy! In 1968, the firm of G.L. Ashworth & Bros. Ltd., took the new title 'Mason's Ironstone China Ltd.' — so the wheel has turned full circle.

Most press notices advertising the introduction of a new product tend to overstate the virtues of the article. That inserted in *The Times* in December 1813 can be regarded as an understatement:

Patent Ironstone-China

The great importance of this article is well worth the attention of the nobility, gentry and the Public, the durability of the composition is beyond any other yet produced, and not being so liable to chip or break, which, together with its being much lower in price than any other china, it is presumed will prove a recommendation for its general utility...

The original advertiser could have had no idea that retailers 160 or

Colour Plate 7. A superbly modelled 'Mason's Patent Ironstone China' vase or ewer after an 'antique' so favoured by Mason. Vases of this type occur decorated in various styles, see Plate 250 and page 113. c.1820-25. 28ins. high. Godden of Worthing Ltd.

more years later would be enjoying regular sales of the same designs, or that the objects of 'general utility' then offered would today grace the cabinets of collectors and be the subject of several illustrated reference books.

Mason factories and subsequent owners

Italics are used to indicate that a factory owner (or owners) was a member of the Mason family

VICTORIA POTTERY
LANE DELPH, FENTON

c.1800	*Miles Mason & George Wolfe*
c.1800-06	*Mason & Co.*
c.1806-43	Samuel Ginder & Co.
c.1844-45	Samuel & Henry Ginder
c.1847-57	James Floyd
c.1860	Wathen & Hudden
c.1862-64	Wathen & Lichfield
c.1864-69	James Bateman Wathen
c.1870-1948	James Reeves

MINERVA WORKS
LANE DELPH, FENTON

c.1800-05	John Lucock
c.1806-16	*Miles Mason*
c.1818-26	Felix Pratt & Co.
c.1826-34	Pratt, Hassall & Gerrard
c.1834-47	Green & Richards
c.1848-59	Thomas Green (died 1859)
c.1860-75	Mary Green & Co.
c.1876-90	T.A. & S. Green
c.1891 to present day	Crown Staffordshire Porcelain Co. Ltd.

SAMPSON BAGNALL'S WORKS
at angle of the road below
MINERVA WORKS

c.1811-22	*William Mason* (works probably run by George and Charles Mason while William was dealing in china, see page 107).
c.1822-25	*Miles Mason* (executors of)
c.1825-26	*George & Charles Mason*
c.1827	Void (or empty according to rate records; works may have been dismantled and combined with the Fenton Stone Works).

FENTON STONE WORKS
PATENT IRONSTONE MANUFACTORY
HIGH STREET
LANE DELPH, FENTON

c.1780-1805	Sampson Bagnall
c.1805-15	Josiah Spode
c.1815-29	*George & Charles Mason*
c.1829-39	*Charles James Mason*
c.1841-43	*Mason & Faraday* (or C.J. Mason & Co.)

c.1845-48	*Charles James Mason* (bankrupt February 1848)
c.1849-52	Samuel Boyle (& Son)
c.1853-60	E. Challinor & Co.
c.1862-91	E. & C. Challinor
c.1891-96	C. Challinor & Co.
c.1897-1932	William Baker & Co. (Ltd.)

DAISY BANK WORKS
LONGTON

c.1797-1802	Samuel Hughes
c.1803-11	Peter & Thomas Hughes
c.1812	Drury & Co.
c.1815-17	John Drury (or Drury & Co.)
c.1818-30	Thomas Drury & Son
c.1831-37	Ray & Tideswell
c.1838-46	Richard Tideswell
c.1851-53	*Charles James Mason*
c.1853-68	Hulse, Nixon & Adderley
c.1869-73	Hulse and Adderley
c.1876-85	William Alsager Adderley
c.1886-1905	William Alsager Adderley & Co.
c.1906 to recent years	Adderley's Ltd.

Chapter Five

The Mason Patent
Ironstone Wares

THIS CHAPTER, WHICH is devoted to listing objects made in Mason's Ironstone and the patterns with which they are decorated, is based not only upon many years of experience in trading in this ware but also on contemporary documents, newspaper notices and accounts.

The most important of the documents are the catalogues of two sales of Mason's stock which were held in London in 1818 and 1822. These catalogues are of the utmost importance, throwing light, as they do, on the large variety of early ware made five and nine years after the patent was granted. They are given in an edited form in the Appendix.

It should be noted that several lots of glass were included in the 1822 sale. As was the practice of the period, manufacturers and retailers often dealt in related objects — glass sellers sold china, china dealers stocked glass, papier mâché trays, etc. The glass items have been deleted to avoid confusion. The rest of the sale comprised 1,538 lots of Mason's earthenware, and of these lots 1,148 were 'bought in' having failed to reach their 'reserve' or the auctioneer's valuation — so only 390 of the 1,538 lots of earthenware offered in 1822 were sold, for a total of £1,119 1s. 6d.

The first sale was held on "Tuesday, December 15th, 1818 and the two following days...by Mr. Christie, at this Great Room, Pall Mall''. The wording on the title page of the catalogue is set out below:

A
CATALOGUE
OF
A MOST VALUABLE AND EXTENSIVE STOCK
OF
ELEGANT AND USEFUL
CHINA
SUITED FOR DOMESTIC PURPOSES
OF ENGLISH MANUFACTURE
Recently consigned from the Manufactory for actual sale, and high deserving the attention of Persons of Fashion and Private Families.
It comprises
A large assortment of complete table and dessert services, composed of a strong and serviceable material, painted in imitation of the rich Japan and other Oriental Patterns; Breakfast, tea and coffee equipages, ornamental Dejeunes and vases for flowers and essence, including about twelve of noble size, suited to fill niches or recesses in Drawing Rooms, superbly ornamented...

It will be observed that Mason's name is not mentioned, nor is 'Ironstone China' by name; but there can be no doubt that the 'strong and serviceable material, painted in imitation of the rich Japan' was Mason's Ironstone China. The inclusion of 'twelve [vases] of noble size, suited to fill niches or recesses in Drawing Rooms' confirms this, as does the description of service patterns which match existing marked specimens.

The second sale, held in June 1822, lasted fourteen days. It was held at 11 Albemarle Street, the London retail shop of George and Charles Mason, "Sole patentees, manufacturers and sellers of Patent Ironstone China", a description taken from London Directories of the 1820-24 period, and was sold by Mr. Harry Phillips, the auctioneer. The catalogue, together with many others of the same period, has been preserved by successive generations and is now published by kind permission of the present Directors of Phillips, Son & Neale, Blenstock House, Blenheim Street, London, W.1.

According to the catalogue, the sale was occasioned by the death of Miles Mason; today the sale and its catalogue description are of the greatest value to collectors, showing the objects and designs produced at the Fenton Patent Ironstone China Manufactory in or just prior to 1822. By comparing objects mentioned in the 1818 Christie catalogue with those in Phillips of 1822, one can gauge the progress made in the intervening years.

This chapter describes the objects and patterns produced in Ironstone China — first the dinner and dessert services, which are the most important products and also those most often encountered (if one includes odd dishes, plates, etc., originally forming part of such services). The remaining articles are listed in alphabetical order, with, where relevant, sample descriptions and prices from the sale catalogues of 1818 and 1822. References are also made to items auctioned by William Wise of Oxford, see Chapter Four, and to items shown in the 1851 Exhibition.

Plate 148. A blue-printed Mason's Patent Ironstone tureen and cover of a 'Blue Pheasants' pattern (see page 128). Impressed Royal Arms mark 'Patent Ironstone China' (see Plate 150a). c.1815-20. Godden of Worthing Ltd.

Plate 149. An early Mason's Patent Ironstone tureen of the 'Oriental Pheasants' design, a coloured in printed pattern on a standard Chinese-shaped tureen form. Printed marks. 10ins. high. c.1815-25. Godden of Worthing Ltd.

Plate 150. An early Mason's Patent Ironstone tureen of a standard form bearing a typical Chinese-styled landscape design. Impressed Royal Arms mark (see Plate 150a). 10ins. long. c.1815-25. Godden of Worthing Ltd.

Plate 151. An early Mason's Patent Ironstone tureen of standard form bearing a rather crudely painted so-called 'Japan' pattern. Impressed name mark. 12½ins. long. Godden of Worthing Ltd.

Plate 150a. Impressed Royal Arms mark on the tureen in Plate 150.

DINNER SERVICES

The Times advertisement of December 1813, quoted on page 119, stresses the main selling points of the newly introduced Patent Ironstone China: "...the durability of the composition is beyond any other yet produced, and not being so liable to chip or break...will prove a recommendation for its general utility..." It is not surprising, therefore, that the earliest Ironstone ware was gaily decorated dinner and dessert services. Surviving specimens prove their general durability but can perhaps be faulted, by present standards, on their thick potting and consequent heaviness. In reality, however, this apparent fault is an asset in dinner ware, for heated ironstone plates, vegetable dishes, etc., retain their heat for far longer than a modern thinly-potted plate — a fact that can readily be proved by an experiment.

In December 1814, Chamberlains — the Worcester porcelain manufacturers — purchased from 'G. & C. Mason, Lane Delph', a dinner service of Patent Ironstone China, pattern 'Birds & flowers'. This purchase is listed in the Chamberlain *Wholesale & Retail Journal*

Plate 152. A rare Mason's Patent Ironstone two-division vegetable dish and cover. Impressed name mark. 11ins. long. c.1815-25. Godden of Worthing Ltd.

125

covering the period 1811-16. The entry is most fortunate as it sets out the individual components of the service, with their prices:

2	Tureens (with covers) & Stands	@ 11/-	£1.	2.0.
4	Sauce tureens & Stands	4/-		16.8.
4	Square covered (vegetable) dishes	5/-	£1.	0.0.
1	Salad bowl	5/6		5.6.
1	20-inch Gravy (dish with well)			13.0.
1	20-inch dish			10.6.
2	18-inch dishes	7/6		15.0.
1	(pierced) Drainer to 18-inch dish			7.6.
2	16-inch dishes	4/6		9.0.
1	(pierced) Drainer to 16-inch dish			4.8.
2	14-inch dishes	3/6		7.0.
4	12-inch dishes	2/-		8.0.
4	10-inch dishes	1/3		5.0.
1	12-inch Baker (deep oval baking dish)			2.8.
1	10-inch Baker (deep oval baking dish)			1.4.
60	Table (dinner) plates	6½		13.0.
24	Twifflers (middle size plates)	5½		11.0.
24	6-inch plates	5		10.0.

Plate 153. An early Mason's Patent Ironstone tureen of pattern number 1 'India Grasshopper' design (see page 128). Printed Ironstone China Warranted mark. 10ins. high. c.1813-20. Godden of Worthing Ltd.

Plate 154. A blue-printed Mason's Ironstone soup plate of willow pattern type, perhaps the Blue 'Chinese landscape' of the 1818 sale catalogue. Printed crowned name mark. Diameter 9½ ins. c.1813-25. Godden of Worthing Ltd.

The sale held by Mr. Christie in December 1818 contained several 'table' or dinner services. Lot 5 describes the contents of a typical service:

One table service, India pheasant pattern; viz. 2 soup tureens covers and stands, 4 sauce ditto, 4 square vegetable dishes, 1 salad ditto, 1 fish ditto, 18 dishes in sizes, 72 table plates, 24 ditto soup and 24 pie ditto [150 separate pieces].

The pattern 'India pheasant' is a typical Anglo-Chinese Mason design and is probably the same as the 'Birds and flowers' sold to Chamberlain in 1814 (see Plates 148 and 156 for patterns of this type).

Plate 155. *A large Mason's Ironstone meat platter from a dinner service. Rather poorly painted in a typical mock-Chinese style. Such platters were made in graduating sizes — from about 9ins. to nearly 24ins. long. Impressed mark. c.1820-30.* Marshall Field & Co., Chicago

Plate 156. *A Mason's Ironstone hexagonal tureen and cover bearing the blue-printed 'Blue Pheasants' pattern. Printed mark. 7ins. high. c.1820-25.* Victoria and Albert Museum (Crown Copyright)

The basic composition of the 1818 service is much the same as that of the 1814 Chamberlain set. The 'fish ditto' (dish) is the same article as the 'drainer' in the Chamberlain set. It is an oval, flat, pierced dish which fits into one of the several large dishes or platters, the surplus liquids draining through the dish below. The typical sizes of the '18 dishes in sizes' are given in the Chamberlain list. These are 20, 18, 16, 14, 12 and 10 inches in length. The number of plates in a dinner service could be adjusted to the customer's requirements, but there are always very many more dinner plates than soup plates — in a ratio of about three to one.

The 1818 Christie sale included dinner services in the following patterns, all with the same composition as that listed above:

Chinese landscape pattern (Plate 154)
Blue and gold border

Plate 157. *Representative pieces from a Mason's Ironstone dinner service painted with gay but originally inexpensive broadly painted 'Japan' designs. c.1825-35.* Mason's Works Collection

Plate 158. An impressed marked Mason's Ironstone six-sided vegetable dish and cover bearing a typical rather broadly painted 'Japan' pattern. Impressed name mark. Diameter 11½ ins. c.1820-25. Godden of Worthing Ltd.

Plate 159, right. A good quality blue-printed Mason's plate in the 'Cambrian Argil' body. Impressed 'Mason's Cambrian Argil' mark. Diameter 9¾ ins. c.1820-25. Victoria and Albert Museum (Crown Copyright)

Table and flowerpot pattern (Plates 143, 164, 181 and 194)
India grasshopper pattern* (Plate 153)
Pagoda pattern in mazarine, red and gold
Mogul pattern (Colour Plate 9, Plates 206 and 260)
Basket Japan
India gold.jar
India water melon
Richly coloured figure pattern
Blue pheasants
Blue Chinese landscape
Rose and rock pattern a la Chinoise
Old Japan pattern in green, pink, mazarine, red and richly gilt
Richly Japanned in red, blue green and gold (similar to Plate 150)

All of these patterns owe their origin to eighteenth century Chinese export porcelain — the type that Miles Mason originally dealt in at London before he started manufacturing porcelain (see Chapter One). The 'Blue Chinese landscape' design is perhaps the old 'Pagoda' design printed in underglaze blue (Plate 154). The 'Blue Pheasants' was also produced by means of an underglaze blue print, sometimes with added gilt borders, gilt handles, etc., and sometimes in the less expensive plain version. Most Mason patterns were 'richly Japanned in red, blue, green and gold', with bold areas of red, and a rich, dark, underglaze mazarine blue. Some of these typical and traditional designs were based on a printed outline which was filled in by semi-skilled painters, so reducing the cost of the finished article.

A table service, Chinese figures, gold edge   R.£18.0.0
A table service, very richly Japanned; hexagonal tureens, gold burnished tops   R.£26.0.0

Several others similar to those in the 1818 sale, decorated with 'rich old Japan pattern' (with reserves of about £25), were also included in the 1822 sale.

*This pattern (see Plate 153) is still produced, but under the name 'Regency' or 'Regency Ducks'.

The normal soup tureen and sauce tureen shapes are based on Chinese export market prototypes, being of elongated octagonal form (see Plates 143, 148-151, 153). This form is repeated in the dishes of various sizes (Plate 155), often but not always with the plates of regular octagonal form.

A second basic dinner service design has hexagonal tureens (see Plates 156 and 157). Some sets listed in the 1822 catalogue are described as 'hexagon shape' and oval tureens are very occasionally found (see Plates 164 and 165). The other sets and those in the 1818 sale, must be presumed to be of the standard octagonal forms. Tureen shapes as Plates 168-171 are later in period.

In the 1822 sale dinner services were also included. The 'R' prices are the reserves as marked in the original catalogue:

A Table service, white (142 pieces)	R.£6. 6.0
A Dinner service, dragon pattern, 142 pieces as per label on tureen	R.£9. 9.0 Unsold at £7.10.0
A Dinner service, in 142 pieces	R.£12.12.0
A Dinner service, gilt and ornamented with flowers, 142 pieces	R.£21. 0.0
A Dinner service, rich Japan pattern, sumptuously gilt	R.£35. 0.0
A Table service, gilt Japan	R.£26. 0.0
A ditto, common Japan	R.£14. 0.0
A Dinner service, hexagon shape, blue birds and flowers (Plate 156)	£11.11.0
A Dinner service, Dresden sprig	R.£26. 5.0
A Dinner service, peacock and flowers, 142 pieces	R.£14.14.0

Plate 160. A very good quality Mason's Ironstone plate with attractive gilt panels on a dark blue ground (see also Plate 298). Impressed name mark. Diameter 8¾ ins. c.1830. Geoffrey Godden, Chinaman

Plate 161. A very poorly painted Mason's Ironstone side, or cheese, plate from a dinner service. Impressed name mark. Diameter 6ins., c.1830-40. Geoffrey Godden, Chinaman

A handsome Table service, rich India devices, hexagon tureens	R.£21. 0.0
A table service, green flowers, only 1 tureen	R.£13.13.0
A dinner service, nosegay pattern	R.£12. 0.0
A table service, Chinese characters on mazarine ground	R.£40. 0.0
A blue table service, Willow (Plate 154)	R.£9. 4.6
A very rich coloured and gilt table service, 142 pieces	R.£35. 0.0
	Unsold at £31.10.0
A Dinner service, Tourney Sprig	R.£11.11.0
A Dinner service, hexagon shape, grasshopper pattern	R.£15. 0.0

Plate 162. Mason's Ironstone plate painted with an unusual divided design in the normal colours. Impressed name mark. c.1815-25. Mr. and Mrs. A.E. Grove Collection

Plate 163. A Mason's Ironstone oval meat platter from a dinner service painted with a rare pattern. Printed crowned name mark. 11ins. by 8½ins. c.1830-40. Geoffrey Godden, Chinaman

Plate 164. A rare oval-shaped Mason's Ironstone covered tureen painted with a good quality Oriental-styled design. Printed and impressed name marks. 13½ ins. long. c.1815-25. Godden of Worthing Ltd.

Plate 165. A rare and good quality Mason's Ironstone tureen, cover and stand, richly decorated in underglaze blue, overglaze red and green enamel with gold enrichments. Impressed name mark. 6½ ins. high. c.1820-25. Godden of Worthing Ltd.

Plate 166. A blue-printed Mason's Ironstone salad bowl with willow pattern type design. The basic form was taken from a Chinese export market shape. Printed crowned name mark. c.1825-35. Godden of Worthing Ltd.

Plate 167. A rare Mason's Ironstone sauce boat decorated with a good quality Chinese-styled pattern, number 2023. Printed crowned name mark. 6¾ ins. long. c.1830-40. Geoffrey Godden, Chinaman

Plate 168. A shaped oval Mason's Ironstone tureen and cover of pattern number 1435. Printed crown name mark. 14¼ ins. long. c.1830-40. Godden of Worthing Ltd.

Plate 169. A shaped oval Mason's Ironstone tureen and cover decorated with a typical Chinese-styled design being a coloured in print. Printed crown mark. 14¼ ins. long. c.1830-40. Sotheby's Belgravia

Plate 170. An unusual and ornately moulded Mason's Patent Ironstone sauce tureen from a dinner service. Printed crowned name mark. 7ins. long. c.1835-40. Godden of Worthing Ltd.

Plate 171. A fine and unusual Mason's Ironstone tureen, cover and stand printed with an attractive design of the 1840s. Printed 'C.J. Mason & Co.' mark. c.1845. Victoria and Albert Museum (Crown Copyright)

Plate 172. An unusual blue-printed Mason's Ironstone dinner plate matching in basic design the tureen and stand shown in Plate 171. Geoffrey Godden, Chinaman

Plate 173. A Morley's Ironstone plate of the 1850s included here to show the similarity to the Mason wares of the 1820s and 1830s. Mason's crowned mark with addition of the word 'Morley's' (see Chapter Seven). Pattern 4/185. c.1848-58. Mr. and Mrs. A.E. Grove Collection

Plate 174. A Mason's Ironstone tureen and dinner plates from a large dinner service. The basic printed outline landscape design (pattern 447) is a variation of that shown in Plate 169. Printed crowned name mark. Tureen 14¼ ins. long. c.1840-50. Sotheby's Belgravia

Colour Plate 8. A decorative 'Mason's Patent Ironstone China' plate from a dinner service, being a coloured in printed design but one of the richest made in the pre-1850 period. Printed mark. c.1840. Diameter 10ins. Mrs. Y. Eldridge Collection

DESSERT SERVICES

As explained at the beginning of the dinner service section, the durability of the new Patent Ironstone China was its most important attribute and dinner and dessert services represented the bulk of the early productions.

The sale catalogue of December 1818 gives the composition of standard Mason dessert services, although this was sometimes modified to suit customers' requirements:

One dessert service Mogul pattern [see Colour Plate 9], viz., 1 centre piece, 2 cream tureens and stands, 12 fruit dishes and 24 plates [sold for £5.18s.0d.]

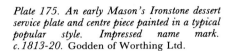

Plate 175. An early Mason's Ironstone dessert service plate and centre piece painted in a typical popular style. Impressed name mark. c.1813-20. Godden of Worthing Ltd.

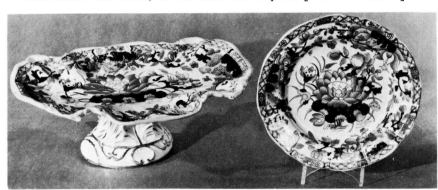

Plate 176. A typical early Mason's Ironstone dessert tureen — two of which were in each full service. This painted pattern with rich blue segments is one of the rarer designs. Impressed name mark. 7¼ins. high. c.1813-20. Geoffrey Godden, Chinaman

The shapes of these dessert ware units are shown in Plates 175-180. Of the twelve fruit dishes, four are usually oblong, four are shaped long dishes with a moulded handle at one end and four are shaped dishes with a moulded handle at one side. The plates are basically of circular form, with a slightly shaped edge, the rim divided into twelve divisions by slight ribs, as can be seen best in Plate 180. The early centre pieces and cream and sugar tureens (now generally known as sauce tureens) are of two basic forms — one with an open arch in the foot (see Plates 176 and 177), the other with solid, rather lower bases to the centre piece and tureens (see Colour Plate 10 and Plates 180 and 197). Other early dessert ware forms are shown in Plates 179 and 181. Pieces from attractively moulded sets are shown in Plates 186 and 187. Other rather rare moulded dessert shapes are shown in Plates 122-126 and 195; the handles are formed as goats' heads, and a reclining cow is used on the tureen covers. A plate from this service bears the rare impressed Royal Arms mark. This shape relates to some porcelains, see page 93. Other rather later dessert shapes are illustrated in Plates 191-193 and 196.

In general, the types of patterns found on dessert services match those on dinner ware (see page 127). The 1818 sale catalogue contained the following dessert sets, each matching in composition that listed above:

Old Japan pattern
Pheasants in colours and gold
Japan, red, purple and gold
India, gold vase pattern
India flower basket Japan
Rock and Rose, Japan and gilt
Gold Thorn
India Grass Hopper

Plate 177. Representative pieces of a Mason's Ironstone dessert service shows typical early shapes painted in a typical style. Impressed name mark. Tureen 7¾ ins. high. c.1815-20. Godden of Worthing Ltd.

Plate 178. Representative pieces of a Mason's Ironstone dessert service painted with an unusual overglaze design. Centre piece 14ins. long. c.1815-25. Mason's Works Collection

Colour Plate 9. Representative pieces from a marked 'Mason's Patent Ironstone China' dessert service showing rather rare forms of the 1820s. The colourful pattern is a standard printed outline design, probably the 'Mogul' pattern of the 1818 sale, see page 128. Centre piece 12½ ins. long. Godden of Worthing Ltd.

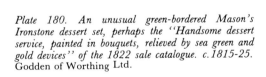

Plate 179. Representative pieces of an impressed-marked 'Mason's Patent Ironstone China' dessert service showing a range of rather unusual forms of the 1820s. Sauce tureen 7ins. high. c.1820-30. Godden of Worthing Ltd.

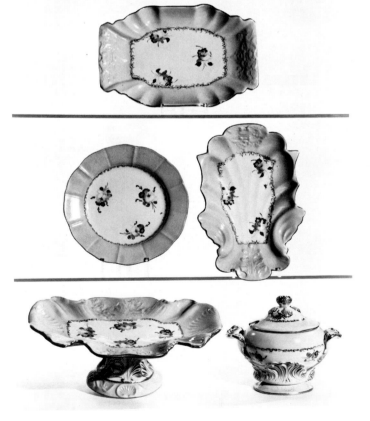

Plate 180. An unusual green-bordered Mason's Ironstone dessert set, perhaps the "Handsome dessert service, painted in bouquets, relieved by sea green and gold devices" of the 1822 sale catalogue. c.1815-25. Godden of Worthing Ltd.

The June 1822 sale contained further dessert services, but these were not always fully listed as the full composition was placed 'on the largest or principal' piece in each service.

A dessert service, beautifully painted in flowers and   R.£18.18.0.
    green ground

Plate 181. Representative pieces from an impressed marked dessert service of the same design as the dinner service tureen shown in Plate 164. Impressed and printed marks. Tureen 6½ ins. high. c.1818-28. Godden of Worthing Ltd.

A dessert service, gilt and painted in flowers	R.£7.10.0.
12 compotier (fruit dishes) and 24 plates	Unsold at £6.15.0.
A dessert service, blue and gold flower border	R.£9.10.0.
A dessert service, blue birds and flowers, 43 pieces	R.£3. 0.0.
A dessert service, blue sprig, 43 pieces	R.£5. 5.0.
A rich Japan dessert service, 43 pieces	R.£8. 8.0.
A dessert set, blue	R.63/-
A dessert service, Japan	R.£5. 5.0.
A dessert service, white	R.36/-
A dessert service, roses and gold edge, 41 pieces	R.£6. 6.0.
A dessert service, Dresden flowers, 37 pieces	R.£7. 7.0.
A handsome dessert service, painted in bouquets, relieved by sea green and gold devices (see Plates 180 or 186)	R.£15.15.0. Unsold at £14.14.0.
A dessert service, Indian landscape, 43 pieces	R.£4. 0.0.
A very beautiful, painted landscape dessert service by S. Bourne (for notes on Bourne, see page 192)	R.£30. 0.0.
A costly dessert service, exquisitely painted in select views by S. Bourne, enriched with burnished gold (see Colour Plate 11, Plate 197 and page 192)	R.35gns.

Plate 182. A Mason's Ironstone dessert centre piece of a characteristic shape. Printed crown mark. 13½ ins. long. c.1825-30. Godden of Worthing Ltd.

Plate 183, below. Two Mason's Ironstone dessert dishes with a moulded floral border design. Decorated with a rich blue ground. c.1820-25. The late Mrs. M. Symes Collection

Plate 184. A blue-printed Mason's semi-china (or earthenware!) dessert centre piece bearing the design and mark shown in Plate 185. 13¾ ins. long. c.1820-30. Godden of Worthing Ltd.

Plate 185. A Mason's semi-china dessert tureen and stand. The tureen and cover turned to show the two blue-printed marks found on this service. Stand 7 by 5¼ ins. c.1820-30. Godden of Worthing Ltd.

Plate 186. A fine Mason's Ironstone dessert dish with relief-moulded border. The centre hand-painted with floral spray. Impressed name mark. 9¾ by 8¼ ins. c.1815-25. Victoria and Albert Museum (Crown Copyright)

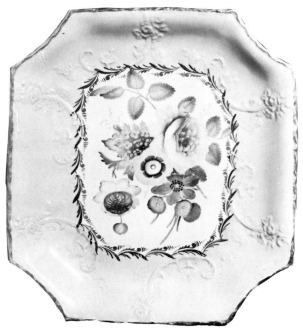

Plate 187. An attractive and good quality Mason's Ironstone dessert plate. The floral moulded border matching Plate 186. Impressed name mark. Diameter 9½ ins. c.1815-25. R.G. Austin, Esq.

140

Plate 188. A rare blue-printed Mason's Ironstone soup plate bearing an English view. Printed crowned mark with retailer's name 'James Laurance'. Diameter 9ins. c.1835-45. Godden of Worthing Ltd.

Plate 189. A very rare and attractive impressed marked Mason's Patent Ironstone china soup plate printed with green border. The owner's crest in the centre. Diameter 9½ins. c.1825. Godden of Worthing Ltd.

Plate 190. A very rare Mason's Ironstone plate, the centre bearing a finely engraved print of the 'Britannia' — the first steam Cunarder, which was launched in 1840. Printed crowned mark. c.1840-45. Author's Collection

Plate 191. Representative pieces from a Mason's Ironstone dessert service of the 1835-40 period. Printed crowned mark. Centre piece 6¼ins. high. c.1835-45. Godden of Worthing Ltd.

Plate 192. A rare Mason's Ironstone dessert dish painted in a typical manner. Printed and impressed marks. c.1820-30. Elsie and John Wenham Collection

Plate 193. A rare Mason's Ironstone footed bowl or dessert centre piece. Printed crowned name mark. 6ins. high. c.1840-45. Godden of Worthing Ltd.

Plate 194. An impressed marked Mason's Ironstone dessert dish of characteristic shape and bearing a popular design. 8¼ by 9½ ins. c.1815-25. Godden of Worthing Ltd.

Plate 195. An ornate moulded Mason's Ironstone dessert centre piece of characteristic form. 13½ ins. long. c.1830-40. Godden of Worthing Ltd.

Plate 196. A rare and elegant Mason's Ironstone handled dessert centre piece. Printed crowned name mark with name and address of the retailer, J. Allsop of 16 St. Paul's Church Yard, London. 9¼ ins. high. c.1840-45. Mr. and Mrs. A.E. Grove Collection

Plate 197. Representative pieces of a part Mason's Ironstone dessert service painted with different British views by Samuel Bourne. See Colour Plate 11 and page 192. c.1820. Phillips

Plate 198. A late Mason's dish bearing a typical design associated with Bandana ware. Printed mark 'Mason's Bandana Ware. 1851. Patentee of the Patent Ironstone China'. 9¾ by 9 ins. c.1851. Mr. and Mrs. A.E. Grove Collection

Plate 199. A rare form of Mason's Ironstone dessert dish or stand decorated with a typical inexpensive so-called 'Japan' pattern. 15½ ins. long. c.1820-30. Godden of Worthing Ltd.

ALPHABETICAL LIST OF OBJECTS LISTED IN THE 1818 AND 1822 SALE CATALOGUES, WITH ITEMS FROM THE OXFORD SALE OF 1826 AND 1851 EXHIBITION

The prices prefixed 'R' are those written in the auctioneer's catalogue before the sale either as a 'reserve', under which the lot should not be sold, or as an indication of the estimated value. In practice, a few lots exceeded their reserve or estimated values, and many were sold for less than these figures. The significance of the reserve prices lies in the fact that they were given either by Mason, as an indication of the value, or by the auctioneer, who would have been familiar with the then worth of the articles. Being the estimate of one person (Mason's or the auctioneer) the prices are perhaps a better indication of the relative values of each lot than the realised prices — for, owing to the unpredictable conditions of auction sales, a lot may fetch far more or less than its true market value.

In the case of items included in the 1822 sale, the reserve prices are given (when only one object or set of articles was included), but in the majority of cases the reserve was not reached and the lot was 'bought in'.

It will be observed that many articles were sold 'with shades'. These were the glass domes normally associated with the Victorian era but which, in fact, came into fashion quite early in the nineteenth century. In November 1821, Pellatt & Green, the London retailers, supplied:

24	French Shades	3½ x 3½	@ 4/-
18	" "	4½ x 5½	6/6
6	" "	6½ x 6½	9/-
2	Large oval shades		16/-

and E. Ring & Co. of Bristol were supplying 'glass shades' at 2s.9d. and 3s.6d. in 1819.

BASINS
1822 Sale
6 basins, covers & stands, painted in flowers   R.£2. 2.0.
4 basins, covers & stands, gilt edge   R.£1. 0.0.
2 broth basins, covers and stands, Japan (and 4 soup plates)   R.30/-

BASKETS
1822 Sale
Pr. fruit baskets, rich Japan   R.18/-
2 violet baskets (see Plate 200)
2 fruit baskets, on feet   R.20/-
2 fruit baskets and stands, Oriental design   R.35/-
A violet basket painted in landscape (with a pair of   R.25/-
    toy jars gilt and painted in flowers)
2 richly painted flower baskets (and 2 lavender   R.27/-
    bottles and shades)

BEAKERS
1818 Sale
...2 flower beakers...
2 dragon octagonal beakers

1822 Sale

A pair of beakers, painted in flowers and a Japan vase   R.£1. 0.0.
A pair of green dragon beakers   R.£1. 1.0.

1851 Exhibition

Zigzag beakers, on bronze (metallic ware, page 202)

BOTTLES
1818 Sale

2 fine large bottles, ornamented, a la Chinoise
2 flat formed bottles

1822 Sale

2 Bottles, mazarine (ground), white figures with   R.£3. 3.0.
    shades and a centre jar, ditto)
2 small hexagon bottles, mazarine, with shades (and   R.27/-
    2 small candlesticks, red ground, with ditto)
2 bottles, India figures and landscape   R.£1.10.0.
2 Lavender Bottles and shades (and 2 richly painted   R.27/-
    flower baskets)

Plate 200. A rare impressed-marked Mason's Ironstone small lidded basket, perhaps one of the "violet-baskets" of the 1822 sale. 3½ ins. long. c.1820-25. Godden Collection

Plate 201. A rare footed bowl or centre piece bearing the standard vase design as Plate 194. The handles link with those on porcelain vases, see Plate 136. Printed crowned mark. 6½ ins. high. c.1820. The late Mrs. M. Symes Collection

BOWLS
1818 Sale

2 Trentham bowls, highly finished
1 very large dolphin-headed bowl, richly embellished
    in colours and gold, damaged
2 dolphin-head bowls, rich in colours and gold

1822 Sale

A salad bowl (and centre piece with cover)   R.25/-
1 large sideboard bowl, Indian pattern   R.£5. 5.0.
A large sideboard bowl   R.£4. 4.0.
A flower bowl, mazarine (ground) and delicate sprigs   R.£1.10.0.
A conservatory bowl   Sold for £2
2 sugar bowls, covers & stands, Japanned   R.£1. 4.0.

Plate 202. Two views of a magnificent Mason's Ironstone bowl with rich blue ground over-painted and gilt with birds on branches. c.1815-25. R. and Z. Taylor Collection

A beautiful flower bowl, mazarine (ground)	R.18/-
5 punch bowls, blue	R.£1.10.0.
2 punch bowls, blue iron-stone	R.15/-
A fine flower bowl and shade	R.£3.13.6.

BREAKFAST SETS

These were enlarged tea services, often with large cups, egg cups, covered muffin or toast dishes (see Plate 203) and sometimes with plates (not included in standard tea services). Other breakfast ware is listed under teasets, as combined 'tea and breakfast' or 'breakfast, tea and coffee sets' were catalogued.

It should be noted that the term 'breakfast set' is now often applied to covered dishes (four segmented and one centre piece, see Plate 262) which fitted into a wooden tray. In contemporary accounts, these sets were termed 'supper sets', q.v., or 'sandwich sets'.

1822 Sale

A breakfast set, white, 82 pieces	R.£2. 0.0.
A breakfast set, white & gold, 76 pieces	R.£5.10.0.
A breakfast service, neat sprig, 100 pieces	
A breakfast service, dragon pattern, 70 pieces	R.£4.10.0.
A breakfast set, coloured flowers, 61 pieces	R.£3.15.0.
12 breakfast cups and saucers, white & gold	R.30/-
A breakfast service, green scroll & gold border, 77 pieces	R.£5. 5.0.
A breakfast set, Indian coloured sprigs, 70 pieces, gold edge	R.35/-
A breakfast service, enamelled roses, 77 pieces	R.£3. 3.0.
A breakfast service, rock pattern, 94 pieces	R.£8. 8.0.
A breakfast set, 55 pieces, dragon, ironstone	R.30/-

1826 Oxford Sale

Breakfast services, with the addition of honey pots, egg pipkins

Plate 205. A charming Mason's Ironstone basket-moulded cup and saucer, the ground painted in yellow. Diameter of saucer 6ins. c.1815-25. Geoffrey Godden, Chinaman

Plate 203. A rare and finely moulded Mason's Ironstone part breakfast service with egg cup and covered muffin or toast dish. The painting and gilding is of very good quality. Impressed name mark. Diameter of plate 7ins. c.1815-25. Godden of Worthing Ltd.

Plate 204. A large and ornate Mason's Ironstone breakfast teapot with moulded basket work to match Plate 203, over-painted in green. Impressed mark 'Patent Ironstone China' in circular form. 8½ ins. high. c.1815-25. Geoffrey Godden, Chinaman

BROTH BASINS
1822 Sale

A pair of broth basins, covers & stands, Japanned blue compartments	R.30/-
6 broth basins and stands, grass hopper, Japan	R.24/-

BULB (OR BOUGH) POTS

These decorative objects with their pierced covers were made by most English porcelain manufacturers in the 1790-1820 period and they were made by Miles Mason in porcelain (see Plate 141 and page 101). They went out of use by about 1820 and are therefore extremely rare in the Ironstone body.

The superb example shown in Plate 206 is unmarked but the basic printed outline design occurs on marked Mason wares and the lion finial is from the same mould as those shown in Plates 117 and 118.

These bulb pots are not mentioned in the 1818 or 1822 sale records.

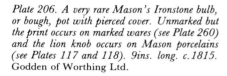

Plate 206. A very rare Mason's Ironstone bulb, or bough, pot with pierced cover. Unmarked but the print occurs on marked wares (see Plate 260) and the lion knob occurs on Mason porcelains (see Plates 117 and 118). 9ins. long. c.1815. Godden of Worthing Ltd.

Plate 207. A rare Mason's Ironstone candlestick decorated in a very typical style. Impressed name mark in circular form. 6ins. high. c.1820-25. R.G. Austin, Esq.

CANDLESTICKS
1818 Sale

2 taper candlesticks, coloured and gilt
4 card candlesticks
2 tall taper candlesticks

1822 Sale

A pair of hand candlesticks with extinguishers and glass shades	R.£2. 2.0.
2 candlesticks, flowers and orange ground, with shades	R.£2. 0.0.
2 candlesticks, buff ground, with shades	R.£2. 2.0.
2 small candlesticks, red ground, with shades (with 2 small hexagon bottles, mazarine)	R.27/-
4 Japan candlesticks, mazarine	R.16/-
4 candlesticks and extinguishers, mazarine, Japan	R.15/-
2 large flat candlesticks, mazarine, with shades	R.£2. 2.0.

A pair of handsome candlesticks, painted in flowers and glass shades ... R.30/-

A pair of reading candlesticks, Dresden flowers, a pentray and an inkstand with glass shade ... R.£1.10.0.

A pair of flat candlesticks and extinguishers, mazarine ... R.25/-

2 candlesticks, green and flowers, with shades ... R.28/-

2 shell candlesticks (with a small ewer & basin, 2 toy watering cans) ... Sold for £1.3.0.

CARD RACKS AND CASES
1822 Sale

2 card racks, mazarine (ground) (Plate 208) ... R.£1.0.0.

A pair of card cases, mazarine and white embossed figures ... R.24/-

A pair of card racks, and a pentray, mazarine ... R.28/-

CHEESE STANDS

Low, circular cheese dishes were sometimes included in dinner services, while other very large examples were probably sold as individual pieces.

1822 Sale

A Stilton cheese stand and cover ... R.£2.4.0.

3 cheese stands (and 6 bakers), rich Japan ... R.£2.0.0.

1826 Oxford Auction Sale

Stilton cheese tubs.

CHOCOLATE CUPS AND STANDS
1822 Sale

2 very rich chocolate cups and stands ... R.£1.10.0.

2 cups & covers, moth on mazarine ground with shades (and two sprinkling bottles) ... R.£1.10.0.

2 rich cups, covers & stands, painted in landscapes and shades ... R.£2.18.0.

COFFEE POTS
1818 Sale

1 coffee pot, antique pattern and shape

2 beautiful antique coffee pots, with shades ... R.35/-

A coffee ewer, richly gilt, from the antique, and glass shade ... R.25/-

A blue and gold coffee ewer and 2 tea canisters ... R.26/-

Plate 208. An attractive blue and gold Mason's Ironstone container, probably the mazarine ground card racks of the 1822 sale. Impressed name mark. 6¾ ins. high. c.1820-25. Godden of Worthing Ltd.

Plate 209. A set of three blue ground Mason's Ironstone containers, perhaps the card racks of the 1822 catalogue. Impressed name marks. 3¾ and 4 ins. high. c.1820-25. Godden of Worthing Ltd.

CORNUCOPIA

1822 Sale

2 flower horns (see Plate 210, for later examples)

CUPS AND SAUCERS

1818 Sale

2 handsome tulip (shape?) cups & saucers

...2 cabinet coffee biggins...

1822 Sale

2 beautiful caudle cups and shades   R.£4. 4.0.

Other normal cups and saucers were components of tea, coffee and breakfast services.

Plate 210. A rare pair of Mason's Ironstone cornucopia in typical colouring. 'Flower-horns' were included in the 1818 sale. Printed crowned marks. 8ins. high. c.1830. Peter Nelson

CUSTARD CUPS

1822 Sale

12 Custard cups and covers, basket pattern   R.14/-
12 Custard cups and covers, grasshopper   R.14/-

1826 Oxford Auction Sale

Custard cups and covers

ESSENCE BOTTLES

1822 Sale

A pair of blue essence bottles

ESSENCE BOWLS

Essence bowls were probably what are now called pot pourri bowls, containing sweet-smelling leaves, dried flowers, etc. Such objects are listed under Pot Pourri, and include 'a large essence jar...'

1822 Sale

A pair of Grecian form essence bowls, with handles,   R.£6. 0.0.
    sumptuously gilt and glass shades

Plate 211. An extremely neatly decorated small ewer and basin richly gilt over a blue ground. Rare printed mark 'Patent Ironstone China' around a circular representation of the Royal Arms. Basin diameter 3 ⅛ ins. c.1815-20.
Dr. M. Tanner

EWER AND BASIN (see also Toilet Sets)
1822 Sale

An ewer and basin, Indian sprig, gilt edge	R.£1. 0.0.
An ewer & basin, enamelled moths & flowers...	
2 rich toilet ewers and basins	R.£3. 3.0.
A mazarine toilet, ewer & basin, with shades	Unsold at £1. 2.0.
3 ewers, blue dragon, from the antique	R.11/-

1851 Exhibition

Ewer and basin and mouth ewer and basin with Oriental figures and a rose border

Toilet ewers and basins

FIGURES AND PORTRAIT BUSTS

Mason figures must surely be the rarest of collector's treasures, but on the evidence of the quality of the few known specimens these Mason essays equal the better known specimens from other famous English factories.

The large pair of unglazed porcelain figures in the City Museum and Art Gallery at Stoke-on-Trent are truly magnificent in detail as well as size. These depict Queen Victoria and Prince Albert and are shown in Plate 212. They bear under the bases the inscription 'Published by C.J. Mason & Co.' and most probably were issued at the time of the Royal marriage in February 1840.

A fine portrait bust is shown in Plate 213 and, although this example is not marked, a seemingly identical specimen is inscribed 'Published by C.J. Mason & Co.' and has been attributed to the Duke of Wellington.

It is to be earnestly hoped that other unglazed or glazed Mason figures or busts will be reported.

Plate 212. A superbly modelled large pair of biscuit or unglazed china figures of Queen Victoria and Prince Albert. Inscribed 'Published by C.J. Mason & Co.' The marriage took place in February 1840. 16ins. high. c.1840. City Museum and Art Gallery, Stoke-on-Trent

Plate 213. A very rare unglazed china bust. This example is not marked but another bears the inscription 'Published by C.J. Mason & Co.' c.1826-30. Dr. D. Rice Collection

FINGER BOWLS
1826 Oxford Auction Sale
Society of Yacht Club finger bowls

These normally bear a printed mark reading 'Patent Yacht Club finger bowl' within a double-line border.

FIREPLACES OR MANTELS

These important objects were not included in the 1818 and 1822 sale catalogues, probably because the manufacture and firing of such large pieces had not been mastered by this period. Several firms made ceramic slabs or tiles which were built into fireplaces, but Mason's appear to be the only firm to have produced purely ceramic mantels.

Examples are illustrated in Plates 214-221. These range in size from miniature models only twelve inches high (perhaps made as samples for retail shops or travellers) to the huge examples six feet wide. Mason fireplaces bear a large printed mark comprising the pre-Victorian Royal Arms and supporters with the wording 'China Chimney pieces. Mason & Co., Patentees, Staffordshire Potteries' arranged above; but this mark (Plate 215) is not visible on examples which are built into the wall.

FISH POND BOWLS
1826 Oxford Auction Sale
Fish Pond Bowls, of extraordinary magnitude
1851 Exhibition
Fish Pond bowls of Anglo-Chinese pattern
Gog and Magog, an Anglo-Indian pattern
The Water Lily, an Anglo-Japanese pattern

Plate 214. A finely moulded and neatly decorated Mason's Ironstone chimney piece. One section of the top reversed to show the mark — shown enlarged in Plate 215. 50ins. high. c.1820-30. Godden of Worthing Ltd.

Plate 215. Detail of the printed mark found on the Mason chimney pieces. 2¾ ins. long.

Plate 216. A finely moulded Mason's Ironstone chimney piece of the same basic form as Plate 214 but decorated in a different style. Printed mark as Plate 215. 62ins. wide. c.1820-30. Sotheby's

153

Plate 217. A rare miniature Mason's Ironstone chimney piece. 12ins. high. c.1830-40. City Museum and Art Gallery, Stoke-on-Trent

Plate 218. A relief-moulded small-sized Mason's Ironstone chimney piece from Charles Mason's house at Fenton. c.1830-40. City Museum and Art Gallery, Stoke-on-Trent

Plate 219. An ornately-moulded and important Mason's Ironstone chimney piece, with hand-painted panels of flowers. 54ins. high. c.1835-45. L.J. Allen, Esq.

Plate 220. A magnificent relief-moulded blue ground Mason's Ironstone chimney piece richly gilt and painted with flower panels. 72ins. wide. c.1835-45. L.J. Allen, Esq.

Plate 221. A relief-moulded Mason's Ironstone chimney piece of the same form as Plate 220 but less richly decorated. 72ins. wide. c.1835-45. L.J. Allen, Esq.

FLOWER POTS

1818 Sale
2 garden flower pots and stands

1822 Sale

A pair of hexagon flower pots and stands, mazarine ground and gold edges	R.£5. 5.0.
2 large flower pots and stands, mazarine (ground)	R.£4. 0.0.
2 blue large flower pots and stands	R.£2. 0.0.
4 small flower pots and stands, mazarine and delicate sprigs	Unsold at £1.18.0.
A pair of flower pots and stands, painted in moths (and an accurate sun dial, with glass shades)	R.25/-
A pair of beautiful hexagonal, flower pots and stands	R.£3.10.0.
A pair of flower pots and stands, painted in birds, with glass shades and 2 match cases	R.£1. 8.0.

1826 Oxford Auction Sale
Siamese Jardinier and Plateaux, adopted by the Horticultural Society, for the culture of bulbous roots &c

These jardinières and stands normally have a relief-moulded design and are in a tinted body. They bear a special self-explanatory mark.

Plate 222. A typical Mason's Ironstone oval foot bath painted in a hasty manner in a pattern seen also in Plate 199. 15 by 12½ ins. c.1825-35. Godden of Worthing Ltd.

FOOT BATHS

Large oval foot baths also occur with typical 'Japan' patterns (Plate 222) which sometimes still have the matching large water jug.

1822 Sale

2 foot pans, white	R.25/-
2 foot pans, blue	R.£1. 0.0.

GARDEN SEATS

The example shown in Plate 223 is unmarked but is probably an example of Mason's garden seats.

1851 Exhibition
Garden seats of an Anglo-Chinese pattern on a sea-ground, with raised solid flowers and gilt panels

Plate 223. *A Mason's-type garden seat after a Chinese prototype. Printed decoration overpainted in light green and other natural colours. Unmarked. 20ins. high. c.1845-51. Geoffrey Godden, Chinaman*

GOBLETS

1822 Sale

2 exquisitely painted satyr goblets	R.£5. 0.0.
2 beautiful painted goblets	R.£4. 4.0.
A pair of very richly painted goblets	R.£4.14.0.

INKSTANDS

1818 Sale

2 inkstands (Plate 224)
2 vase shaped ink stands
2 cabinet inkstands

1822 Sale

2 Inkstands, green ground and flowers, gilt	R.24/-
A shell ink stand, red ground (1 toy watering can and 2 teapots with glass shades)	R.£1.12.0.
A shell ecritoire and pair of match cases, blue and gold	R.32/-
A shell ink stand and 2 paper cases, flower border	R.23/-

Two very rare shell-shaped inkstands are shown in Plates 225 and 226.

JARDINIERES (see also Flower Pots)

1818 Sale

2 Jardinieres & Stands	13/-

Plate 224. *An early Mason's Ironstone inkstand painted in typical colours. 6¾ins. long. c.1815-20. Godden of Worthing Ltd.*

Plate 225. A very rare Mason's Ironstone inkstand, perhaps the 'shell inkstand' of the 1822 sale catalogue. 3ins. high. c.1820-25. Geoffrey Godden, Chinaman

Plate 226. A very rare Mason's Ironstone double-shell inkstand with loose ink containers. This is almost of porcelain quality. Impressed name mark. 5¼ins. long. c.1820-25. R.G. Austin, Esq.

Plate 227. An elegant Mason's Ironstone inkstand decorated in typical style. Printed crowned mark. 8¼ins. long. 1825-30. Godden of Worthing Ltd.

Plate 228, right. A small Mason's Ironstone inkwell painted in a typical style. Impressed name mark. Diameter 4½ins. at base. c.1820-30. E.H. Chandler Collection

Plate 229. A fine and complete Mason's Ironstone inkstand decorated in deep blue, red and green and richly gilt. 13¼ins. long. c.1835-45. Bonhams

JARS

Some articles described here as jars would today be termed vases.

1818 Sale

2 elegant mitre shaped jars and covers, sumptuously gilt
  (see Plate 231)

1 handsome sideboard jar, dragon handles and
  sumptuously gilt (see Plate 275)

2 large bottle shaped perfume jars   R.£1. 4.0.

2 tall octagonal embossed Chinese covered jars

1 drawing room lion's-head perfume jar

1 splendid dragon jar, a la Chinoise

2 small griffin octagonal jars

2 tall Roman shaped jars   R.£1. 0.0.

1 costly Hall jar, elegant Chinese design

2 strawberry jars and covers

2 fine hexagonal Hall jars and covers, enamelled in
  compartments and sumptuously gilt

1 richly executed jar, Chinese subjects, on mazarine
  ground

2 curious antique jars, handsomely gilt, etc.

2 octagonal jars & cover

1 ditto embossed jar & cover

2 rose and apple jars and covers, octagonal bronze
  and gold

2 costly jars, a la Chinoise, beautifully pencilled and
  gilt

2 bell jars, lions heads

2 small griffin octagonal jars

2 three handle jars

Plate 230. A superb two handled pot probably painted by Samuel Bourne (see page 192). See Plate 231 for covered example. 8¾ ins. high. c.1820-25. Delomosne & Son Ltd.

Plate 231. A fine Mason's Ironstone covered jar, perhaps the "elegant mitre shaped jars and covers" of the 1818 catalogue. Bearing the 'Water-lily' printed design. Printed crowned mark. 13¾ ins. high. c.1820-25.
Northampton Museum

Plate 232. An unusual large Ironstone covered jar bearing a typical Mason's printed design coloured in by hand. Printed mark depicting the Fenton Stone Works, see page 202. 16ins. high. c.1840-45. R. and Z. Taylor Collection

2 rose and apple handled octagonal perfume jars
2 strawberry jars and covers

1822 Sale

A pair of jars, Chinese landscape and figures	R.25/-
A pair of jars and covers, Japanned flower and gilt ram's head and edges	R.£3.10.0.
A pair of shaped jars and covers, Japanned and gilt flowers	R.£5.0.0.
A noble lofty jar with cover surmounted with griffins and blue ground, beautifully enamelled in bird and flowers	R.£9. 9.0.
A lofty essence jar and cover, dragon handles, and top painted in flowers	R.£3. 3.0.
A pair of shaped jars and covers, gilt and painted flowers	R.£2. 2.0.
A pair of essence jars and covers	R.30/-
A pair of jars with dragon handles	R.35/-
A handsome essence jar, green ground and flowers (and 2 match cases in landscapes)	R.£3. 3.0.
3 jars, mazarine and gold chased figures, with shades	£5. 5.0.
1 fine hexagonal Hall jar	R.£7.10.0.
1 superb square very large Hall jar, mazarine and Indian devices (auctioneer's note: "chipd a little but may be regilt")	R.£17.17.0.

160

A Trentham plaid jar	R.35/-
2 elegant griffin jars, painted in fruit and flowers, sumptuously gilt	R.£6. 6.0.
A rose and apple Jar	R.£2. 2.0.
2 Indian flower Jars, mazarine	R.£2. 2.0.
A large hydra top jar, mazarine, birds and flowers	R.£9. 9.0.
2 Chinese jars & covers, no reserve, sold for	17/-
2 hexagon tall jars and covers, Japan	R.£2. 2.0.
2 Jars, sprigs, on mazarine (ground), one faulty	Unsold at £1. 1.0.
A fine Hall jar, Oriental design	Unsold at £6.10.0.
A Hall jar, lion head handles	R.£2.10.0.
2 serpent handled jars	R.42/-
A splendid Hall jar, from an improved Indian model	R.£16.16.0.
A pair of jars neat sprig, on blue ground	R.£3. 3.0.
A pair of jars, painted in landscape and glass shades	R.£2. 0.0.
A noble essence jar, painted in flowers on a celest ground relieved by burnished gold	R.£21. 0.0.
A pair of blue jars, raised figures on blue ground, glass shades	R.£2. 0.0.
A pair of Jars, Japanned, flower and dragon handles	R.£1. 4.0.
A rich pagoda formed hall jar	R.£6. 6.0.
A very fine Hall jar, mazarine hydra top	R.£9. 9.0.
A handsome mantel jar, beautifully painted in shells	R.£2.10.0.

1851 Exhibition

Jars with raised enamel mandarin figures and sea-dragon handles. Large jars and covers of Anglo-Indian pattern. There are also some open jars. Jars covered; dragon handles of Anglo-Indian and Anglo-Japanese patterns, with raised solid flowers, etc.

Three jars and covers, with Anglo-Indian grounds

Jars: the old India crackle, with red India red grounds

JUGS
1822 Sale

A handsome jug, painted in landscape and hunting subject	R.£2. 2.0.
4 Antique shape jugs	R.14/-
5 Jugs from the Antique and 5 kitchen jugs	R.16/-
2 large jugs, gold plaid and flowers	R.30/-
6 jugs, pheasant and flowers from the Antique (see Plate 243)	R.14/-
6 jugs, blue ironstone	R.13/-
6 jugs, blue earthenware	R.13/-
8 stone figured jugs	R.£1. 0.0.
3 jugs from the Antique fancy patterns	R.30/-
A suite of 4 jugs in flowers	R.30/-
8 Jugs, blue bird & flower	
12 Jugs and covers, blue bird, etc.	R.30/-
4 Antique form jugs, grasshopper pattern	R.11/-
5 large jugs, embossed flower	R.15/-
6 coloured jugs (and 12 mugs)	R.27/-
3 rich India pattern jugs	R.25/-

8 uncovered jugs and 5 covered ditto, blue	R.35/-
6 hunting jugs and 5 mugs [It is interesting to see that relief-moulded hunting jugs were reintroduced in 1979.]	R. 24/-
6 Jugs, gold jar pattern	R.25/-
3 Jugs, Japan	R.25/-
4 hexagon jugs, mazarine and gold bands	R.£2.10.0.
6 jugs, gold jar, and 4 ditto, grasshopper	R.26/-
2 large jugs, richly Japanned	R.£2. 2.0.
2 very rich water jugs	Sold for £1. 3.0.
10 jugs, embossed flowers and figures	R.£1. 3.0.
Fine hunting jugs, stone	R.12/-
Fine jugs from a beautiful Chinese original	R.30/-
Six jugs, blue Ironstone	R.13/-
12 ditto, blue earthenware	R.13/-
A pair of water jugs, mazarine and broad gold edge	R.32/-

1851 Exhibition

Jugs of old India, Japanese and gold patterns of the original shape, also Anglo-Indian and melon pattern; with Oriental figures and gold ornaments

Jugs, showing various patterns in Bandana ware

Antique jugs of Japanese pattern and gold ornaments

Plate 233. Two small Mason's Ironstone jugs painted in a very typical style. 5¾ and 2½ ins. high. c.1815-25. A.M. Broad Collection

Plate 234, right. A standard shape of Mason's Ironstone jug but decorated in a particularly rich style, boldly gilt on a deep blue ground. Impressed name mark. 8¾ ins. high. c.1815-25. Godden of Worthing Ltd.

LUNCH SERVICE
1822 Sale

A lunch set, of basket pattern, gold edge, 68 pieces (the Plates are not gilt)	R.£4.10.0.
35 Lunch plates, rich brown and gold border	R.£4.10.0.

Plate 235. An unusual and early form of Mason's Ironstone jug painted on a deep blue ground in a typical style. Impressed name mark in circular form. 5¾ ins. high. c.1815-25. Godden of Worthing Ltd.

Plate 236. A neatly potted Mason's Ironstone jug, well-painted in a typical style. Impressed name mark. 8¾ ins. high. c.1815-25. Godden of Worthing Ltd.

Plate 237. A rare and large punch jug bearing a well-known Chinese-styled figure subject design. 10ins. high. c.1820-30. S. O'Toole Collection

Plate 238. A Mason's Ironstone jug of unusual shape and pattern on a dark blue ground. Printed crowned name mark. 7¼ ins. high. c.1840-45. Dr. and Mrs. P. Stovin.

Plate 239. A large Mason's Ironstone jug of unusual form, broadly painted on a dark blue ground. 10¼ ins. high. c.1835-40. R.G. Austin, Esq.

Plate 240. A fine quality relief-moulded Mason's stoneware jug. Perhaps one of the 'stone figured jugs' of the 1822 sale catalogue. Printed crowned mark. 7¾ ins. high. c.1820-25. Worthing Museum

Plate 241. An unusual relief-moulded Mason's jug in a pale blue earthenware body. Printed mark depicting the 'Fenton Stone-Works' with the initials 'C J M & Co' and the description 'Granite China'. 8¼ ins. high. c.1835-40. Godden of Worthing Ltd.

Plate 242. A rare, if heavy, form of Mason's covered jug. 12ins. high. c.1840-45. Miss.F.R. Webster

164

Plate 243. Two typical Mason's Ironstone jugs. The factory names for these forms being 'Hydra' (left) and 'Fenton' (right). c.1840. Mason's Works Collection

Plate 244. A Mason's Ironstone jug of rather unusual form, the printed outline design not fully painted in. Printed crowned name mark with name of a New York retailer — 'T.T. Kissam'. 7ins. high. c.1840-45. Godden of Worthing Ltd.

Plate 245. A selection of Mason's Ironstone jugs showing a range of typical shapes and patterns. Printed crowned name marks. c.1835-45. The late Mrs. M. Symes Collection

MATCH BOXES, CASES, POTS

These are probably what we would now call spill vases which do not feature in the sale records under this name.

The examples shown in Plate 246 are painted with conventional and traditional Mason designs which obviously outnumber other styles, but this is not to say that other more refined designs were not made. To illustrate this general point, Plate 246a shows a delightful spill vase painted with an amusing figure subject (in the style of the vases shown in Plates 273 and 274). This vase is painted with a green ground and has an attractive gilt border to the panel. It bears the early impressed name mark 'Mason's Patent Ironstone China' in circular form but in general appearance this spill vase could well be mistaken for a porcelain example from one of our leading factories.

1822 Sale

2 match boxes (and 3 paper cases) mazarine ground	R.30/-
A pair of match cases, Dresden flowers and glass shades	R.£1. 0.0.
2 match pots, roses on black ground (and an antique coffee pot with shade)	R.£1.12.0.
2 match cases, delicately finished, with shades	R.£1. 7.0.
1 pair of match cases, blue and gold (with a shell ecritoire)	R.32/-
2 match cases and shades, mazarine	R.22/-

Plate 246. A selection of early impressed marked 'Mason's Patent Ironstone China' spill vases or match pots painted with typical 'Japan' patterns. Tallest example 5¾ ins. c.1815-25. Godden of Worthing Ltd.

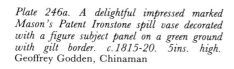

Plate 246a. A delightful impressed marked Mason's Patent Ironstone spill vase decorated with a figure subject panel on a green ground with gilt border. c.1815-20. 5ins. high. Geoffrey Godden, Chinaman

Plate 247. Two basic forms of simple Mason's Ironstone mug shapes, decorated in typical styles. Printed crowned name mark. 4¾ and 3 ins. high. c.1820-30. Mrs. G. Allbright Collection

MUFFIN DISHES

Circular covered muffin dishes were made to go with the scarce breakfast services, and one example is included in Plate 203.

MUGS
1822 Sale
9 hunting Mugs	R.12/-
12 mugs, ironstone	R.14/-

MYRTLE POTS
1822 Sale
2 large Myrtle pots and stands, mazarine	£4. 4.0.

NEAPOLITAN EWER
1826 Oxford Auction Sale

"The Neapolitan Ewer rivals the best work of Dresden manufactory." This description and that in *John Bull* of 23rd March, 1828: "The sets of fine jars of English make are the finest we ever saw,

Plate 248. Two fine quality Mason's Ironstone mugs richly gilt over a deep blue ground. Impressed name marks. 5½ and 3¼ ins. high. c.1820. The late Mrs. M. Symes Collection

Plate 249. A rare Mason's Ironstone mug form rather broadly decorated in a typical style. 5½ ins. high. Mrs. S. O'Toole Collection

Plate 250. A magnificent large Mason's Ironstone ewer. Richly gilt, the figure panel probably painted by Samuel Bourne (see page 192). 28ins. high. c.1820-25. Mason's Works Collection

Plate 251. A rare and superb quality Mason's Ironstone ewer in the Continental style. The large scenic panel most probably painted by Samuel Bourne (see page 192). Impressed name mark. 27ins. high. c.1820-25. Sotheby's

and are superior to foreign productions, we understand the models cost five hundred pounds'', probably relate to the ornately modelled large ewers, illustrated here in Colour Plate 7 and in Plates 250 and 251.

ORNAMENTS
1818 Sale
2 low bat-head ornaments
2 Pan's head ornaments, landscapes in compartments of mazarine (ground) and splendidly gilt

PAPER CASES
1822 Sale
2 paper cases, raised figures on mazarine	R.15/-
3 paper cases, rich, with shades	R.38/-
3 richly painted paper cases, with shades	R.£2.10.0.
3 paper cases, rich landscapes	R.30/-
3 paper cases, painted birds	R.£2. 0.0.

PASTILLE JARS OR BURNERS
1818 Sale
2 Etruscan jars for pastilles
2 essence burners
2 Etruscan jars for pastilles

1822 Sale
A pair of essence jars, gilt and painted in birds and flowers, faulty	R.30/-
2 pastille burners, with glass shades	R.55/-
A pair of essence burners, mazarine	R.32/-
A pair of ditto (blue & gold) essence burners and 2 cups and covers	R.30/-

PEN TRAYS
1822 Sale
2 shell pen trays (2 hand candlesticks and 2 glass shades)	R. 24/-

PLATES
Many other plate shapes and designs are shown in the dinner service and dessert service sections.

1822 Sale
6 very rich plates	R.£4.12.0.
12 plates, richly painted in various arms & crests	R.£6. 0.0.
7 handsome dessert plates, Melange	R.35/-
22 Lunch plates, gilt Japan	R.25/-
35 Lunch plates, rich brown and gold border	R.£4.10.0.
12 rich Melange plates, no reserve — sold for	9/-
17 ice plates, Japan	R.£2.10.0.
6 plates, birds and shells on gold border	R.30/-
8 rich plates, arms	R.£2. 0.0.

1851 Exhibition
Specimens of plates in the Oriental style of pattern, on registered shapes and Anglo-Japanese. (The 'registered' shape plate is shown in Plates 145 and 146.)

A plate, a dish, a tureen, a covered dish, a tall coffee cup and saucer and a sugar-basin, made of the white patent Ironstone china, as used in the hotels of the United States of America

Plate 252. A Mason's Ironstone plate printed in underglaze blue with a rare Chinese-styled design. Impressed name mark. Diameter 9½ ins. J.K. des Fontaines Collection

Plate 253. A Mason's Ironstone dinner plate with eight indentations around the rim, rather broadly painted in a typical Oriental style. Impressed name mark. Diameter 10¼ ins. c.1815-20. Private Collection

POT POURRI BOWLS AND VASES
1822 Sale

A pot pourri, ram's head, mazarine	R.£2. 2.0.
A large essence jar, Japanned & gilt (see Plate 255)	R.£2. 2.0.
A rich pot pourri	R.36/-
1 pot pourri, rich Japan	R.38/-

Plate 254. A large and rare impressed-marked 'Mason's Patent Ironstone China' pot pourri painted with flowers on a pale yellow ground. 14ins. high. c.1820-25. Godden of Worthing Ltd.

171

Plate 255. A rare Mason's Ironstone pot pourri bowl complete with the inner cover. Decorated in a typical style. Impressed name mark. 9½ ins. high. c.1820-25. Godden of Worthing Ltd.

Plate 256. A very rare large blue-printed Mason's Semi-China pot pourri type vase decorated with the 'Fountain' pattern (see also Plates 184 and 185). Blue printed mark 'Mason's semi-china warranted'. 13ins. high. c.1820-30. R. and Z. Taylor Collection

Plate 257. A good quality Mason's Ironstone pot pourri bowl with typical pierced cover. Printed circular name mark incorporating the Royal Arms. Diameter 4¾ ins. c.1820-25. R.G. Austin, Esq.

Plate 258, left. A fine relief-moulded C.J. Mason vase with pierced cover, perhaps for pot pourri. Printed name mark depicting the Fenton Stone Works with 'Granite China' below. 15½ins. c.1840-45. Mrs. F.R. Webster

Plate 259, right. A simple Mason's Ironstone covered pot pourri vase broadly painted in the typical 'Japan' style. Impressed name mark. 7ins. high. c.1820-25. City Museum and Art Gallery, Stoke-on-Trent

PUNCH BOWLS

Large size bowls are very often called 'punch bowls' although they probably usually held fruit or served a purely decorative use. Some such examples were listed in the 1822 sale catalogue as large sideboard bowls, Indian pattern. Two such examples, illustrated in Plates 260 and 261, are very much in the style of the earlier Chinese export market bowls which were shipped into this country during the second half of the eighteenth century and which Miles Mason must have stocked in his London shop.

Plate 260. A colourful Mason's Ironstone punch, or 'sideboard', bowl decorated with a well known coloured-over printed design. Printed crowned mark. Diameter 13ins. c.1815-25. Godden of Worthing Ltd.

Plate 261. A colourful Mason's Ironstone punch, or sideboard, bowl decorated in the type of style of the late eighteenth century Chinese export market bowls. Printed crowned name mark. Diameter 12½ins. c.1820-25. Miss K. Baker Collection

SPRINKLERS (see also Watering Cans)

Sprinklers were small watering can-like objects of toy size, intended for sprinkling lavendar water, etc.

1822 Sale

A pair of blue sprinklers, gilt handles, embossed figures and glass shades	R.£2. 0.0.

SUNDIAL

1822 Sale

An accurate sundial (and a pair of flower pots and stands painted in moths, with glass shades)	R.25/-

SUPPER SETS

Supper sets, made up of four covered dishes which fit round a central covered bowl, are today often called breakfast services in error. A typical example is illustrated in Plate 262. Such sets were also known as 'sandwich sets'. Although supper, or sandwich sets were not included in the 1818 sale, such articles were made by 1815 as is evidenced by Chamberlain's (of Worcester) account books: 'A Table service and Sandwich, white Patent-Ironstone. £12.14.0,' purchased from George & Charles Mason in February 1815.

Plate 262. A very rare complete Mason's Ironstone supper service decorated with the blue-printed 'Blue Pheasants' pattern (see page 128). Supper sets of this type were included in the 1822 sale. Printed crowned name mark. Diameter of complete set 22ins. c.1820-25. Mason's Works Collection

1822 Sale

A white supper set	R.20/-
A supper service, centre and 4 quadrants and covers, Japanned flower, gilt	R.£4. 0.0.
A supper set, richly gilt, 10 pieces	R.£3.10.0.
A supper set, rich Japan, gold edge	R.30/-
A blue supper set (see Plate 262)	R.25/-
An oval set, Japan, gilt, with mahogany tray	R.£2.12.0.
A square supper set, rich Japan	R.£2.10.0.
A square supper service, finished Japan	R.£3.10.0.
A square supper set, 8 pieces, snipe pattern	R.£2. 0.0.
A square supper set, willow Japan, 12 pieces	R.£3.10.0.
A supper set, 5 pieces and tray, Rose Japan	R.£3. 3.0.

TABLET

1851 Exhibition

A monumental tablet, made of Ironstone, and lettered under the glaze

TEA CADDIES

1818 Sale

2 square caddies

2 tea caddies, groups of flowers and gold lace border

2 caddies, mazarine ground & gold

1822 Sale

4 square canisters (tea caddies?) Japan, with shades	R.£2. 0.0.
A pair of Chinese tea caddies	R.30/-
2 rich caddies and shades	R.42/-

TEA KETTLES

1818 Sale

2 cabinet tea kettles

Plate 263. A large Mason's Ironstone blue-printed 'Pagoda' pattern teapot (see Chapters One and Two). Blue-printed mark 'Patent Ironstone China Warranted'. 10½ ins. long. c.1820-30. R.G. Austin, Esq.

TEAPOTS

1818 Sale

1 Cabinet teapot

TEASETS, etc.

1818 Sale

One breakfast, tea and coffee service, corn flower sprig and gold lines, viz. 12 bowls and saucers, 12 tea cups and saucers, 15 coffee cans, 12 breakfast plates, 1 teapot and stand, 1 salt (sugar) box, 1 cream ewer, 1 pint basin, 2 bread and butter plates, and 2 butter tubs and stands

1 breakfast, tea and coffee set, vine embossed

1822 Sale

A tea and breakfast set, 56 pieces	
A tea service, Dresden sprig, 68 pieces	
A dejeune (tea set) gold edge, Japan	R.£2. 2.0.
A dejeune (tea set) festoon flowers & sprig	R.15.0.
A teaset, Japan, 57 pieces	R.£4. 4.0.
A teaset, coloured flowers, 45 pieces	R.30/-
A breakfast & tea service, India sprig, 111 pieces	R.£4. 4.0.
A dejeune, Indian garden	R.50/-
A breakfast service, dragon pattern, 70 pieces	R.£2.15.0.
A tea service, white, 45 pieces	R.15/-
A ditto, yellow & gold border, 45 pieces	R.£1. 5.0.

Plate 264. A neatly potted and attractive Mason's Ironstone trio from a teaset (see also Plate 265). c.1815-20. Phillips

Plate 265. The teapot, covered sugar bowl and milk jug from the tasteful teaset which included cups and saucers as Plate 264. Impressed name mark in circular form on teapot. Teapot 5¼ ins. high. c.1815-20. Phillips

Colour Plate 10. Representative pieces of an impressed marked 'Mason's Patent Ironstone China' dessert service of the early 1820s, hand-painted with flowers within a richly gilt dark-blue border. Sauce tureen 6½ ins. high. Godden of Worthing Ltd.

Colour Plate 11. An impressed marked 'Mason's Patent Ironstone China' dish from the part dessert service shown in Plate 197. Inscribed 'Interior of the Hall of Kenilworth Castle, Warwickshire', almost certainly painted by Samuel Bourne and part of the scenic service offered in 1822, see page 192. 10¼ ins. by 9ins. Geoffrey Godden, Chinaman

Plate 267. A neatly potted small size Mason's Ironstone teapot painted with flowers. Richly gilt spout and handle. Impressed name mark. 5¼ ins. high. c.1815-20. Sotheby's

Plate 266. A charming and neatly potted covered sugar bowl matching in shape that shown in Plate 265 but here decorated in a more traditional style. Impressed name mark inside cover. 5ins. high. 1815-20. Godden of Worthing Ltd.

Plate 268. A very rare oval Mason's Ironstone tray for an early morning teaset, decorated in a traditional manner. This object with its moulded basket-work edge suggests that some of the small sized matching tearwares, as Plates 266 and 267, were originally part of such tray sets. Impressed mark 'Patent Ironstone China' with Royal Arms as Plate 150a. 16¾ by 13¼ ins. c.1815-20. Geoffrey Godden, Chinaman

Plate 269. A very rare Mason's Ironstone bourdaloue (or lady's chamber pot) decorated in a traditional style. Impressed name mark. 8¾ ins. long. c.1815-20. Godden of Worthing Ltd.

TOILET SETS
1818 Sale
1 elegant toilet ewer and basin, antique form & pattern

1822 Sale

2 chamber sets, white	R.26/-
2 blue and white pheasant toilet suites, 16 pieces	R.10/-
6 ditto jugs and a toilet suite, dragon pattern	R.10/-
A ditto (pheasant and flowers) toilet suite, 8 pieces	
A chamber slop pail and cover, painted in flowers, gilt edges and ornaments	R.£2. 0.0.
A chamber slop pail & cover, blue birds and flowers	R.16/-
A chamber service, Chinese figures, with (glass) carafe and tumblers	R.25/-
2 chamber sets, white, with (glass) carafes and tumblers	R.25/-
2 new form blue chamber sets, with (glass) carafes and tumblers	R.£2. 0.0.
2 chamber sets, green leaf border, with (glass) carafes and tumblers	R.35/-
A chamber service, very richly Japanned, with carafes and tumblers (glass)	R.£2. 0.0.
A chamber set, basket Japan, with carafe and tumbler (glass)	R.£1. 0.0.
2 chamber sets, jar pattern	Sold for £1.11.6.
2 chamber services, gold jar pattern	R.35/-

1826 Oxford Auction Sale
Complete chamber services with additional pieces, such as foot pails, slop jars &c. &c.

Plate 270. An early Mason's Ironstone chamber pot, painted with a standard 'Japan' pattern. 6ins. high. c.1815-20. Godden of Worthing Ltd.

TOY OR MINIATURE PIECES
1818 Sale
1 toy ewer, basin, jug and mug, for a cabinet
4 toy Dresden pattern cups and saucers
2 toy tea kettles
2 toy jars & covers

1822 Sale
2 toy ewers and basins, mazarine, with shades	R.27/-
4 toy spouted mugs, rich Japan (and 2 candlesticks, Tourney sprigs and shades)	R.35/-
1 toy watering can (a shell inkstand, red ground and 2 teapots with glass shades).	R.£1.12.0.
A pair of toy chamber candlesticks and 2 buckets with glasses	R.23/-
A pair of toy hand candlesticks, a pen tray and sprinkling pot, gold edges and flowers	R.25/-
A pair of toy jars, gilt and painted in flowers (and a violet basket painted in landscape)	R.25/-
A toy jug (with a violet basket painted in landscapes, and inkstand and sprinkler)	R.£1. 0.0.
2 toy jugs and a sprinkler, Japan flowers, 3 glasses and 4 toy candlesticks	R.£2. 0.0.
A toy ewer and basin, painted in landscape, 2 pairs of candlesticks and glass shades	R.25/-
1 toy teapot, 2 inks and 3 shades	R.24/-
A small ewer & basin, 2 toy watering cans and 2 shell candlesticks	Sold for £1. 3,0.

1828 Advertisements (see page 113) mention 'diminutive specimens which could relate to these numerous miniature or 'toy' pieces: "Ornaments of every description that can be manufactured in China from the minutest article calculated to adorn pier table and cabinets..."
See Colour Plate 12.

TUREENS
Tureens were normally part of dinner services, two being included in most sets. They were rarely sold as individual pieces.

1822 Sale
2 soup tureens and stands, rich brown and gold border   R.£3.10.0.

UNMERAPOORA TEA EXTRACTORS
The rare rather ungainly pots normally bear a formal floral design in the so-called 'Japan' style. They bear a special printed mark comprising the words 'MASON'S Unmerapoora Tea Pot' within a double-lined oval.

One may reflect that they did not seem to be very popular — a mere short-lived novelty.

1826 Oxford Auction Sale
A supply of Unmerapoora tea extractors, which have entirely superseded the Rockingham teapot.

Plate 271. A rare blue ground Mason's Ironstone Unmerapoora tea extractor as mentioned in an 1826 sale advertisement. 7¼ ins. high. c.1825-35. R. and Z. Taylor Collection

URNS
1822 Sale

A pair of handsome urns on pedestals, richly gilt and glass shades	R.£2. 0.0.
A pair of flower urns, richly gilt and painted and 2 glass shades	R.35/-
A set of fine Grecian shape urns, painted in birds and flowers sumptuously gilt and 5 shades	R.£6.10.0.
A handsome essence urn, blue ground, enriched by moths, flowers and gilt decoration	R.£4. 4.0.
A ditto, its companion	R.£4. 4.0.
A pair of urns, beautifully painted in landscapes, and glass shades	R.£2. 2.0.

VASES (see also Jars and Bottles)
1818 Sale

2 Lizard-handled vases	18.0.
2 Three handled fluted vases	
1 sideboard vase, dragon handles, sumptuously gilt	
2 oak leaf low vases and covers	
2 Three handle dragon vases	

1822 Sale

A pair of hexagon vases, gilt Chinese buildings, figures, flowers and moths	R.£2.15.0.

Plate 272. Three rare and superb Mason's Ironstone vases richly gilt over a blue ground and painted by Samuel Bourne (see page 192). Impressed marked. 11½ and 7¾ ins. high. c.1820-25. Sotheby's

Plate 273. A rare orange-ground Mason's Ironstone small vase, with gilt handles. Impressed name mark. 6ins. high. c.1815-20. Geoffrey Godden

Plate 274. An unusual yellow-ground Mason's Ironstone covered vase painted with figures in landscape. Impressed name mark. 9½ins. high. c.1815-20. Photo Chichester Antiques

A pair of biscuit vases, with bandeau of flowers and glass shades	R.35/-
A suite of 3 ditto, with shades	R. 35/-
A splendid Neapolitan vase, painted by S. Bourne (see Plate 251)	R.£30. 0.0. Unsold at £25. 4.0.
2 Hexagon vases, mazarine, 1 faulty	R.£10. 0.0.
2 Chimney vases, Chinese pattern	R.£1. 0.0.
2 ditto Japanned	R.25/-
A set of 3 vases, fruit and green ground, with shades	R.£3.15.0.
2 vases, views in Rome	R.£4. 4.0.
A very beautiful Italian formed vase, painted by S. Bourne, superbly gilt and burnished.	R.35gns. Unsold at 33gns.
A Pagoda vase, Japan	R.£5.15.6.
A set of 5 vases, painted shells and landscapes, red ground	R.£8.8.0.
A splendid Hall jar, mazarine and oriental devices	R.£12.12.0.
An Italian formed vase, superior painting, richly burnished and finely modelled	R.£18.18.0.
5 two handle vases, enamel sprig, on mazarine ground	R.£2.10.0.
A hexagon temple jar	R.£1. 8.0.
A dragon vase and cover, Indian devices	R.£3.13.6.
A two handled Etruscan formed flower vase, highly finished in flowers and gold, with shade	Unsold at £2.14.0.
A Pagoda vase, for vestibule	Unsold at £3.12.0.
2 vases, green ground, fruit, and shades	R.£4. 4.0.
A pair of handsome vases, richly gilt and painted in flowers, and 2 blue bottles in birds, and glass shades	R.30/-
A noble vase, formed from the antique, beautifully painted in landscapes and figures by Bourne, and sumptuously gilt	R.£21. 0.0. Unsold at £17. 6.6.
A pair of ornaments in the style of the Portland vase and shades	R.£2.10.0.
3 handsome vases, painted in landscape, and shades	R.£4. 4.0.
2 vases, flies (painted) on mazarine ground, and shades	28/-
Five vases and covers, Japan	R.40/-
2 vases and covers, green dragon	R.30/-
2 vases, views in Rome	R.£4. 0.0.
3 vases, painted in landscapes	R.£3.10.0.
A vase, painted in shells	R.£2.10.0.
2 Grecian shape vases, flowers and green ground, with shades	R.£3. 3.0.
A handsome two-handle vase, mazarine and shade	R.£2. 2.0.
2 handsome Satyr vases, painted in landscapes and shades	R.£4.10.0.
A handsome one-handled vase, fruit and green ground	R.30/-
2 rich vases, fruit and green ground	R.£2.10.0.
A pair of four-handled vases, mazarine	R.£2. 2.0.
2 Spanish (shape?) vases, mazarine	R.£2. 2.0.
2 Satyr vases, flowers and red ground	R.£3. 3.0.

Plate 275. A large Mason's Ironstone vase richly gilt over a deep blue ground. Perhaps the "sideboard vase — dragon handles sumptuously gilt" of the 1818 sale catalogue. 18¾ins. high. c.1815-20. Godden of Worthing Ltd.

Plate 276. A pair of blue-ground Mason's Ironstone vases over-painted and gilt in a typical manner. 13½ins. high. c.1815-20. Godden of Worthing Ltd.

Plate 277, left. A very simple blue-ground Mason's Ironstone vase over-painted and gilt in a typical manner. 12½ins. high. c.1815-20. R. and Z. Taylor Collection

Plate 278, right. A large blue-ground Mason's Ironstone vase, richly decorated in a typical style. 24ins. high. c.1815-20. Bonhams

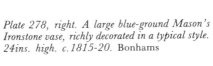

183

Plate 279. A large covered Mason's Ironstone hall vase with dragon handles decorated with formal floral design. 26½ ins. high. c.1815-25. Sotheby's Belgravia

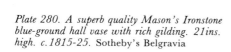

Plate 280. A superb quality Mason's Ironstone blue-ground hall vase with rich gilding. 21ins. high. c.1815-25. Sotheby's Belgravia

Plate 281. A large impressed-marked 'Mason's Patent Ironstone China' vase painted with a typical Japan pattern, shown with a miniature ewer Vase 15ins. high. c.1815-25. Godden of Worthing Ltd.

Plate 282. A good quality Mason's Ironstone blue ground vase with gilded relief motifs. 21ins. high. c.1820-25. Godden of Worthing Ltd.

Plate 283. Three small size Mason's Ironstone vases, each painted with typical so-called 'Japan' pattern in blue, red, green and gold. Centre vase 7¼ins. high. c.1815-20. Godden of Worthing Ltd.

185

Plate 284. A set of three Mason's Ironstone vases decorated in the 'Japan' style. The left-hand example reversed to show the alternative panel. Printed crowned mark. 8½ and 7 ins. high. c.1840. Godden of Worthing Ltd.

Plate 285. A Mason's Ironstone covered vase bearing a typical coloured-in printed design. Printed crowned name mark. 16ins. high. c.1835-45. J.S. West Collection

Plate 286. Two Mason's Ironstone covered vases of characteristic form decorated with typical printed designs. Printed crowned name mark. 16ins. high. c.1835-45. Sotheby's Belgravia

Plate 287. One of a pair of Mason's Ironstone covered vases bearing a typical coloured-in printed design. Printed crowned name mark. 15ins. high. c.1840. Godden of Worthing Ltd.

Plate 288. A rare Mason's Ironstone vase after an Oriental original decorated with underglaze-blue printed motifs. Printed crowned name mark. 9⅜ ins. high. c.1840. Victoria and Albert Museum (Crown Copyright)

Plate 289. Two large Mason's Ironstone hall or alcove vases decorated in the fashionable Chinese style. 58 and 56½ ins. high. c.1840. City Museum and Art Gallery, Stoke-on-Trent

Plate 290. A large Mason's Ironstone covered hall or alcove vase with rare yellow ground decorated with typical printed designs. Printed mock-Chinese seal mark. 37¾ ins. high. c.1840-45. Sotheby's Belgravia

Plate 291. A Mason's Ironstone vase of the same form as that shown in Colour Plate 6, richly decorated in the Oriental style. Printed mock-Chinese seal mark. 17¼ ins. high. c.1840-51. Sotheby's Belgravia

VEGETABLE DISHES

Ordinary covered vegetable dishes were included in dinner services (Plates 143, 152 and 158). The 'vegetable dishes for hot water' listed here are rarely found. The base is deep and was intended to be filled with hot water. A shallow dished section fitted over this to hold the vegetables, the middle section was kept hot by contact with the hot water in the base, and a cover fitted over the middle section enclosing the heat.

1822 Sale

2 vegetable dishes for hot water	R.£3. 0.0.
2 vegetable dishes, Japan	R.30/-
2 vegetable dishes for hot water, gold jar pattern (and a rag-out dish & cover)	R.£2. 2.0.
2 vegetable dishes for hot water (2 cheese stands and 6 bakers) grasshopper (pattern), Japan	28/-
2 hexagon vegetable dishes for hot water and 6 bakers, nosegay pattern	R.30/-

WAFER CUP
1822 Sale

Wafer cup and cover (with 2 inkstands)

WATERING CANS
1818 Sale

2 Watering cans

1822 Sale

1 Toy watering can (1 shell ink and 2 teapots with glass shades)	R.£1.12.0.
2 sprinkling bottles (2 cups and covers, moths on mazarine ground, with glass shades)	R.30/-

Plate 292. A small Mason's Ironstone covered jug — perhaps one of the 'sprinkling bottles' of the 1822 sale. Such bottles and watering cans held lavender water and other sweet smelling liquids. Impressed name mark. 6¾ ins. high. c.1820. Godden of Worthing Ltd.

WINE COOLERS

1822 Sale

2 white ice pails	R. 16/-
A pair of wine coolers, gilt mask heads and ornaments (see Plate 293)	R.£2. 2.0.
A pair of Ice pails, covers and liners, gilt and painted in flowers	R.£3. 0.0.
A wine cooler, gilt and Japanned flowers	R.30/-
Pair of blue Ironstone coolers	R.14/-
2 ice pails, covers and liners, grasshopper and flowers, gilt edge	R.£2. 2.0.
2 fluted top wine coolers, willow (and 2 Stilton cheese stands)	R.£2. 0.0.
2 ice pails, richly gilt	R.£3.10.0.
2 wine coolers, elegantly gilt	R.£2. 2.0.
A pair of ice pails, Japan	R.£3. 0.0.
2 ice pails, flowers in compartments, on blue border, richly gilt	R.£4. 4.0.
2 porous wine coolers and 24 (glass) wines	R.30/-
2 ice pails, blue, and 2 wine coolers, white	R.25/-
2 richly gilt ice pails	R.£4. 0.0.

Plate 293. A superb quality Mason's Ironstone wine, or fruit, cooler, hand-painted with flowers. The 1822 sale catalogue included a "pair of wine coolers, gilt mask heads and ornaments". c.1820-25. Mason's Works Collection

Plate 294. A fine quality blue-ground Mason's wine, or fruit, cooler richly painted and gilt in a typical Mason's style. 11½ ins. high. c.1815-20. Sotheby's Belgravia

2 ice pails, peacock Japan	£2. 0.0.
A pair of ice Pails, very richly Japanned	R.£3. 3.0.
Two ice pails, rich Japan	R.£4. 4.0.
2 coolers, plaid Japan	R.£2.10.0.
A pair of blue Ironstone coolers	R.14/-
A pair of wine coolers, rich Japan	R.£2.10.0.

SUMMARY OF MASON PATTERNS LISTED IN 1818 AND 1822 SALE CATALOGUES

The colourful Chinese-styled 'Japan' patterns, with their rich underglaze blue and overglaze reds and greens and gilt enrichments, were the designs most favoured for the many dinner and dessert services listed in the catalogues of 1818 and 1822. Typical examples were:
'Mogul' pattern (Colour Plate 9)
'Table and Flower Pot' pattern (Plate 143)
'India Grasshopper' pattern (Plate 153)
'Rose and Rock' pattern (perhaps as Colour Plate 5)
and others listed as 'Old Japan' or merely as 'Japan, red, purple and gold'.

These and similar bold, colourful designs were the staple patterns employed by the Masons on their Patent Ironstone China, not only on dinner and dessert ware but also on a host of other objects: jugs in sets of graduating sizes (Plates 242-245); spill vases (Plate 246); punch bowls (Plates 260 and 261); vases, and so on.

A popular design based on a Chinese original was the 'Dragon' pattern, which was produced in different colours — blue, green, red, etc., and was used to decorate services, jugs and vases.

Another popular style had a deep underglaze blue ground with gilt floral designs added over the glaze, producing a very rich effect and showing the fine quality of the Mason gilding. Some very fine blue-ground ware was delicately enamelled with birds, etc., in place of the formal gilt floral designs. Such objects were far more expensive than the repetitive 'Japan' patterns with their broad areas of colour — Lot 887: "A handsome Essence Urn blue ground, enriched with Moths, flowers and gilt decoration". Very many objects are listed in the 1818 and 1822 catalogues as having a rich mazarine blue ground (see Plates 234, 235, 275-278, 280, 294 and Colour Plate 10).

Many objects were painted with flowers, ranging from simple, inexpensive sprig patterns: "A breakfast service, neat sprig, 100 pieces", to the finer, naturally-depicted flowers described as 'Dresden flowers': "A dessert service, Dresden flowers, 37 pieces".

Ware was sometimes decorated to special order, rare examples having regimental arms and similar devices. The "12 plates, richly painted with various arms crests" may well have been samples kept in the London shop so that the various styles could be viewed by the customer. Apart from special orders taken at the London shop or sent direct to the manufactory, it must be remembered that some untypical designs could have been added by London decorators or by other manufacturers for the sales included several lots of white ware, and Chamberlain of Worcester purchased white Ironstone direct from the Mason factory at Fenton.

The only artist mentioned by name in the catalogues of the 1818 and 1822 sales is Samuel Bourne, and the references relate to landscape subjects:

A very beautiful, painted landscape dessert service, by S. Bourne. [Lot 309, 1822 sale. Reserve £30. Unsold at £29.18s.6d.]
A costly dessert service exquisitely painted in select views by S. Bourne, enriched with burnished gold. [See Colour Plate 11 and Plate 197 for dessert wares of this type — perhaps even one of the services offered in 1822.]
A noble vase, formed from the antique, beautifully painted in landscapes and figures by Bourne, and sumptuously gilt. [Lot 866, 1822 sale. Reserve £21. Unsold at £17.6s.6d. See Plate 251 for an example of this type.]

There is a further lot, but no subject is mentioned:

A splendid Neapolitan vase, painted by S. Bourne. [The superb vases illustrated in Plates 250 and 251 are almost certainly by Bourne.]

The first edition of L. Jewitt's *Ceramic Art of Great Britain,* 1878 gives some information on this little known artist:

Mr. Samuel Bourne, of Norton-in-the-Moors, Staffordshire, who had been apprenticed to Messrs. Wood & Caldwell this partnership terminated in July 1818, to learn the art of enamel-painting, and who attained by his industry and talents a high reputation, entered the service of Mr. Minton, in 1828, as chief designer and artist, and continued to render the firm occasional services until 1860 [this date is corrected to 1863 in the 1883 revised edition] when the infirmities of increasing years necessitated his retirement.

The Fenton 1851 census return describes ''Samuel Bourne, Painter-artist'' as aged sixty-two, and his place of birth as Norton, Staffordshire. (His son, also Samuel Bourne, is listed as having been born at Fenton and aged twenty-nine in 1851.) The place of birth tallies with Jewitt's information, and there can be little doubt that this Samuel Bourne is the S. Bourne referred to in the 1822 Mason sale catalogue. The census return shows that he was born in or about 1789, so at the time of the 1822 sale he would have been approximately thirty-three.

It is possible that Samuel Bourne may have been employed by Miles Mason, decorating his porcelain (as opposed to the post-1813 Ironstone china), from perhaps the age of twenty in about 1809, see Plates 125 and 126. The rather free landscape painting on post-1813 Ironstone ware, such as the two vases shown in Plates 273 and 274, may have been executed by Bourne. Some of the more elaborately decorated articles included in the 1822 sale could well have been painted by this artist, like ''A set of 5 vases, painted shells and landscapes, red ground''. Almost certainly the vases illustrated in Plate 272 are by this talented painter.

Samuel Bourne painted a watercolour of George Miles Mason, his wife and three children. He also painted several topographical views which were later engraved and one appears in John Ward's 1843 work *The Borough of Stoke-upon-Trent.* His painting on Mason's Ironstone wares is not signed.

MODERN PRODUCTS

I show in Plates 295-297 a selection of modern Mason's Ironstone productions showing typical shapes and patterns which are available in

Plate 295. A selection of modern Mason's productions decorated with the colourful 'Double Landscape' design in the style of earlier Mason's Ironstone wares. Mason's Ironstone

Plate 296. A selection of modern Mason wares decorated with the printed 'Oriental' design coloured-in by hand. Mason's Ironstone

Plate 297. A selection of modern Mason wares in the Chartreuse pattern. Mason's Ironstone

retail shops today and which attract buyers seeking traditional English pieces for their homes.

Remember that in the main these decorative wares are made and purchased to be used as were the original Mason's Patent Ironstone pieces over a hundred and fifty years previously.

Even today one can see the Oriental influence in these designs, reflecting perhaps Miles Mason's early career selling Chinese porcelains in London during the later part of the eighteenth century. They also reflect the time honoured traditional appeal of Oriental designs.

The plate shown in Plate 298 is the second of a special issue of Christmas plates which commenced in 1975; this example depicts a printed view of Holyrood House, Edinburgh. It is interesting to see that the border to this 1976 plate is the same as the c.1830 example shown in Plate 160. The mark on this recent example is shown in Plate 298a — note the inclusion of the wording 'Made in England' in the standard Mason mark.

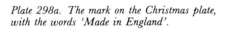

Plate 298. Mason's Christmas plate depicting Holyrood House. Issued in 1976. The border design is a reissue of one produced over one hundred and forty years earlier, see Plate 160. The mark is reproduced in Plate 298a. Diameter 10ins. Author's Collection

Plate 298a. The mark on the Christmas plate, with the words 'Made in England'.

Colour Plate 12. A selection of 'toy' or miniature items in Mason's Patent Ironstone China. Many toy pieces were included in the 1818 and 1822 sales. The larger vase which is 8ins. high is included for comparison only. c.1815-25. Godden of Worthing Ltd.

Chapter Six

Mason Marks and Dating

PORCELAINS

AS WE HAVE seen in Chapter Two the Liverpool porcelains made by the Wolfe, Mason, Luckcock partnership are not marked.

After 1800 when Miles Mason started production on his own account in Staffordshire a simple name mark 'M. MASON' was sometimes impressed into the body. His 1804 advertisement (see page 54) included the notation: ''N.B. The articles are stamped on the bottom of the large pieces to prevent imposition''.

Only the larger pieces were marked. A complete teaset as originally sold would probably only have been marked on the teapot, its stand, the covered sugar bowl, some of the milk jugs and the two plates. Consequently the now separated teacups, coffee cups or coffee cans, saucers and the waste bowl will be unmarked. Identification of these pieces therefore rests on their relation in shape, body and pattern to the marked pieces, in other words to a familiarity with key marked examples.

The illustrations in this work show a good cross section both of shapes — most of which are unique to this factory, as well as patterns, and these should enable the reader to attribute these Mason porcelains correctly.

It should be noted that the standard impressed mark 'M. MASON' very often occurs on the foot rim of teapots, sugar bowls and creamers (see Plate 72) and not on the flat slightly recessed base. It also occurs, though rarely, on the outside edge of a teapot base so that it is visible without turning the pot up, see Plate 78.

Some pieces bear various small impressed signs which were probably the individual potter's tally marks for piece rate payment. One quite commonly found example takes the form of a small circle — as if the potter had a retracted ball point pen which he pressed into the base of the article. This mark is shown on the left.

The basic 'M. MASON' mark sometimes appears to be framed in an oblong outline but this is merely the outline of the matrix or die used to impress the name into the porcelain and the presence or otherwise of this outline is of no significance.

This impressed 'M. MASON' mark is, in my experience, only found on porcelains of the c.1804-13 period and then not on all pieces.

Some authors have quoted as a mark the full name 'MILES MASON', but I have seen this only on blue-printed Pagoda-styled designs of the 1807-13 period, in conjunction with a mock-Chinese seal mark, all printed in underglaze blue. On some of these patterns, the seal device appears without a name. As other manufacturers also used seal devices of this type, the shapes should be closely compared with the marked forms. This mark, reproduced below, does not appear to have been used on the early versions of the blue-printed Pagoda design before about 1807. Great care is necessary in attributing the Pagoda-type designs bearing the seal mark alone without the name, and both the shape and the printed design should be carefully checked against pieces illustrated in this book.

Pattern numbers can be a very important guide to identification especially when the painted number can be checked against a known Miles Mason design. The following patterns are included in this book:

Pattern 2	Enamelled simple floral design	Plate 51
Pattern 3	Enamelled simple floral design	Plates 52, 54 and 55
Pattern 22	Enamelled formal vase of flowers design	Plates 56 and 57
Pattern 43	Formal floral and leaf design in gold and platinum	Plate 90
Pattern 48	Blue Pagoda print with gilt border	Plate 45
Pattern 49	Blue Pagoda print with gilt border	Plate 41
Pattern 83	Enamelled rose and trellis design	Plate 70
Pattern 84	Enamelled variation on pattern 83	Plate 71
Pattern 91	Narrow formal leaf border	Plate 94
Pattern 100	Dessert pattern, wide gilt and enamelled scroll and floral design	Plates 113, 114 and 115

Note, however, that the majority of Miles Mason porcelains featured in this work do not bear a pattern number. It is often worthwhile to check the inside of lids for the Mason pattern numbers. The numbers are normally painted in a neat manner, sometimes prefixed 'N' or 'No' but at other times only the numerals were painted.

The later, post-1813 porcelains made by Charles James Mason and George M. Mason do not appear to have been marked and they seldom bear a pattern number. On account of their later period these porcelains bear little resemblance to the earlier Miles Mason porcelains and much research remains to be carried out on the post-1813 products. Some pieces of this later type are illustrated in Plates 98-101 and 121-126.

EARTHENWARES

It must also be remembered that Miles Mason and his sons produced the normal run of earthenware, of pearlware type. Blue-printed ware, including large dinner services, was made and may bear the printed marks: 'SEMI-CHINA / WARRANTED'. The name 'MASON'S' was rarely placed above this mark, see Plate 185.

When the brothers George M. Mason and Charles James Mason formed a working partnership on the retirement of their father in 1813, they used many different marks incorporating the initials 'G. & C.J.M.' or the fuller particulars 'G.M. & C.J. Mason'. Examples relate to the 1813-26 period, but such marks do not often occur on Ironstone ware.

The printed mark 'W. MASON' appears on a fine-blue printed earthenware platter formerly in the Meigh Collection (see my *Illustrated Encyclopaedia of British Pottery and Porcelain*, Barrie & Jenkins, 1966, Plate 389). This and other similarly marked specimens belong to the period 1811-24.

IRONSTONE

From the introduction of 'Mason's Patent Ironstone China' in 1813 (see Chapter Four) various 'Patent Ironstone' marks were used. On plates and large articles, the full description 'Mason's Patent Ironstone China' normally appears in one or two lines; on small items, the name 'Mason' is often omitted and the words 'Patent Ironstone China' are arranged in circular form. Although within a few years the description 'Ironstone China' was taken up by other manufacturers, the word 'Patent' should only occur on Mason ware or on ware made after 1850 by successive firms, such as Ashworth's (see Chapter Seven). The use of these impressed Mason marks would seem to have ceased by about 1830, and so an impressed mark always indicates an early example.

Apart from the normal 'Mason's...' or 'Patent Ironstone China', the following more unusual marks of identification may be found on some rare pieces, especially dinner service tureens: an ornate printed Royal Arms' mark, see above; an impressed Royal Arms device with the word 'Patent' in the central shield (Plate 150a); 'Mason's Cambrian Argil' (Plate 159) on the printed earthenware, apparently of the early 1820s (Mason is recorded as purchasing Cambrian clay in the 1819-21 period), and occasionally the inscription 'Patent Ironstone Warranted' is found printed in blue or black.

The standard blue or black printed Mason's 'Patent Ironstone China' mark with the crown was in use by 1815, but the impressed marks are those normally found on pre-1820 Ironstone. For a few years, the impressed marks and the new crowned printed marks were used concurrently, the two marks occurring on the same piece; but by about 1830 the use of the printed mark would seem to have superseded the former impressed markings completely. This printed mark was used over many years, with several variations, on Ironstone ware. In some specimens from the 1840s the word 'Improved' was introduced (often replacing the word 'Patent'), and in the 1840s the outline of the crown became angular. This later version is seen well on the base of the

1851 Exhibition vase shown in Colour Plate 6, the mark being reproduced below beside the earlier more rounded crown. These printed marks were sometimes filled in or coloured over with various overglaze colours. In rare cases the crown and the word 'Mason's' appear alone, especially on the later Bandana wares.

Standard printed mark.

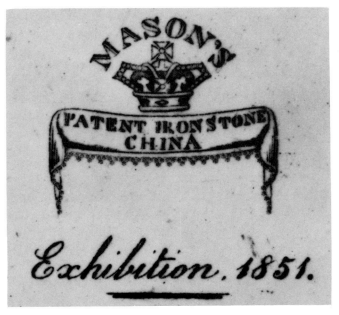

Later mark with angular crown.

It must be understood that very many slight variations of the basic crowned Mason's Patent Ironstone marks occur, for most Mason standard designs were based on a printed outline and the mark formed part of each engraved copper plate. In effect we have one mark to each printed design. For this reason too the colour of the mark will reflect the colour of the basic printed outline, so that we will have an underglaze blue mark on a blue design. Complications arise when an old design was reissued at a later period, for if the original copper plates were reused the old former mark will also appear. Ashworths also used the basic printed crowned mark after 1861.

With regard to other marks incorporating the name 'Mason', the reader should bear in mind the fact that G.L. Ashworth & Bros. (Ltd.) used this name in the latter part of the nineteenth century and up to 1968, when the firm was retitled Mason's Ironstone China Ltd. As successors to the original firm, they were — and are — quite entitled to use this registered trade name, although it is confusing to some new collectors.

It is noteworthy that the early impressed marked specimens of 'Mason's Patent Ironstone China' do not generally have painted pattern numbers. As a general rule, it may be considered that specimens bearing a painted pattern number are post-1830, and certainly those numbers in excess of one hundred are of this later period. High numbers such as B 9799 are, of course, of the Ashworth period and often indicate a twentieth century origin. The next series

prefixed 'C' is confined to the present century, C 5000 having been reached in 1978.

Examples bearing impressed date marks such as 1.10 are also obviously of a post-Mason period — in the case just cited the piece would have been potted in January 1910.

The incorporation of the word 'England' shows a date subsequent to 1891 so obviously the mark reproduced left is not a true Mason mark but one used after 1891 by Ashworths (see Chapter Seven.). The words 'Made in England' denote a present century dating, as will design registration numbers above 365,000.

Returning to nineteenth century marks. The words 'FENTON / STONE WORKS' appear printed within an octagonal double-lined frame on ware from c.1825 onwards, sometimes with a painted pattern number added below the main printed mark. Specimens bearing this mark are not of the finest quality and are normally purely utilitarian pieces decorated with standard gay Japan patterns based on printed outlines.

Some special types of Mason products bear marks individual to that family. For example the chimney pieces bear a large elaborate Royal Arms mark as shown in Plate 215. Similarly the Patent Yacht Club finger bowl (see page 152), the Unmerapoora Tea Extractor (Plate 271), Mason's Siamese Jardinier and the Patent Butter Frigefacter, bear special printed marks. Other special printed marks appear on Mason Bandana Ware of the late 1840s and early 1850s (Plate 198) and on the rare Bronzed Metallic Wares made by C.J. Mason in 1850. Some pieces marked 'Royal Terra Cotta Porcelain' are considered to be Mason although there does not seem to be any firm evidence for this belief. This mark is reproduced on the left.

In 1826, the partnership of G.M. and C.J. Mason was terminated and the firm of C.J. Mason & Co. came into being. Several printed marks were used incorporating the initials 'C.J.M. & Co.' or, more rarely, 'C.J. Mason & Co.' The elevation of the factory is sometimes incorporated in these marks, which belong to the 1826-45 period. One of two addresses might be included — 'Fenton Stone Works', describing the works depicted, or 'Lane Delph'. The description 'Granite China' is incorporated in several marks of this period.

202

On some specimens of Ironstone of the 1840 period a rather large Chinese-type seal mark appears printed in underglaze blue, and this is almost certainly a Mason's mark, see Plate 291.

From 1845 to his bankruptcy in 1848, Charles James Mason continued the Fenton Stone China Works, producing Ironstone ware on the old traditional lines. The basic printed crowned mark was also used, and it is difficult, if not impossible to distinguish the ware made in this final period from that made by C.J. Mason & Co., from 1820-45. As explained in Chapter Four, Mason survived the bankruptcy to continue production on a limited scale until c.1853. These late products, including the ware shown in the 1851 Exhibition, were in all probability indistinguishable from the ware of the 1840s.

In carrying out the research needed to prepare this volume, I have been astounded to discover how high a proportion of seemingly Mason Ironstone ware does not bear a factory mark. In some services, only a few pieces are marked. Consequently, when the services are divided, many individual pieces may be found unmarked. Many vases and other ornamental articles are also without marks, and yet other pieces are marked in unusual and easily overlooked positions such as inside covers and inside the top flange of vases. This is not to say that all unmarked Ironstone-type wares were made by Mason — this would be very wide of the mark, for well over a hundred other British firms made this popular type of ceramic and many of their productions were also unmarked. However, study of the first 294 illustrations in this book should enable the reader to distinguish the Mason shapes and designs from those of the many imitators.

Chapter Seven

Mason-type Wares — The Other Manufacturers

I HAVE ALREADY explained that the Masons were by no means the first potters to produce a durable compact earthenware, but there can be no doubt that they publicised and popularised the material — in much the same way that Josiah Wedgwood's perfecting of the creamware body and marketing of it under the new name 'Queen's ware' caught the public's fancy some forty-five years earlier.

Just as other potters copied Wedgwood's Queen's ware, so numerous manufacturers strove to produce ware similar to Mason's new Ironstone. It has been stated that the Masons were protected by their patent rights; but in practice, very similar bodies could be produced from materials differing from the Mason patent specification. There being no copyright on the Mason style of colourful 'Japan' patterns, the only real protection that Mason's patent gave them was over the use of the words 'Patent Ironstone' in describing and marking their ware. The most valuable aspect of the patent was to give publicity to Mason's ware and to suggest to the public that the body was entirely new.

In the following pages, details are given of some of the British firms that are known to have manufactured Ironstone-type ware. This alphabetically arranged list is probably not complete. Examples by little-known potters may come to light as interest in this ware increases. Remember that Ironstone-type wares were also made elsewhere, particularly in America where potters closely copied in style the marks, shapes and patterns of the British wares. Other marks found on Ironstone-type ware are also listed, and these include the Registration Marks used between 1842-83, and from 1884, as well as unidentified marks.

Before Charles James Mason introduced the description 'Ironstone' for his new ware in 1813, the standard name for this type of heavy, compact and durable body was 'Stone China', a description used in the marks of Spode, Davenport, Hicks & Meigh, Ridgway and some lesser-known firms. The term 'Opaque China' was also widely used, but this body is normally a standard white earthenware unrelated to the heavy Stone China. Opaque china and similar descriptions were merely sophisticated and sometimes inaccurate trade terms for earthenware.

The term 'Ironstone' was first used by C.J. Mason in 1813. When this name is preceded by the word 'Patent' on early pre-1830 objects, it may be considered to relate to genuine Mason ware; but existing examples prove that other potters soon adopted the new description, without the prefix 'Patent', to describe their own ware made in the Mason tradition.

The term 'Granite China' was adopted before 1842, as it occurs on marked 'Brameld' ware (q.v.). The name 'Granite' became very popular, especially on ware exported to North America. It was much used by late nineteenth-century manufacturers and occurs with great frequency in trade advertisements.

The address 'Staffordshire' in the following list refers to the district known as the Staffordshire Potteries. This was made up of seven separate towns: Burslem, Cobridge, Fenton, Hanley, Longton, Stoke and Tunstall — all now combined to form the city of Stoke-on-Trent.

William Adams & Sons (Potters) Ltd., Tunstall and Stoke, Staffordshire, 1769-present day (a division of the Wedgwood group since 1966).

This well-known firm produced a wide range of good quality ceramics: basalt, jasper, creamware, parian, porcelain and standard earthenware, as well as Ironstone-type ware. Various marks were used on the Ironstone-type ware from about 1830 onwards. These normally comprise or incorporate the name 'ADAMS' or the initials 'W.A. & S.'. However, the firm changed its title from time to time and from c.1866-99 traded as William & Thomas Adams, during which period the marks incorporated the name 'W. & T. Adams' or the initials 'W. & T.A.' The addition of the word 'England' on any Adams mark (or other mark) normally signifies a date after 1891*. The date '1657' incorporated in several Adams' marks is the claimed date of the firm's establishment. In 1851, William Adams employed 165 men, seventy-one women, sixty-five boys and twenty-six girls. Sample marks are reproduced below. The trade-name 'MICRATEX' has been used for an especially strong Ironstone-type body since 1963.

* It does not necessarily follow that marks without the word 'England' pre-date 1891, as this indication of origin was only required on wares exported to overseas markets. It also happens that the word 'England' was sometimes used by some potters slightly before 1891.

205

Henry Alcock & Co. (Ltd.), Elder Pottery, Cobridge, Staffordshire, c.1861-1910.

Jewitt, writing of Henry Alcock & Co. in the revised 1883 edition of his *Ceramic Art of Great Britain,* noted:

> At these extensive works, which have recently been much enlarged (formerly carried on by John Alcock), Henry Alcock & Co. manufacture white Granite ware, under the names of 'Ironstone china' and 'Parisian porcelain', exclusively for the American markets, and also the common descriptions of printed wares.

The Henry Alcock ware bears marks incorporating the initials 'H.A. & Co.' or the name in full. From 1910-35 the firm was retitled The Henry Alcock Pottery, and the marks include this new title. See also following entries.

John Alcock, Elder Road, Cobridge, Staffordshire, c.1853-60.

John Alcock made a good range of Ironstone wares including registered shapes. Examples are normally clearly marked.

Henry Alcock & Co. succeeded John at the Elder Pottery (see previous entry).

John & George Alcock, Cobridge, Staffordshire, c.1839-46.

This partnership produced good quality Ironstone-type ware. Impressed mark: 'ORIENTAL / STONE / J. & G. ALCOCK.' Other printed marks incorporated the initials 'J. & G.A.

John & Samuel Alcock (Junr.), Cobridge, Staffordshire, c.1848-50.

This firm succeeded John & George Alcock (see previous entry) and continued the old lines and patterns, which included 'flowing blue' designs. Marks include 'J. & S. Alcock Jr.', and the description 'Oriental Stone' was favoured.

Richard Alcock, Central Pottery, Market Place, Burslem, c.1870-82.

Fragments of an Ironstone plate discovered on an 'archaeological' site in California have borne two marks relating to Richard Alcock.

Firstly we have an impressed mark in circular form reading: 'RICHARD ALCOCK. / BURSLEM' with 'Staffordshire' below and the numerals '76' which almost certainly relate to the date of manufacture. In conjunction with this impressed mark appears the printed mark incorporating the Royal Arms device with the wording 'ROYAL PATENT / IRONSTONE / RICHARD ALCOCK / BURSLEM. ENGLAND.' This is an example of the word 'England' appearing in marks before 1891.

Samuel Alcock & Co., Cobridge and Burslem, Staffordshire, c.1828-59.

Samuel Alcock & Co. manufactured a large range of decorative and fine quality porcelain and earthenware. The name has not, in the past, been associated with Ironstone but recently finds on the factory site include fragments marked: 'ALCOCK'S / INDIAN IRONSTONE' with, in some cases, other standard Alcock marks which incorporate the initials 'S.A. & Co.' or the name in full. Several such marks incorporate an ornate armorial bearing (Plate 299). One site fragment bearing the impressed 'Alcock's Indian Ironstone' mark has also the date '1839'. A general review of Samuel Alcock's products is given in my book *British Porcelain, an Illustrated Guide* (Barrie & Jenkins, 1974).

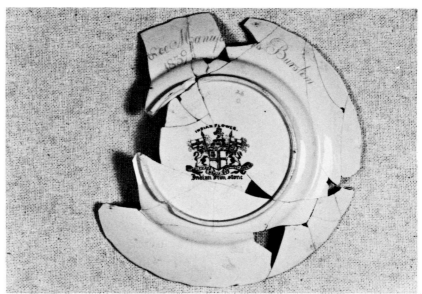

Plate 299. The front and reverse of a plate found on the site of Samuel Alcock's factory showing the armorial device to be found on some of his productions. Dated 1839. City Museum and Art Gallery, Stoke-on-Trent

Jon Anton (Ltd.), Longton, Staffordshire, c.1968-74.

Jon Anton was mainly known for porcelains but Ironstone wares were also made and the standard marks incorporate the name in full.

G.L. Ashworth & Bros. (Ltd.), Hanley, Staffordshire, c.1861-1968 (subsequently continued under the new style 'Mason's Ironstone China Ltd.').

Ashworth have been the largest producers of Ironstone since 1861. The firm acquired Mason's original moulds, patterns, etc., through the partnership between Taylor Ashworth and Francis Morley, the latter having purchased them — some on his own account and some through his later partnerships, the last of which, between Morley and Taylor Ashworth (c.1858-61), led to the formation of G.L. Ashworth & Bros.

The April 1861 Hanley census returns show that at that period Taylor Ashworth, then aged only twenty-two, employed two hundred and fifty men, one hundred women, fifty boys and fifty girls. These figures may have been approximate, as the numbers are strangely even, but they do show that the Ashworth concern was quite large. There is no mention of a partner with Ashworth, a fact that suggests that the Morley-Ashworth partnership had terminated by this period — that is, prior to 1862, the date which has been given by other authorities.

The original Mason engraved designs, incorporating the 'Mason's Patent Ironstone' printed marks, have been extensively used to the present day. Various new marks have also been issued, but these still retain the original wording. Some 'Mason' marks had the name 'Ashworth' added, but these are rather rare. The addition of the word 'England' to a Mason mark indicates an Ashworth parentage after 1891. The wording 'Made in England' is a twentieth century variation (see Plate 298a).

Some Ashworth-Mason ware of early twentieth century date has month and year numerals impressed to show the date of potting. These date numerals take the form 6.07 for June 1907, 7.08 for July 1908, and so on.

Ashworth also produced earthenware other than Ironstone, bearing various printed marks incorporating the initials 'G.L.A. & Bros.' or 'A. Bros.'. Sample Ashworth marks are reproduced.

The *Art Journal* featured an article on Mason and his Ironstone China, in 1867, which included a review of the current Ashworth products:

...Messrs. Ashworth Brothers continue, to the fullest extent, the manufacture of the 'Patent Ironstone China'...and produce all Mason's best patterns in services, etc. from the original moulds...These they produce in immense quantities, both for home and foreign markets, about one-third of their whole productions being export...The 'Ironstone China', from its extreme hardness

and durability...is specially adapted, in its simpler styles of decoration, for services used in large steamship companies, hotels, clubs, colleges, and other places where hard usage has to be undergone; while in its more elaborate and rich style — and it is capable of the very highest degree of finish — it is eminently fitted for families of the highest ranks. It is much used in the houses of the nobility and higher classes. No climate effects this ware...

Although the trading title remained the same for the remainder of the century a change of ownership took place in December 1883 when John S. Goddard purchased the company from the Ashworths and continued it with the help of Ashworth's manager, Charles Brock. Taylor Ashworth joined the Old Hall Earthenware Company Ltd. in 1884.

The largest proportion of Ashworth's output comprises useful ware — dinner, dessert or tea services, with some jugs, vases, etc., decorated with traditional Mason-style designs. A notable exception occurred just before the outbreak of the 1914-18 war when experiments were carried out to produce decorative glaze effects after the Chinese 'rouge flambe' ware. An Austrian chemist, Dr. Basch, was engaged by

Plate 302. An Ashworth's two-handled loving cup, the printed design washed over in green. Printed Mason's crowned name mark. 7ins. high. c.1862-75. Godden of Worthing Ltd.

the then Managing Director, Mr. J.V. Goddard. Numerous experimental pieces were produced and the new ware was christened 'Lustrosa' — but, reputedly, not a piece was marketed due to the outbreak of the war, Dr. Basch's return to Austria and Mr. Goddard's entry into the armed forces. Experimental pieces of Ashworth 'Lustrosa' ware are still preserved in the works museum. Examples were shown at an exhibition held in the Louvre in 1914, and the official catalogue states that these pieces were designed by J.V. Goddard.

On a visit to the Ashworth-Mason factory, I was shown the numerous processes of manufacture and the production of the traditional Mason Ironstone designs. In some cases, these designs have been slightly simplified or amended to bring them into line with modern taste; but in all cases, the spirit of the original design has been preserved. Many will regret, however, the retirement of the old bottle-shaped kilns in favour of the smaller gas-fired ovens into which trolley loads of ware are run without the need of the old protective saggars.

Passing as one does from one process to another, seeing the various skilled hands through which the clay forms must progress before they become fit objects for the table, the ultimate reaction is one of bewilderment that the finished articles can be sold so cheaply. In this world, so many objects seem grossly overpriced; but no one who has seen a pottery in action can ever regard fine ceramics as anything but an inexpensive luxury.

Plate 303. Representative pieces from an Ashworth's part breakfast service. Printed Mason's crowned name mark. Pattern 1426. c.1865-85. Godden of Worthing Ltd.

Plate 304. A fine Ashworth soup tureen and stand in the traditional Mason's style. Pattern B 1834. Printed Mason's crowned name mark. 11ins. high. c.1865-75. Godden of Worthing Ltd.

Plate 305, right. An Ashworth Ironstone bowl showing the reuse of a traditional Mason's design. Printed Mason's crowned name mark with the post-1891 addition of the word 'England'. Diameter 10ins c.1900. Godden of Worthing Ltd.

Plate 306. A decorative and colourful Ashworth Ironstone plate of pattern B 1955. Printed Royal Arms mark. Impressed mark 'Ashworths Real Ironstone China'. Diameter 10ins. c.1875-90. W. Baker Collection

As I have stated previously the Ashworth firm adopted the new name of Mason's Ironstone China Ltd. in the summer of 1968.

In the past the Ashworth products have been neglected by many collectors but are now, rightly, commanding respect. Some examples are extremely rich and decorative, see Colour Plate 13.

W. Baker & Co. (Ltd.), Fenton, Staffordshire, c.1839-1932.

The early ware of this firm was often unmarked, and the marks 'W. Baker & Co.' or 'Baker & Co.' are rarely found. A late printed mark of the post-1893 period when 'Ltd.' was added to the firm's title, is reproduced. The firm was a large one, employing over five hundred people in 1851, and six hundred and fifty in 1861.

Barker & Son, Burslem, Staffordshire, c.1850-60.

The impressed mark 'BARKER & SON' is recorded on Ironstone-type ware, and the initial mark 'B. & S.' occurs on a printed design 'Missouri', registered at the Patent Office on 5th June, 1850 in the name of Barker & Son, Hill Works, Burslem. The partnership employed 265 people in 1851 and was, consequently, a large concern.

Barrow & Co., Longton, Staffordshire, c.1853-56.

This firm, which was also listed as Barrow & Taylor, of Market Street, Longton produced Ironstone wares which bear an impressed or relief-moulded mark incorporating the Royal Arms with supporters, also the words: 'IRONSTONE CHINA / BARROW & CO'.

Bates & Bennett, Cobridge, Staffordshire, c.1868-95.

The first printed mark reproduced may have been used by this firm, but the initials could relate to any one of sixteen other Staffordshire partnerships of the 1820-80 period. An earlier 'B.B.' mark with the pre-Victorian Royal Arms is also reproduced.

Bates, Walker & Co., Burslem, Staffordshire, c.1875-78.

This partnership working the famous Dale Hall works in succession to Bates, Elliott & Co., 1870-75, produced a good general selection of pottery including Ironstone china. One mark incorporates the kneeling boy with vase trade mark with the year '1790' and the initials 'B W & Co.'

Batkin, Walker & Broadhurst, Lane End, Staffordshire, c.1840-45.

Good quality Ironstone-type ware was made by this short-lived firm under the description 'Stone China'. Printed marks incorporate the initials 'B.W. & B.'

Colour Plate 13. Representative parts of a colourful Ashworth's Ironstone dinner service bearing both impressed and printed name marks. Potting date marks for September 1892, pattern number 3623. Tureen 11½ ins. high. Godden of Worthing Ltd.

Beardmore & Edwards, Longton, Staffordshire, c.1856-58.

The initial mark 'B. & E.' occurs, rarely, on blue printed ware. No other Staffordshire partnership used these initials before Bradbury & Emery of c.1889-1902.

J. & M.P. Bell & Co. (Ltd.), Glasgow, Scotland, c.1842-1928.

This firm produced a very large range of earthenware and porcelain. Their exhibits at the 1851 Exhibition included:

> Dinner services in stoneware: Blue printed . . .
> Toilet services in stoneware . . .
> Tea services and jugs in stoneware and porcelain . . .

Patterns mentioned by name include 'Italian lakes'; 'Warwick Vase'; 'Diana'; 'Convolvulus'.

Most of Bell's ware bears marks incorporating the initials 'J.B.' or 'J. & M.P.B. & Co.'. 'Ltd.' was added to the firm's style, and initial marks, from 1881. A bell device was also used as a mark, and it occurs impressed or printed.

Further information on this important firm may be found in Jewitt's *Ceramic Art of Great Britain* (see bibliographic note) or in J.A. Fleming's *Scottish Pottery,* 1923.

The Belleek Pottery Ltd., Belleek, Co. Fermanagh, N. Ireland, c.1863-present day.

This factory is mainly known for its delicate, thinly potted porcelain ware, often based on marine forms: objects vastly different from one's image of Ironstone. However, Ironstone or Granite-type ware was made and L. Jewitt in the first (1878), edition of his *Ceramic Art of Great Britain* especially notes:

> Besides the speciality of these works (the 'Belleek China') Messrs. McBirney & Armstrong manufacture to a large extent white granite ware services of every variety, and of excellent quality both in body, in glaze, and in printed, painted, enamelled, and gilt decorations. Many of the patterns are of more than average excellence, and in every respect the Irish earthenware equals the ordinary commercial classes of Staffordshire wares . . .

Belleek earthenware is rare. It may be marked with the words 'BELLEEK Co. FERMANAGH' and a crowned harp device or with the standard hound, tower and harp mark with the name 'BELLEEK' below. A catalogue of Belleek ware, dated 1904, includes useful earthenware but no Ironstone.

Birks Brothers & Seddon, Cobridge, Staffordshire, c.1877-86.

This firm employed the Royal Arms device above the wording 'IMPERIAL IRONSTONE CHINA, BIRKS BROS. & SEDDON'.

Bishop & Stonier, Hanley, Staffordshire, c.1891-1939.

This partnership succeeded Powell, Bishop & Stonier (c.1880-90), and various types of earthenware, including Ironstone, were produced. The marks incorporate the name 'Bishop & Stonier' or the initials 'B. & S.'.

Edward F. Bodley & Co. (& Son), Burslem, Staffordshire, c.1862-98.

Edward F. Bodley & Co. worked the Scotia Pottery at Burslem from 1862-81. Various kinds of earthenware were produced and marked with the name or initials 'E.F.B.'. The name 'Scotia Pottery' also occurs. Much Bodley Ironstone was exported.

In 1881, the firm's style was amended to Edward F. Bodley & Son and the New Bridge Pottery at Burslem was taken over. Advertisements feature 'Genuine Ironstone China', which was manufactured between 1881 and 1898 and would bear marks incorporating the initials 'E.F.B. & Son' or 'E.F.B. & S.'. A further mark incorporates the address, 'New Bridge Pottery', arranged in a Staffordshire knot as below.

T. & R. Boote Ltd., Burslem, Staffordshire, c.1842 into the present century as tile manufacturers.

This firm made a wide selection of earthenware and parian ware in the middle of the nineteenth century; but by 1880 the firm had confined its attention to tiles and to Ironstone or 'Granite Ware' marketed under the title 'Royal Patent Ironstone'. The printed marks incorporate the firm's name or the initials 'T. & R.B.'. Much of Boote's Ironstone and Granite ware was made for overseas markets, and a great quantity was made for North America.

Booth & Meigh, Lane End, Staffordshire, c.1828-37.

The mark 'IRONSTONE / B & M' is recorded, and some writers have attributed it to Bagshaw & Meir of c.1802-08, but the name 'Ironstone' could not have been used at so early a period. These initials probably relate to Booth & Meigh, c.1828-37, or to Brougham & Mayer of Tunstall, c.1853-55.

Thomas Booth & Co. (& Sons), Tunstall, Staffordshire, c.1868-76.

T. Booth & Co. produced earthenware and Ironstone-type bodies, as did their successors Thomas Booth & Son, c.1872-76. Initial marks were used: 'T.B. & Co.' or 'T.B. & S.', 'T.G.B.' or 'T.G. & F.B.'.

G.F. Bowers (& Co.), Tunstall, Staffordshire, c.1842-68.

George Frederick Bowers is mainly known for his good quality porcelain and standard earthenware, but Ironstone-type ware was made and is marked: 'IRONSTONE / CHINA / G.F. BOWERS'.

Brameld (& Co.,) Swinton, Yorkshire, c.1806-42.

The Bramelds owned and managed the Swinton pottery (more popularly called Rockingham) from 1806 to its closure in 1842. The pottery is mostly known for its standard earthenware and fine porcelain, but Ironstone bodies were also made (see Plate 307). Printed marks incorporate the name of the printed pattern with the description 'GRANITE CHINA' (an early use of this term), 'STONE CHINA' or 'FINE STONE'. The initial 'B' occurs rarely in these printed marks. The impressed name 'BRAMELD' or 'BRAMELD & CO.' may also appear on this Swinton or Rockingham ware. For information see *The Rockingham Pottery* by A.A. Eaglestone and T.A. Lockett, revised edition 1973, and Dr. Alwyn and Angela Cox's joint work *The Rockingham Works,* Sheffield, 1974.

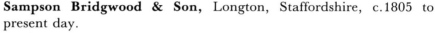

Plate 307. A rare blue printed impressed marked 'Brameld' stone china Rockingham plate with printed mark 'Parroquet, Fine Stone, B'. Diameter 8½ ins. c.1830. Godden Collection

Sampson Bridgwood & Son, Longton, Staffordshire, c.1805 to present day.

The early Bridgwood earthenware is unmarked. In the middle of the nineteenth century, a large range of earthenware and porcelain was produced. In Jewitt's account of this firm, written in or before 1878, he records:

> In earthenware they produce largely the white Granite for the United States, Australian and Canadian trade, and they also produce for the home market. One of their specialities is what is technically called 'Parisian Granite' (stamped 'Limoges'), which is of fine, hard, durable body and excellent glaze. In this ware tea, breakfast, dinner and toilet services are largely produced; many are of excellent design...The Parisian granite bears the impressed stamp, an oval, with the word 'Limoges', and in the centre 'P.G.' (for Parisian Granite). It also bears the printed mark of an elaborate shield of arms with mantling, sceptres, etc., and the words 'Porcelaine Opaque, Bridgwood & Son'.

Initial marks as shown were also used.

Bridgwood & Clarke, Burslem and Tunstall, Staffordshire, c.1857-64.

This firm produced Ironstone or 'Granite' ware mainly for the American market. Their ware bears the names in full or the initials 'B. & C.' with descriptions such as 'Opaque China' or 'Porcelain Opaque'. This firm was continued by Edward Clarke (& Co.).

Brougham & Mayer, Tunstall, Staffordshire, c.1853-55.

The printed mark of the words 'Ironstone' and 'Brougham & Mayer' occurs, rarely, with a garter-shaped device.

William Brownfield (& Son(s)), Cobridge, Staffordshire, c.1850-91.

William Brownfield produced large quantities of fine earthenware (and porcelain from 1871), and over 450 people were employed in 1861. The Brownfield pottery is not known for its Ironstone, but such ware was certainly produced. William Brownfield's son was taken into partnership in 1871 and from this period '& Son' was added to the firm's style and marks. The plural form dates from 1876. Marks comprise the name 'Brownfield', the initials 'W.B.', or 'W.B. & S.' (after 1871). From 1891-98, the firm was titled Brownfields Guilds Pottery Society Ltd.; and from 1898-1900, Brownfield Pottery Ltd.

Henry Burgess, Burslem, Staffordshire, c.1864-92.

Henry Burgess potted at the Kilncroft Works, Sylvester Square, Burslem. Good Ironstone-type wares were produced and bear clear name marks.

Burgess & Leigh (Ltd.), Burslem, Staffordshire, c.1867-present day.

This famous firm has produced a large range of earthenwares which especially in recent years has included Ironstone wares. These often bear the trade name 'BURLEIGH WARE'.

The original partnership of Burgess & Leigh became a limited company in 1889.

Samuel & John Burton, Hanley, Staffordshire, c.1832-45.

This partnership at New Street, Hanley, produced general earthenwares, using the description 'Pearl China', as well as some Ironstone wares. Various marks incorporate the initials 'S & J B'.

Plate 308. An impressed marked 'Careys' stone china tureen stand with fine underglaze blue print of York Cathedral. Printed mark 'Carey's Saxon Stone China'. 14½ by 12¾ ins. c.1825-35. Godden of Worthing Ltd.

Thomas & John Carey, Lane End, Staffordshire, c.1823-42.

John Carey started potting at Lane End in about 1813. The Careys produced very good quality standard earthenware, often decorated with fine blue printed designs. The standard mark is the word 'CAREY'S' with or without an anchor; but one mark incorporates the description 'SAXON STONE CHINA'. A finely printed tureen stand is shown in Plate 308.

Cartwright & Edwards (Ltd.), Longton and Fenton, Staffordshire, c.1869-present day.

Cartwright & Edwards worked the Borough Pottery at Longton from c.1869. The Victoria Works were taken in 1912 and the Heron Cross Pottery at Fenton in 1916. Advertisements of the 1880s mention ''IRONSTONE CHINA, AND EARTHENWARE of every description for the home, colonial and foreign markets''. Marks feature or include the initials 'C. & E.'. Ltd. was added to the firm's style and to some marks from c.1907. A wide range of ware has been produced, including bone china. The present trade style is 'Cartwrights of England', being one of several firms in the Grindley of Stoke group.

Charles Challinor, Tunstall, Staffordshire, c.1848-65.

Charles Challinor potted in High Street, Tunstall. Name marks could relate to this firm or to the later firm of Charles Challinor & Co.

Charles Challinor & Co., Fenton, Staffordshire, c.1892-96.

This company succeeded E. & C. Challinor in 1892. Name marks occur on Ironstone-type wares.

E. Challinor & Co., Fenton, Staffordshire, c.1853-62.

This firm produced good quality blue printed earthenware, examples of which are recorded with the name mark 'E. CHALLINOR & CO'. E. & C. Challinor succeeded (see next entry).

E. & C. Challinor, Fenton, Staffordshire, c.1862-91.

This firm succeeded E. Challinor & Co. (see previous entry). Printed or impressed marks incorporate the name 'E. & C. CHALLINOR' or the initials 'E. & C.C.', sometimes below the Royal Arms.

Edward Challinor, Tunstall, Staffordshire, c.1842-67.

Edward Challinor, worked the Pinnock Pottery at Tunstall (and the Unicorn Pottery from 1862-67). Good quality earthenware, including Ironstone-type ware, was produced and marked with the initials 'E.C.' or the name 'E. CHALLINOR'. This pottery should not be confused with E. Challinor & Co. of Fenton (q.v.), although there were firms having this style at Tunstall in 1851 and in 1853-54.

Chamberlain & Co., Worcester, c.1786-1852.

I have already shown, that as early as 1814 — one year after the original Ironstone patent was granted — Chamberlain & Co., the Worcester porcelain manufacturers, had ordered Ironstone ware from Mason.

It would appear that at least by the 1840s they had themselves begun the manufacture of a similar type of hard, durable ware which they sold under the popular term 'Stone China'. However, this is now extremely scarce and was perhaps only made for a short period as an experiment.

A special mark has been recorded incorporating the name of an American importer:

MR. BILLSLAND, IMPORTER, 447 BROADWAY.

CHAMBERLAINS

WORCESTER

MANUFACTURERS TO THE ROYAL FAMILY.

STONE-CHINA

This printed mark would appear to be of the 1840-50 period. The trade name 'GRANITE CHINA' was also used. The Chamberlain firm was succeeded by Kerr & Binns in 1852.

Edward Clarke (& Co.), Burslem and Tunstall, Staffordshire, c.1865-87.

This firm succeeded Bridgwood & Clarke (q.v.). Similar ware was produced, and the marks incorporate the name 'EDWARD CLARKE'

or 'EDWARD CLARKE & Co'. A Tunstall address indicates a date prior to 1878, a Burslem address a date between 1878 and 1887.

Clementson Bros. (Ltd.), Hanley, Staffordshire, c.1865-1916.

Clementson Bros. succeeded Joseph Clementson, 1839-64 (see next entry). Good quality Ironstone and 'Royal Patent Stoneware' was made and sold with several marks incorporating the style 'Clementson Bros.'. 'England' was added to most marks between 1891-1916. Much Clementson Ironstone was exported to Canada, and from the 1840s Francis Clementson had an important retail establishment in Canada.

Joseph Clementson, (Shelton) Hanley, Staffordshire, c.1839-64.

Good quality Ironstone· and standard earthenware was made by Joseph Clementson. One design registered in 1842 has a printed mark incorporating the initials 'J.C.' and the description 'GRANITE WARE'. Other ware is marked with the name in full, with or without the word 'IRONSTONE' or 'STONE CHINA'. In 1861, Joseph Clementson employed 149 men, 63 women, 146 boys and 76 girls.

Clementson, Young & Jameson, (Shelton) Hanley, Staffordshire, 1844.

This short-lived partnership produced Ironstone, as is proved by a design registered in October 1844. The mark incorporates the initials 'C.Y. & J.' and the description 'Ironstone'. Clementson & Young (c.1845-47) succeeded, and probably made Ironstone-type ware marked with their name or initials.

James & Ralph Clews, Cobridge, Staffordshire, c.1818-34.

This partnership produced very good quality earthenware, often blue printed and intended for the American market as well as home consumption. Stone china was also produced and this description is incorporated in several marks with the name 'Clews'. One is a particularly close copy of the printed Spode mark reproduced on page 251, except that the name 'Clews' replaces 'Spode'. The term 'Dresden Opaque China' was also used.

Cochran & Fleming, Glasgow, Scotland, c.1896-1920.

This Scottish firm produced 'ROYAL IRONSTONE CHINA', using this description with their name and the Royal Arms device or the seated figure of Britannia.

Cockson & Chetwynd (& Co.), Cobridge, Staffordshire, c.1867-75.

Ironstone ware, marked with the Royal Arms and having the description 'Imperial Ironstone China' and the names of the partnership, was produced between 1867-75. Similar ware and marks were used by the succeeding partnership of Cockson & Seddon (c.1875-77) with, of course, the new name replacing the former.

Copeland)
Copeland & Garrett) See Spode

Cork & Edge Burslem, Staffordshire, c.1846-60.

This firm produced a large range of ornamental and useful earthenware, much of which was exported to North America. Trade terms 'STAFFORDSHIRE STONE WARE' and 'PEARL WHITE IRONSTONE' were employed on marks with the names 'CORK &

EDGE' or with the initials 'C. & E.'. This partnership was succeeded by Cork, Edge & Malkin (c.1860-71). Marks were employed with these names or with the initials 'C.E. & M.'.

W. & E. Corn, Burslem, Longport, Staffordshire, c.1864.

W. & E. Corn traded from Burslem from c.1864-91 and at the Top Bridge Works, Longport, from 1891-1904. Early ware was marked with the initials 'W. & E.C.' or 'W.E.C.'. Jewitt, writing in or before 1878 noted that "Messrs. W. & E. Corn are exclusively devoted to the production of white graniteware for the United States and other foreign markets". From c.1900, printed marks incorporating the trade name 'Porcelaine Royale' were employed.

Crown Clarence Pottery, Longton, Staffordshire, late 1960s.

Ironstone wares were made by this firm at King Street, Longton in the late 1960s before the firm was acquired by Jon Anton (q.v.). The marks incorporate the trade name 'Crown Clarence'.

H. & R. Daniel, Stoke and Shelton, Staffordshire, c.1823-41.

Daniel produced very fine quality porcelain, richly decorated, of which few examples are marked. The firm also produced Ironstone and stone china. The rare impressed mark 'DANIEL'S REAL IRONSTONE' has been recorded. Simeon Shaw, in his *History of the Staffordshire Potteries*, 1829, stated that in 1826 Daniel produced their stone china in Shelton: "the shapes and patterns being of the improved kind, so much preferred by the public..."

An existing pattern and price book confirms that Daniel produced stone china dinner and dessert and tea services, as well as toilet sets. Recorded patterns reach number 1946. A typical entry reads: "1925. Japan Groups of flowers blue outlines, blue & green leaves, gold fibres & gold lines."

Plate 309. A marked Davenport stone china jug very much in the Mason tradition. 5¾ ins. high. c.1820. Godden of Worthing Ltd.

Plate 310. An impressed marked Davenport blue-printed Ironstone plate of the 'Friburg' pattern. Diameter 10½ ins. Potting numbers for 1844. Godden Collection

Printed tea ware patterns mentioned by name include Birds, Broseley, Indian Figure, Peacock, Swiss Girl, Barbeaux, Gothic, Fruit and Flowers, Strawberry.

Printed dinner ware designs were termed Chinese Scenery, Oriental Vases, Birds, Fruit and Flowers, Strawberry, and Barbeaux.

It is interesting to note that articles made in stone china were more expensive than the same object in the standard earthenware body.

Davenport (Ltd.), Longport, Staffordshire, c.1793-1887.

This firm produced a very fine range of porcelain, earthenware, stoneware and even glass. Neatly potted and tastefully decorated stone china was produced from c.1805 to about 1820 (see Plate 311). Direct copies of the later Mason Ironstone ware were seldom attempted, although a variation of the standard Mason jug shape does occur with the Davenport name mark (see Plate 309). Advertisements show that Davenport Ltd. produced Ironstone-type ware up to the 1880s; much was exported. Early marks incorporated the names 'REAL STONE CHINA', 'REAL IRONSTONE CHINA' or 'IRONSTONE'. An impressed mark of the 1840-60 period has the words 'Davenport.

Plate 311. Representative pieces of a 'Davenport Stone China' dessert service, decorated with a standard design favoured by some other firms. Printed 'Stone China' marks. Basket 10½ ins. long. c.1810-20. Godden of Worthing Ltd.

Ironstone China' surrounding the anchor device. The date of manufacture of much of the mid-nineteenth century Davenport earthenware can be discovered by careful examination of the standard impressed 'Davenport' and anchor mark, for the last two numerals of the year were placed each side of the anchor. The plate shown in Plate 310 is datable to 1844 by this device (see sample mark on page 221). Other pieces sometimes have the month and year of manufacture impressed, i.e. 6.67 for June 1867.

The standard book on this factory is T.A. Lockett's *Davenport Pottery & Porcelain 1794-1887* (David & Charles, 1972).

L.L. Dillwyn, Swansea, Wales, c.1831-50.

Lewis Llewelyn Dillwyn owned the famous Swansea Pottery in Wales from 1831-50. Among the varied pottery he produced was some Ironstone-type ware which bears descriptive marks 'CYMRO STONE CHINA'. Other printed marks use the term 'STONE WARE' with the initial 'D' or the name 'DILLWYN & CO.' The standard reference book on Swansea ceramics is E. Morton Nance's *The Pottery and Porcelain of Swansea and Nantgarw,* 1942.

Thomas Dimmock & Co., (Shelton) Hanley, Staffordshire, c.1828-59.

Dimmock were important producers of a large range of earthenware, but this is little known today. Ironstone-type ware was made under the description 'Stone Ware'. Printed marks incorporate the initial 'D' and can be mistaken for similar 'D' marks as employed by Davenport's and by L. Dillwyn of Swansea. However, some Dimmock ware also bears an impressed monogram device which is a great help in identifying this Company's products. The device is reproduced.

Ducroz & Millidge, Retailers, London, c.1835-54.

Many printed marks bear the name marks of 'DUCROZ', 'DUCROZ & Co.' (c.1827-35) or the later partnership of Ducroz & Millidge (c.1835-54).

Basic Dimmock mark, found impressed or incorporated in printed marks

CHINESE TREE

These London retailers claimed, on several elaborate printed marks, that they were manufacturers but this was untrue and some examples also bear the marks of the true manufacturers, sometimes Masons.

Dudson Bros. (Ltd.), Hanley, Staffordshire, c.1898-present day.

This important Staffordshire pottery firm has, and still continues to produce Ironstone type vitrified stonewares and hotel type wares of good quality. Various printed marks incorporate the name 'DUDSON'.

Dunn, Bennett & Co. (Ltd.), Burslem, Staffordshire, c.1875-present day.

This firm, originally of the Boothen Works, Hanley, produced good Ironstone ware. Jewitt, writing in the revised 1883 edition of his *Ceramic Art of Great Britain,* noted:

> Messrs, Dunn, Bennett & Co. here manufacture earthenware and ironstone china in all the usual services, both for the home and American markets. Their productions are of a high quality, and having houses both in London and New York, they are in a position to cater successfully for both countries.

The firm's advertisements of the 1890s mention 'IRONSTONE CHINA', specially adapted for ships, hotels, restaurants and coffee house use. Early marks incorporated the initials 'D.B. & Co.', often with a beehive device. 'Ltd.' was added to marks late in 1907. Subsequent marks include the term 'Vitreous Ironstone' with the company's name in full. Their ware enjoys a large sale at the present time. In 1968 the company was merged with Doulton, now being part of Royal Doulton Tableware producing vitrified tableware for the hotel and catering trades.

Edge, Malkin & Co. (Ltd.), Burslem, Staffordshire, c.1871-1903.

Edge, Malkin & Co. succeeded Cork, Edge & Malkin (see Cork & Edge). Advertisements of the 1880s mention "IRONSTONE-CHINA AND EARTHENWARE, plain, printed, enamelled and gilt dinner, tea and toilet ware, in white ivory and other coloured bodies..." The standard printed mark incorporates the initials 'E.M. & Co.' on a ribbon under a dog device. The full name or initials also occur as impressed marks.

James Edwards (& Son), Burslem, Staffordshire, c.1842-82.

From 1842, James Edwards traded under his own name until, in 1851, '& Son' was added to the style. Good class Ironstone-type ware was manufactured and sold under the descriptions 'Ironstone China', 'Real Ironstone' or 'Stone China', with the name of the firm or the initials 'J.E. & S.'.

John Edwards (& Co.), Fenton, Staffordshire, c.1847-1900.

John Edwards first potted at Longton, moving to Fenton in about 1853. In 1861, 170 persons were employed. Marks on Ironstone-type ware include the name 'John Edwards', 'England' being added after 1891. Jewitt noted in 1878: "The goods now produced are semi-porcelain and white granite for the American market."

Elsmore & Forster, Tunstall, Staffordshire, c.1853-71.

This firm worked the Clayhills Pottery at Tunstall, where general earthenware as well as Ironstone-type ware was produced. One of the

best-known lines has a raised wheat design. This basic pattern was registered in November 1859. Marks incorporate the name of the partnership, often with the Royal Arms. Elsmore & Son succeeded this firm c.1872-87.

English Ironstone (Pottery) Ltd., Shelton, Staffordshire, c.1972-74, title amended to **English Ironstone Tablewares Ltd.** in 1974.

This Company, a branch of Washington Pottery (Staffordshire) Ltd. produced wares marked with this name in the early 1970s.

Everard, Glover & Townsend, Longton, Staffordshire, c.1837-45.

This partnership, which also traded as Everard, Townsend & Co. produced Ironstone-type wares which were normally marked with printed marks incorporating the initials 'E G & T'.

Ferrybridge Pottery, Nr. Pontefract, Yorkshire, c.1792-present day.

Prior to 1804, this pottery was known as the Knottingley Pottery. A succession of owners worked it and many different marks were used, basic details of which are given in my *Encyclopaedia of British Pottery and Porcelain Marks,* 1964.

In 1856, Lewis Woolf purchased the Ferrybridge Pottery, and in the following year his sons built the adjoining Australian Pottery — both works trading under the style 'Lewis Woolf & Sons'. Several printed marks incorporate the initials 'L.W.' or the addresses 'Ferrybridge and Australian Potteries'. The name 'Ferrybridge' also occurs as a mark, sometimes with the 'd' reversed.

Jewitt, writing in or before 1878 (*Ceramic Art of Great Britain*), stated that the marks included:

> a shield, with the words OPAQUE GRANITE CHINA in three lines, supported by a lion and unicorn, and surmounted by a crown. This mark is also impressed. . . The mark at the present time [that is, in the late 1870s] is that of the lion and unicorn with shield and crown and the words 'Ferrybridge and Australian Potteries' sometime impressed, and at others printed on the goods, with the names of the bodies, as 'granite', 'stone china', etc.

The first mark mentioned would seem similar, apart from the crown, to that found on fragments at the Swillington Bridge Pottery (q.v.). Jewitt also records that the two factories employed some five hundred hands.

In about 1884 the works passed to Poulson Brothers, then to Sefton & Brown (c.1897-1919) and from then to T. Brown & Sons (Ltd.).

Stephen Folch (& Sons), Stoke, Staffordshire, c.1819-30.

A long but damaged Folch Ironstone china dinner service was sold at Christie's in 1967. The shapes were very similar to the standard Mason Ironstone dinner ware shapes as depicted in Plate 143.

The mark, printed in underglaze blue on this service, took three forms. Firstly, the key mark comprised an elaborate version of the Royal Arms with the Prince of Wales' feathers behind and, under this device, the wording 'GENUINE FOLCH'S STONE CHINA' appeared in a ribbon. Other pieces bore the same arms mark with two different styles of wording below — either 'IMPROVED IRONSTONE CHINA' or 'IMP^d IRONSTONE CHINA, STOKE WORKS'. These do not include the key word 'Folch's', but all pieces were clearly from the same service and the work of one manufacturer — so these marks can be added to those used by Stephen Folch during the period c.1819-30. Some marks incorporate the longer title 'Folch & Sons'.

According to a trade account dated October 1819, Folch's ware was moderately priced: covered soup tureens and stands at 11s., plates at 3½d. However, it would seem that Folch's Stoke factory produced a wide range of decorative Mason-style Ironstone china, much of which has not been correctly attributed to this manufacturer.

Ford & Challinor, Tunstall, Staffordshire, c.1865-80.

Ford & Challinor (also listed as Ford, Challinor & Co.) occupied the Lion Works at Tunstall. Various types of earthenware, including Ironstone-type wares were produced and sometimes bear name or initial marks.

Forester & Hulme, Fenton, Staffordshire, c.1887-93.

This partnership produced some standard quality Ironstone-type wares. Their name mark is recorded.

Jacob Furnival & Co., Cobridge, Staffordshire, c.1845-70.

Ironstone-type ware occurs with the initial mark 'J.F. & Co.', which may relate to this firm.

Jacob & Thomas Furnival, (Shelton) Hanley, Staffordshire, c.1843.

Ironstone-type stone china made by this firm bears the Royal Arms device with the initials 'J. & T.F.'. The partnership was succeeded by Thomas Furnival & Co. (c.1844-46) and this later ware bears initial marks 'T.F. & Co.'. Thomas Furnival's ware was, to a great extent, exported to America. Some American authorities have attributed the 'T.F. & Co.' marks to Thomas Ford & Co., but the Patent Office registration mark and the contemporary records prove that the firm concerned was Thomas Furnival & Co.

Thomas Furnival (& Sons), Cobridge, Staffordshire, c.1851-90.

Thomas Furnival's early ware bears the impressed name mark 'FURNIVAL'. From c.1871, '& SONS' was added to the firm's style. Various marks incorporate the initials 'T.F. & Sons' or the name in full. Ironstone-type ware was made, advertised as 'white granite', as well as standard earthenware.

Furnivals (Ltd.), Cobridge, Staffordshire, c.1890-1968.

Furnivals succeeded Thomas Furnival (& Sons) (see previous entry). 'Ltd.' was added to the firm's style and to most marks in 1895. In January 1919, the style was changed to 'FURNIVALS (1913) LTD.'. Good quality Ironstone-type ware was made by all these firms, using marks similar to the four examples reproduced.

In 1967 Furnivals was taken over by Barratts of Staffordshire Ltd., but the factory was closed in December 1968. The trade name and some patterns were purchased by Enoch Wedgwood (Tunstall) Ltd., early in 1969.

Thomas Gater & Co., Furlong Lane, Burslem, Staffordshire, c.1885-94.

Marked examples of Ironstone from this Burslem firm have been reported.

Gelson Bros., Hanley, Staffordshire, c.1868-75.

This firm produced various earthenwares at the Cobden Works in High Street. Thomas Gelson & Co. succeeded in the period 1876-78.

Godwin Rowley & Co., Burslem, Staffordshire, c.1828-31.

Blue printed Ironstone-type ware appears bearing the description 'STAFFORDSHIRE STONE CHINA' with a crown device and the initials 'G.R. & Co.'.

Thomas Godwin, Burslem, Staffordshire, c.1834-54.

Good quality stone china ware occurs with the name 'THOS. GODWIN, BURSLEM'.

Thomas & Benjamin Godwin, Burslem, Staffordshire, c.1809-34.

T. & B. Godwin manufactured a wide range of earthenware decorated with fine quality transfer printed designs. Some Ironstone-type ware was made under the description 'Stone China', and printed marks incorporate the initials 'T. & B.G.'.

Thomas Goodfellow, Tunstall, Staffordshire, c.1828-59.

Thomas Goodfellow made general earthenware, including Ironstone-type ware bearing the name mark 'T. GOODFELLOW'.

Griffiths, Beardmore & Birks, Lane End, Longton, Staffordshire, c.1830.

This partnership is listed in the Lane End (Longton) rate record for March 1830. The names match the initials 'G.B. & B.' found on 'STAFFORDSHIRE IRONSTONE CHINA' with the pre-Victorian Royal Arms device.

W.H. Grindley & Co. (Ltd.), Tunstall, Staffordshire, c.1880-present day.

This firm represents one of the later manufacturers of Ironstone-type ware. Their ware is clearly marked. The present style is 'Grindley of Stoke'.

Hackwood, Shelton and Hanley, Staffordshire.

Several potters with the surname Hackwood worked in the Staffordshire Potteries in the nineteenth century producing good quality earthenware of various descriptions. A printed mark of an urn with swag containing the words 'IRONSTONE CHINA' occurs on ware bearing the impressed name mark HACKWOOD, c.1830-40.

Ralph Hall (& Co.) or (& Son), Tunstall, Staffordshire, c.1822-49.

Ralph Hall produced a range of very good quality earthenware bearing fine printed designs, sometimes expressly made for the American market. Marks from 1822-41 incorporate the name 'R. Hall' or 'R. Hall & Son'. From c.1841-49 the style became Ralph Hall & Co., during which time marks included the initials 'R.H. & Co.' or the fuller name 'R. Hall & Co.' Podmore, Walker & Co. succeeded this firm (q.v.).

Ralph Hammersley (& Son), Burslem and Tunstall, Staffordshire, c.1860-1905.

Ralph Hammersley's advertisements list ''IRONSTONE CHINA & GENERAL EARTHENWARE...specially adapted to the home and colonial trade, also the United States of America and continental markets. Real Ironstone china in shapes suitable for Hotels, ships, etc. etc...'' Early marks incorporated the initials 'R.H.'. In 1883, the firm's style was amended to Ralph Hammersley & Sons, and marks then incorporated the initials 'R.H. & S.'.

C. & W.K. Harvey (Charles Harvey & Sons), Longton, Staffordshire, c.1835-53.

Harvey made good quality earthenware, including Ironstone. The Ironstone often bears the Royal Arms device with the description 'REAL IRONSTONE CHINA' and the initials 'C. & W.K. Harvey'. Holland & Green succeeded this firm (q.v.).

J.E. Heath Ltd., Burslem, Staffordshire, c.1950-present day.

J.E. Heath Ltd. of the Albert Potteries at Burslem produce a quality of hotel type ware much of which is exported. In February 1963 the trade name 'Flintstone' was introduced.

Joseph Heath, High Street, Tunstall, Staffordshire, c.1841, 1845-53.

A Joseph Heath is recorded at the Newfield Pottery, Tunstall, in 1841 and at High Street, Tunstall, from 1845-53. Ironstone-type ware bearing the name 'J. Heath' probably relates to this Tunstall potter.

Joseph Heath & Co., Newfield Pottery, Tunstall, Staffordshire, c.1828-41.

Good quality general earthenware was made, sometimes with North American transfer printed views. Marks include 'J. Heath & Co.'; 'J.H. & Co.' or 'I.H. & Co.'. (In many nineteenth century marks the initial 'J' appears as 'I', which was normal practice of the period.)

Hicks & Meigh, (Shelton) Hanley, Staffordshire, c.1804-22.

Hicks & Meigh were among the first producers of stone china as made by Davenport and Spode. The ware is of good quality, boldly decorated on fine imposing shapes (see Plates 313-321). The name mark was rarely used. Most of their stone china bears the pre-Victorian Royal Arms device with the wording 'Stone China' below. A numeral is often added below these words.

STONE CHINA.
No.13

Plate 313. A finely moulded Hicks & Meigh stone china tureen from a richly decorated dinner service. Printed Royal Arms mark (page 227). 13½ ins. high. c.1810-20. Godden of Worthing Ltd.

Plate 314. A good quality well-potted Hicks & Meigh stone china tureen, cover and stand from a complete dinner service. Printed Royal Arms mark. 11ins. high. c.1815-22. Godden of Worthing Ltd.

Plate 315. A blue-printed Hicks & Meigh stone china dinner plate from a large service. Printed Royal Arms mark with 'No.21' below. Diameter 10ins. c.1815-22. Geoffrey Godden, Chinaman

Plate 316. A fine Hicks & Meigh soup tureen decorated with a printed design coloured in by hand. Printed Royal Arms mark with 'No.8' below. 15ins. long. c.1815-22. Godden of Worthing Ltd.

Plate 317. A good quality Hicks & Meigh of the same form as Plate 316. Printed Ironstone Warranted mark with 'No.5'. 12ins. high. c.1815-22. Godden of Worthing Ltd.

Plate 318. An unusual Hicks & Meigh stone china tureen and cover. Printed Royal Arms mark with 'No.23' below. 12ins. high. c.1815-22. Godden of Worthing Ltd.

Plate 319. A good quality Hicks & Meigh stone china meat plate from a dinner service. Printed Royal Arms mark with 'No.71' below. Diameter 10½ ins. c.1815-22. Geoffrey Godden, Chinaman

Plate 320. Representative pieces from a colourful Hicks & Meigh stone china dessert service. Royal Arms mark with 'No.7' below. Centre piece 13ins. long. c.1815-22. Godden of Worthing Ltd.

Plate 321. A decorative Hicks & Meigh dessert service with one piece reversed to show the standard Royal Arms mark, in this case with 'No.69' below. The tureen shape matches the larger soup tureen shown in Plate 318. Diameter of plate 9ins. c.1822-35. Godden of Worthing Ltd.

Hicks, Meigh & Johnson, (Shelton) Hanley, Staffordshire, c.1822-35.

This partnership, which succeeded Hicks & Meigh (see previous entry), produced the same class of good quality stone china. In 1833, this firm employed some six hundred work people. Marks include the two devices shown, normally with the design number added below. The firm's initials 'H.M. & J.' (appearing as 'H.M. & I.') were rarely used on printed marks. It is interesting to see the following comment in a letter written to Henry Davenport in 1825: "I am sorry to say that everybody prefers Hicks & Co's No.9 to any of ours..."

Plate 322. A Hicks, Meigh & Johnson Ironstone china tureen decorated in the traditional 'Japan' style. 6½ins. high. c.1822-35. Godden of Worthing Ltd.

Plate 323. A Hicks, Meigh & Johnson part dinner service bearing a popular coloured in printed pattern found also on other wares (see Plate 311). Blue-printed 'Stone China' mark with crown. Tureen 10½ins. high. c.1822-35. Christie's

Plate 324. Representative pieces from a Hicks, Meigh & Johnson dinner service bearing a colourful design on typical shapes. Printed Royal Arms mark. c.1822-35. Sotheby's Belgravia

Plate 325. A Hicks, Meigh & Johnson-type stone china tureen decorated in a typical 'Japan' styled design. Printed mark 'Real Stone China'. 9½ins. high. c.1822-35. Godden of Worthing Ltd.

Plate 326. A good quality Hicks, Meigh & Johnson plate, the pattern related to that shown in Plate 324 but here on a different plate shape. Printed Royal Arms mark with '156' below. Diameter 9ins. c.1822-35. Geoffrey Godden, Chinaman

Colour Plate 14. Representative pieces from a 'Spode Stone China' dessert service showing typical forms of the 1815-20 period, although fruit coolers are rare in the stone china body. This popular printed design is taken from Chinese export market wares. Pattern 2118. Fruit cooler 12 ¼ ins. high. Godden of Worthing Ltd.

Holland & Green, Longton, Staffordshire, c.1853-82.

Holland & Green succeeded C. & W.K. Harvey (q.v.). Their Ironstone-type ware was marked with the Royal Arms and the firm's name or 'H. & G., late Harveys'. The descriptive term 'Real Ironstone China' was used.

Hollinshead & Kirkham, Tunstall, Staffordshire, c.1876-90 at Woodland Street Pottery; c.1890-1956 at Unicorn Pottery.

This well-known firm produced a large range of earthenwares including Ironstone. One mark incorporates the initials 'H & K' with the wording 'Late J Wedgwood' relating to the Woodland Street works which this firm occupied from 1876-90.

Hope & Carter, Burslem, Staffordshire, c.1862-68.

This famous partnership produced a good range of earthenwares including Ironstone-type wares at the Fountain Place Works, which was later taken over by Ashworths.

Thomas Hughes, Burslem (and Longport), Staffordshire, c.1860-94.

Thomas Hughes produced 'GRANITE' and 'IRONSTONE CHINA' largely for the North American market. His ware was marked with the name in full, often with the Royal Arms device.

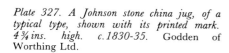

Thomas Hughes & Son (Ltd.), Longport, Staffordshire, c.1895-1957.

This firm produced a good range of Ironstone ware over a long period. Their ware is normally plainly marked with the name. 'Ltd.' was added to the firm's title in about 1910.

Reuben Johnson, Hanley, Staffordshire, c.1817-38.

Printed marks occur depicting the name 'JOHNSON / HANLEY' over the description 'Stone China.' These are believed to relate to this potter and to Phoebe Johnson, who continued from c.1823-c.1838. A typical jug is shown in Plate 327.

Plate 327. A Johnson stone china jug, of a typical type, shown with its printed mark. 4¾ ins. high. c.1830-35. Godden of Worthing Ltd.

Johnson Bros. (Hanley) Ltd., Hanley, Staffordshire, c.1883-present day.

Johnson Bros. (Hanley) Ltd. are among the largest producers of

233

twentieth century Ironstone-type ware. Their marks are clear and self-explanatory. The firm is now a division of the Wedgwood Group.

Keele Street Pottery Co. (Ltd.), Longton, Staffordshire, c.1915-67.

This twentieth century firm produced Ironstone-type wares as well as general earthenwares. The marks incorporate the initials 'K.S.P.'.

J.K. Knight, Foley, Fenton, Staffordshire, c.1846-53.

John King Knight succeeded the Knight, Elkin & Co. (c.1826-46) partnership. He made stone china as well as other earthenware. Marks incorporate the initials and name 'J.K. Knight', or sometimes 'I.K. Knight'.

Liverpool

The 'Herculaneum' factory may well have produced good quality stone china type ware during the closing years of its existence — during the management of Case & Mort (c.1833-36) and then of Mort & Simpson (c.1836-40). This Liverpool stone china ware may bear the impressed 'Liver bird' mark, and specimens will probably be found in North America and in the other export markets enjoyed by this great seaport factory. The full story of the important Herculaneum Pottery is given in Mr. Alan Smith's *Illustrated Guide to Liverpool Herculaneum Pottery,* 1970.

Livesley Powell & Co., Hanley, Staffordshire, c.1851-66.

Livesley Powell & Co. produced a good range of earthenware and china. The firm was an important one, employing over 408 people in 1861. Some marks incorporate the description 'Ironstone China' with the name in full or the initials 'L.P. & Co.'. Powell & Bishop succeeded this company in 1866 (q.v.).

J. Maddock, Burslem, Staffordshire, c.1842-55.

John Maddock succeeded the Maddock & Seddon (c.1839-42) partnership. Good quality earthenware was produced, with tasteful printed motifs. Various fancy printed marks occur with the initial 'M' introduced to one side. The description 'Stone China' occurs below the main mark (see example).

John Maddock & Sons (Ltd.), Burslem, Staffordshire, c.1855-present day.

This important firm produced a large range of durable earthenware. Jewitt, in *Ceramic Art of Great Britain,* records that the firm "manufacture white graniteware for the American markets to a large extent". Various marks have been employed incorporating the name 'Maddock' or 'John Maddock & Sons'. 'Ltd' was added to the firm's style after 1896 — a fact which assists in dating specimens. Trade names include 'Ironstone China', 'Royal Vitreous' and 'Stone China', as well as other descriptions for different non-ironstone bodies.

Maddock & Gater, Dale Hall Pottery, Burslem, Staffordshire, c.1874-75.

Ironstone wares bearing the name of this Dale Hall partnership have been reported.

Maddock & Seddon, Burslem, Staffordshire, c.1839-42.

The firm produced good quality ware, including stone china. Marks incorporate the initials 'M. & S.', often placed one above the other at the side of a mark — similar in position to the 'M' on the later J. Maddock mark reproduced.

Masons

See Chapters One to Five for history, and Chapter Six for marks.

Mason's Ironstone China Ltd.

From the summer of 1968, the new trading title adopted by the former firm of G.L. Ashworth & Bros. Ltd. (q.v.).

J. Maudesley & Co., Tunstall, Staffordshire, c.1862-64.

Printed marks occur on 'Stone ware' incorporating the initials 'J.M. & Co.', which are believed to relate to this firm.

Note: The following three entries refer to English potters and should not be confused with American firms bearing the name 'Mayer', several of which produced Ironstone ware.

Thomas Mayer, Stoke and Longport, Staffordshire, c.1826-38.

Many different Mayers were potting in Staffordshire from the late eighteenth century onwards. Thomas Mayer of the Cliff Bank Works at Stoke (c.1826-35) and then at Brook Street, Longton (c.1836-38), produced very good quality earthenware, often transfer-printed with tasteful designs, many of which were made for the American market. The American eagle appears in several marks. Ironstone-type ware was also made. Marks include the name 'T. Mayer', sometimes with the place name 'Stoke'.

Thomas & John Mayer, Longport (Burslem), Staffordshire, c.1841.

Thomas & John Mayer are recorded at the Dale Hall Works, Longport, in 1841, but the partnership may well date back to 1838, when Thomas Mayer entries ceased at Longport. The partnership may have continued until 1843. The name mark 'T. & J. Mayer, Longport' occurs on Ironstone.

T.J. & J. Mayer, Longport (Burslem), Staffordshire, c.1842-55.

Thomas, John & Joseph Mayer succeeded Thomas & John Mayer. A wide range of ware, including good parian, was produced and shown at the exhibitions of 1851, 1853 and 1855. Ironstone-type articles bear marks 'T.J. & J. Mayer' or 'Mayer Bros.', often with the address 'Dale Hall Pottery, Longport'. Succeeding firms working this famous pottery were:

Mayer Bros. & Elliott (c.1856-58)
Mayer & Elliott (c.1858-61)
Liddle, Elliott & Son (c.1862-70)
Bates, Elliott & Co. (c.1870-75)
Bates, Walker & Co. (c.1875-78)
Bates, Gildea & Walker (c.1878-81)
Gildea & Walker (c.1881-85)
James Gildea (c.1885-88)

Meakin & Co., Cobridge, Staffordshire, c.1865-82.

The products of this firm (also known as Meakin Brothers & Co.) were, according to Jewitt (*Ceramic Art of Great Britain*), confined to white granite ware for the American market. He records that the works were capable of producing about 2,500 crates of ware per year for this market.

Alfred Meakin (Ltd.), Tunstall, Staffordshire, c.1875-1974.

Alfred Meakin's advertisements of the 1880s feature 'IRONSTONE CHINA, WHITE GRANITE, suitable for North America, South America, West Indies, the Colonies, etc.'. Various self-explanatory marks were employed, and 'Ltd.' was added to the title in about 1897. Marks include the trade description 'Royal Ironstone China'. From c.1913 the firm was retitled 'Alfred Meakin (Tunstall) Ltd.' but marks record only the name 'Alfred Meakin'. In 1974 this firm was acquired by Myott & Son Co. Ltd., now Myott-Meakin Ltd.

Charles Meakin, Burslem and Hanley, Staffordshire, c.1876-89.

Charles Meakin worked the Trent Pottery at Burslem from c.1876-82. From 1883-89, Charles Meakin potted at the Eastwood Pottery at Hanley. His Ironstone-type granite ware was exported to North America. The mark comprises his name below the Royal Arms; 'Hanley' was added below the name from 1883 but sometimes this was replaced by the word 'England' especially on export wares.

Henry Meakin, Cobridge, Staffordshire, c.1873-76.

Henry Meakin made Ironstone-type earthenware which was marked with his name and initial below the Royal Arms device and the words 'IRONSTONE CHINA'.

J. & G. Meakin (Ltd.), Hanley, Staffordshire, c.1851-present day; a division of the Wedgwood group from 1970.

This important firm produced in the second half of the nineteenth century (245 persons were employed in 1861) a good range of Ironstone-type granite ware which was largely exported to North America. The marks are self-explanatory, including the firm's name and the description 'Ironstone China'. The registered trade name 'SOL' with a rising sun dates from 1912 and is used on many modern marks.

Lewis Meakin, Shelton (Hanley), Staffordshire, c.1853-55.

Lewis Henry Meakin potted at Cannon Street, Shelton, where he produced various earthenwares.

Charles Meigh (& Son), Hanley, Staffordshire, c.1835-49 and 1851-61.

Charles Meigh succeeded his father Job in 1835, although he had managerial command over the 'Old Hall Works' before this date. A vast quantity of good quality earthenware, which included Ironstone-type ware, was produced by Charles Meigh. Various marks incorporate the name or the initials 'C.M.'. An impressed mark

Plate 328. A decorative Charles Meigh tureen, cover and stand decorated with a printed pattern coloured in by hand. Impressed 'Indian Stone China' mark, pattern number 402. 10½ ins. high. c.1835-49. Geoffrey Godden, Chinaman

Plate 329. A good quality Charles Meigh dessert service dish, decorated with a version of the printed design shown in Plate 328. Impressed 'Indian Stone China' mark, pattern number 422. 12 by 9½ ins. c.1835-49. Geoffrey Godden, Chinaman

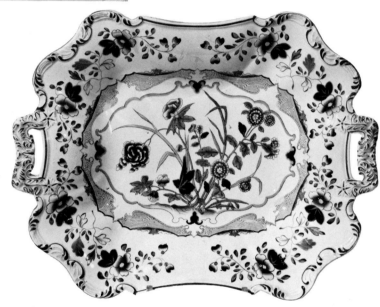

incorporates the description 'Improved Stone China' (see example) or 'Indian Stone China' see Plates 328 and 329.

From 1849-51, Charles Meigh was in partnership under the style 'Charles Meigh, Son & Pankhurst'. This partnership was succeeded in 1851 by Charles Meigh & Son. Marks then included the initials 'C.M. & S.' or the name in full. In March 1861, the firm became Old Hall Earthenware Co. Ltd. (q.v.).

John Meir & Son, Tunstall, Staffordshire, c.1837-97.

John Meir & Son produced a wide range of good quality earthenware, often decorated with underglaze blue printed designs. The marks are numerous and incorporate the name 'MEIR', 'MEIR & SON', 'J. MEIR & SON' or the initials 'I.M. & S.' or 'J.M. & S.'. Descriptions such as 'Stone China' or 'Ironstone' were used in the marks. The son was Henry Meir (born c.1812), who ran the firm for the greater part of its duration. In 1851, two hundred people were employed.

Plate 330. Representative pieces from a Minton-type 'Improved Stone China' dinner service, decorated with a coloured in printed design. Printed mark with initial 'M'. Pattern number 964. c.1825-35. Sotheby's Belgravia

Mellor, Taylor & Co., Burslem, Staffordshire, c.1881-1904.

L. Jewitt, in the revised 1883 edition of his *Ceramic Art of Great Britain,* wrote of this firm: "...Mellor, Taylor & Co., who continue to produce the usual articles in hard durable 'granite' or 'Ironstone china' for the American markets. Goods are also to some extent, produced for the home trade." The mark of the firm was "the royal arms in plain shield, with crown and wreath, exactly copied from the reverse of the half crown of Queen Victoria, surrounded by the words MELLOR, TAYLOR & CO. ENGLAND, WARRANTED STONE CHINA". A further mark is reproduced.

Mellor, Venables & Co., Burslem, Staffordshire, c.1834-51.

Mellor, Venables & Co. produced a fine range of printed earthenware, including Ironstone-type ware. Much was exported to North America, and several designs — including the Arms of the different American States — were engraved.

Many different marks were employed incorporating the name 'Mellor Venables & Co.' or the initials 'M.V. & Co.' with descriptions such as 'Royal Patent Ironstone'. The firm was succeeded by Venables & Baines, c.1851-53.

Henry Mills, Hanley, Staffordshire, c.1892.

The mark shown is believed to relate to the short-lived works of Henry Mills, although it could have been used by a Henry Mills who potted at Shelton from 1841-50.

Minton (various titles), Stoke, Staffordshire, c.1793-present day.

The Minton firms are mainly known for their superb porcelain, but many different types of earthenware were also produced. During the Minton & Boyle period (c.1836-41), marks incorporated the initials 'M. & B.'. The initials 'M. & H.' occur on marks during the Minton & Hollins period (c.1845-68), but 'M. & Co.' was widely used from c.1841-73. The single initial 'M' was incorporated in some printed marks which are probably of Minton origin — see Plate 330. The later Minton ware does not include the Ironstone body. Minton are now part of the Royal Doulton Group.

Morley & Ashworth, Hanley, Staffordshire, c.1858-61.

As related in the entry for G.L. Ashworth, the Morley & Ashworth partnership succeeded Francis Morley & Co. (see next entry). This partnership is a vital link in the preservation of the original Mason moulds, designs, etc., which Francis Morley had acquired. Ashworth succeeded this partnership in 1861. The standard marks incorporate the name in full or the initials 'M. & A.'.

Francis Morley (& Co.), Shelton, Hanley, Staffordshire, c.1845-58.

Francis Morley had great experience of the pottery trade. He married the daughter of William Ridgway, and a link exists between Francis Morley and Hicks, Meigh & Johnson, the celebrated producers of stone china (q.v.). Francis Morley acquired the Mason designs, moulds, etc., and passed them on to the succeeding Morley & Ashworth partnership (see previous entry). The many marks incorporate the initials 'F.M.', or 'F.M. & Co.', or the name in full.

Myott-Meakin Ltd., Tunstall, Staffordshire, c.1974-present day.

This recent amalgamation between Myott, Son & Co. (Ltd.) and Alfred Meakin Ltd. of Tunstall has produced Ironstone-type wares under the 'Myott' or 'Myott-Meakin' trade names.

New Bridge Pottery

See Edward F. Bodley & Co.

Old Hall Earthenware Co. Ltd., Hanley, Staffordshire, 1861-86.

This firm, the first limited liability company in the ceramic industry, was formed in March 1861, succeeding Charles Meigh (& Son) (q.v.). Good earthenware was produced. Trade descriptive names used include 'Indian Stone China' — sometimes arranged in triangular form reading 'Stone China Indian', 'Imperial Parisian Granite' and 'Opaque Porcelain', the last name being used on normal earthenware and not on Ironstone ware. Marks incorporate the initials 'O.H.E.C.' or 'O.H.E.C.(L)', the name 'Old Hall', or the full title of the company.

The firm was succeeded by the Old Hall Porcelain Works Ltd. (c.1886-1902).

J.W. Pankhurst & Co., Hanley, Staffordshire, c.1850-82.

James Pankhurst and John Dimmock traded as J.W. Pankhurst & Co. from 1852. Good quality Ironstone-type stone china was made, mainly for the American market, and was marked with the Royal Arms above the description 'Stone China' and the firm's name.

George Phillips, Longport, Staffordshire, c.1834-48.

This potter produced good earthenware between 1834 and 1848. Marks often include his name with the place name 'LONGPORT'. The example reproduced relates to the pattern 'Friburg', registered in November 1846.

Thomas Phillips & Son, Burslem, Staffordshire, c.1845-46.

The name 'T. PHILLIPS & SON, BURSLEM' occurs on some marks found on earthenware of Ironstone-type. Other potters with this surname include Edward Phillips of Shelton (c.1855-62), Edward & George Phillips, Longport (c.1822-34), and George Phillips, Longport (c.1834-48).

Pinder, Bourne & Co., Burslem, Staffordshire, January 1862-82.

Pinder, Bourne & Co. succeeded Pinder, Bourne & Hope (c.1851-62) of Nile Street, Burslem. A large range of earthenware includes Ironstone-type stoneware. The name 'IMPERIAL WHITE GRANITE' occurs on some marks, sometimes with the American eagle. The full name or the initials 'P.B. & Co.' was incorporated in marks. Doulton purchased the firm in 1878, but it was continued under the old style until 1882.

Plymouth Pottery Co. Ltd., Plymouth, Devon, c.1856-63.

Jewitt, in his *Ceramic Art of Great Britain* mentions this firm and the mark — the Royal Arms with the initials 'P.P. Coy. L.' and the description 'STONE CHINA' — but he was far from enthusiastic about the products.

Podmore, Walker & Co., Tunstall, Staffordshire, c.1834-59.

The products of this important firm were often marked with the name 'WEDGWOOD'. Enoch Wedgwood was, indeed, a partner and his name was found to be most useful. Good earthenware, including Ironstone-type ware titled 'IMPERIAL IRONSTONE CHINA' and 'PEARL STONE WARE', was made and exported to many countries. Many marks were employed with the initials 'P.W. & Co.', 'P.W. & W.', 'WEDGWOOD' or 'WEDGWOOD & CO.'. A large export market was enjoyed by this firm. The firm was large, employing 164 men, 133 boys, 60 women and 57 girls in 1851. From c.1860 the firm was retitled Wedgwood & Co. Ltd. (q.v.).

This 'Wedgwood' mark occurs on ware registered by Podmore, Walker & Co. in 1849. It proves that the name 'Wedgwood' was then used by this firm.

Pountney & Co. (Ltd.), Temple Backs, Bristol, c.1849-1970.

Pountney & Co. were preceded by Pountney & Allies (c.1815-35) and by Pountney & Goldney (c.1836-49). These Bristol firms produced a fine range of decorative earthenware, including stone china and 'Granite'. Marks used include 'BRISTOL POTTERY', 'P', 'P. & A.', 'P. & Co.' or the firms' names in full. 'Ltd.' was added to the style and marks from c.1889. The firm subsequently moved to Redruth, Cornwall, and now trades under the title Cauldon Bristol Potteries (Cornwall) Ltd.

Powell & Bishop, and **Powell, Bishop & Stonier,** Hanley, Staffordshire, c.1876-91.

The partnership of Powell & Bishop was of short duration, c.1876-78, being then succeeded by Powell, Bishop & Stonier. Two factories were in use. The Church Works at High Street, Hanley, were devoted to the manufacture of Ironstone-type granite ware which, according to Jewitt in *Ceramic Art of Great Britain,* "they produce of excellent quality and in every variety of style, both plain, embossed, and otherwise decorated...for the United States and Canadian markets". Marks incorporate the initials 'P. & B.' or 'P.B. & S.', the names of the partnership, or one of the two trade marks reproduced below.

Pratt & Simpson, Fenton, Staffordshire, c.1878-83.

This firm's advertisements feature "semi-porcelaine, white Granite, printed, and all kinds of earthenware, suitable for Colonial and foreign markets". Printed marks incorporate the initials 'P. & S.'.

Rathbone Smith & Co., Tunstall, Staffordshire, c.1883-97.

Rathbone Smith & Co. of the Soho Pottery in High Street, Tunstall produced a general range of earthenwares including Ironstone-type wares which were marketed under the description 'Imperial Stone'. The various marks incorporate the name in full or the initials 'R.S. & Co'.

Read & Clementson, (Shelton) Hanley, Staffordshire, c.1833-53.

This Shelton partnership produced good quality richly-decorated stone china ware (see Plate 331). Printed marks like the one shown incorporate the initials 'R. & C.'. Read, Clementson & Anderson continued in 1836, their marks incorporating the initials 'R.C. & A.'.

J. Reed, Mexborough, Yorkshire, c.1839-73.

James Reed, of the Rock Pottery (renamed Mexborough Pottery in c.1849), produced a wide range of useful earthenware, often bearing

Plate 331. A rare Read & Clementson stone china plate bearing a coloured in painted design 'Japan Beauty'. Printed initial mark. Diameter 10½ ins. c.1833-35. Godden of Worthing Ltd.

the impressed 'REED' name mark; but various printed marks also occur incorporating the description 'STONE CHINA' and the name 'REED'. John Reed succeeded his father in c.1849. Sidney Woolfe & Co. worked the Pottery from 1873-83.

Job Ridgway & Sons, (Shelton) Hanley, Staffordshire, c.1808-13.

Job Ridgway was the founder of several stone china firms, which subsequently all produced very fine Ironstone and stone china as well as other earthenware and porcelain. The sons mentioned in the firm's title were John and William, each of whom later owned separate factories (see subsequent entries).

The early Job Ridgway & Sons ware was rarely marked. The impressed name 'RIDGWAY & SONS' occurs, and also the initials 'J.R. & S.', sometimes with a beehive device.

John & William Ridgway, (Shelton) Hanley, Staffordshire, c.1814-30.

Job Ridgway's two sons, John and William, took over their father's Cauldon Place works, and also the Bell Works. Their various kinds of ware are difficult to fault in design or workmanship (see Plates 332, 333 and 334). Many marks incorporate the initials 'J.W.R.', 'J. & W.R.', or 'J. & W. Ridgway'.

Plate 332. A simple but good quality stone china soup plate from a dinner service by John & William Ridgway. Printed shield-shaped mark. Diameter 10ins. c.1814-20. Godden of Worthing Ltd.

Plate 333. A John & William Ridgway 'fancy stone china' tureen, cover and stand. The small tureen turned to show the printed mark. Tureen 11ins. high. c.1820-30. Godden of Worthing Ltd.

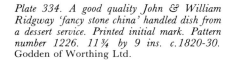

Plate 334. A good quality John & William Ridgway 'fancy stone china' handled dish from a dessert service. Printed initial mark. Pattern number 1226. 11¾ by 9 ins. c.1820-30. Godden of Worthing Ltd.

John Ridgway (& Co.), (Shelton) Hanley, Staffordshire, c.1830-55.

John Ridgway separated from his brother, c.1830, and continued his father's celebrated Cauldon Place Works, where the finest porcelain and earthenware was produced (Plate 335). Many printed marks were used, often featuring the Royal Arms and the initials 'J.R.', 'J.R. & Co.' (from 1841) or the name in full. The descriptions 'Real Ironstone China', 'Superior Stone China' or 'Imperial Stone China' were sometimes used, and high pattern numbers are normally found on John Ridgway pieces — numbers often in excess of 1,000.

Plate 335. A John Ridgway tureen and cover, the stand reversed to show the Royal Arms mark with the wording 'Imperial Stone China' above. Tureen 13ins. high. c.1830-40. Godden of Worthing Ltd.

William Ridgway (& Co.), (Shelton) Hanley, Staffordshire, c.1830-54.

William Ridgway, after the separation from his brother John, worked the Bell Works and the Church Works. Fine earthenware and stoneware was produced. The hand-painted ornamental ware was often unmarked, but the transfer-printed useful ware bears marks, including the name 'W. Ridgway' or 'W. Ridgway & Co.' (from c.1834), or the initials 'W.R.' or 'W.R. & Co.' (from c.1834). Descriptive names 'OPAQUE GRANITE CHINA' and 'QUARTZ CHINA' were used. An impressed mark occurs comprising the Royal

Plate 337. William Ridgway & Co. granite china plates and a dessert dish of pattern 267. Dish 9ins. long. c.1834-54. Sotheby's Belgravia

Arms, supporters and a shield, similar to that reproduced on page 254 but with the initials 'W.R. & Co.' and sometimes with the printed Royal Arms reproduced here (see also Plates 336 and 337).

William Ridgway, Son & Co., Hanley, Staffordshire, c.1838-48.

This variation of the William Ridgway Company produced the same type of ware as the parent firm. Marks incorporate the initials 'W.R.S. & Co.' or the firm's style in full.

Ridgway & Morley, (Shelton) Hanley, Staffordshire, c.1842-45.

Ridgway & Morley succeeded Ridgway, Morley, Wear & Co. (see next entry). Good quality earthenware was produced, which included

Plate 336. The underside of a William Ridgway plate showing the printed Royal Arms mark and above the impressed mark with the wording 'Opaque Granite China. W.R. & Co' within the shield. c.1834-54. Godden of Worthing Ltd.

'Improved Granite China' and 'stone ware'. Marks incorporate the initials 'R. & M.' or the name of the firm in full. Francis Morley continued on his own from 1845. He purchased most of Mason's moulds and designs, passing them on through the Morley & Ashworth partnership of c.1849-62 to the present holders, the Ashworth firm recently retitled 'Mason's Ironstone China Ltd.' Several original Mason engraved copper plates are still preserved through Francis Morley's far-sighted purchase in the 1840s.

Successive Ridgway firms were:
    Ridgways c.1879-1920
    Ridgways (Bedford Works) Ltd. c.1920-52

Ridgways & Adderley Ltd.
Booths & Colcloughs Ltd.   } 1952-55
Ridgway, Adderley, Booths & Colcloughs Ltd. }
Ridgways Potteries Ltd. c.1955 to present day

These have from time to time reissued some of the old Ridgway patterns, which sometimes bear versions of the original mark. Later reissued marks should include the words 'England' or 'Made in England', not found on the originals.

Ridgway, Morley, Wear & Co., (Shelton) Hanley, Staffordshire, c.1835-42.

This firm succeeded the Shelton Works of Hicks, Meigh & Johnson (q.v.). The new partnership continued to produce very good quality stone china, richly decorated in the Mason style. Many different marks incorporate the initials 'R.M.W. & Co.' or the name in full. The description 'Improved Granite China' was used.

Robinson, Wood & Brownfield, Cobridge, Staffordshire, c.1838-41.

This partnership succeeded Robinson & Wood in 1838, working the famous Cobridge Works which had been erected in 1808.

The large platter shown in Plate 338 is from a complete dinner service and bears the mark, below a crown: 'OPAQUE STONE CHINA. R W & B'. Other marks may well be employed incorporating these initials.

Plate 338. A rare and attractive Robinson, Wood & Brownfield 'Opaque Stone China' platter or meat dish originally from a large dinner service. Printed initial mark. 19½ by 15½ ins. c.1838-41. Geoffrey Godden, Chinaman

Seacombe Pottery, Seacombe, near Liverpool, c.1851-70.

This little-known pottery was established by the Staffordshire potter John Goodwin in 1851. The first kiln was fired in June 1852 and good general earthenware as well as 'Ironstone China' was produced, mostly decorated with underglaze blue prints in the Staffordshire tradition. In fact, Goodwin took with him to Liverpool engraved copper plates he had previously used in Staffordshire. The works had closed by October 1871. Marks include the name 'J. Goodwin' or 'Goodwin & Co.' with the address 'Seacombe Pottery, Liverpool'. A typical Ironstone mark is reproduced, and it is interesting to see that the registration mark relates to a printed design registered by John Goodwin in 1846, while he was working the Crown Pottery at Longton. This fact suggests that similar Ironstone-type ware was produced by John Goodwin in Staffordshire prior to 1851 — but such examples would not, of course, bear the Liverpool address. A large export business was carried on, and in the 1850s the firm had a retail establishment in Toronto. The printed design 'Lasso' was a very popular one in the American markets.

The *Journal of Ceramic History,* no.10 of 1978, Stoke-on-Trent City Museums, contains a very detailed paper on the Seacombe Pottery, by Helen Williams.

Anthony Shaw (& Sons), Tunstall and Burslem, Staffordshire, c.1850-1900.

Jewitt, writing in his *Ceramic Art of Great Britain,* revised 1883 edition, noted:

> The Mersey Pottery was established in 1850 by Anthony Shaw, and is now, since 1882, carried on as 'Anthony Shaw & Sons'. Goods, specially adapted for the various American markets are made, the specialities being white graniteware and cream-coloured wares for the United States...In 1855 Mr. Shaw was awarded a medal at the Paris Exhibition. The mark formerly used was the Royal Arms, with ribbon bearing the words STONE CHINA, and beneath, in three lines, WARRANTED. ANTHONY SHAW, BURSLEM. That at the present time has the words WARRANTED. ANTHONY SHAW & SONS, OPAQUE STONE CHINA, ENGLAND. The works were rebuilt on a very extensive scale in 1866.

Various name marks were used: 'SHAW', 'A. SHAW', or 'ANTHONY SHAW'. From 1882, '& Son' or '& Sons' may be added to the name; but from c.1898 to 1900 '& Co.' takes the place of '& Sons'.

South Wales Pottery, Llanelly, Wales, c.1839-58.

W. Chambers established the South Wales Pottery in 1839, producing a wide range of earthenware, including 'PEARL WHITE IRONSTONE'. Marks include the name 'Chambers', 'South Wales Pottery' or the initials 'S.W.P.'. From 1854 to 1858 the pottery was continued by Coombs & Holland, then by Holland & Guest, and finally by Guest & Dewsberry to c.1927.

Spode, Stoke, Staffordshire, c.1784-1833.

Josiah Spode was possibly the second potter to have produced stone china. He is said to have purchased Turner's patent rights on the then new body in about 1805 (see page 258); but Leonard Whiter, in his book *Spode: A History of the Family, Factory and Wares from 1733-1833,* 1970, suggests that this Spode body was newly introduced in 1814 — a view

Plate 339. A superb 'Spode Stone China' covered vase decorated with a rich 'Japan' pattern. The whole having the appearance of fine translucent porcelain. Printed 'Spode Stone China' mark with pattern number 2247. 24ins. high. c.1820. Christie's

Plate 340. Representative pieces from a 'Spode New Stone' dinner service of an unusual and attractive design — pattern number 3435. Large meat platter 19ins. long. c.1825. Godden of Worthing Ltd.

partly supported by an account of a Royal visit to the firm's London showroom as reported in *The Times* of 4th July, 1817. My own view — at present, supported only by the style of the ware, the patterns and the shapes — is that it was first produced several years before the Royal visit of 1817, and before 1814.

Be this as it may, the Spode firm produced very fine stone china, proving that this hard, durable body could be finely potted and decorated in tasteful designs fit for any drawing rooms and dining rooms. Superb dessert and dinner services were made by Spode and decorated with Chinese-type patterns (see Colour Plate 14 and Plates 339-346). One gains the impression that Spode was striving to capture

Plate 341. A selection of 'Spode New Stone' wares showing typical designs, all being printed outlines coloured in by hand. Printed marks. c.1820-30. Godden of Worthing Ltd.

Plate 342. A rare form of 'Spode Stone China' dinner service tureen bearing a standard printed design coloured in by hand. Printed mark. 11½ ins. high. c.1825. Christie's

Plate 343. A large 'Spode New Stone' tureen, cover and stand decorated in a typical style. Pattern number 2038. Printed mark with retailer's name 'James Kerr & Sons of Dublin'. c.1825. Sotheby's

Plate 344. An impressed marked 'Spode New Stone' three-piece vegetable dish, the bottom section of which held hot water to keep the contents above hot. 12ins. long. c.1820. Godden of Worthing Ltd.

Plate 345. A marked 'Spode Stone China' tureen from a lengthy dinner service decorated with a standard Spode design — pattern number 2054. Printed mark. 7¾ins. high. c.1820. Godden of Worthing Ltd.

the vast market formerly served by imported Chinese porcelain, the importation of which certainly fell sharply as the new English stone china came into prominence. It must be admitted that this change was assisted by the raising of import duties on Chinese porcelain; but at the same time, Spode stone china was finer in the potting and far less liable to chip than the Oriental porcelain. Spode made many replacements and additions to Chinese porcelain services, and these have withstood the passing of time better than the originals.

No stone china is as fine in quality as the Spode examples, which are thinly-potted and excellently finished. Many fine pieces were made: ice pails, trays, baskets and bowls, as well as the more normal components of dinner, dessert and tea services.

As noted above, Spode was favoured with Royal patronage. Wedgwood's salesman, Josiah Bateman, reported in October 1817 of the effect of the Royal visit:

> . . .Since the Queen went to Mr. Spode, the Stone China is much inquired for and is got more into repute — indeed a dealer cannot be without it, and a great deal is sold.

The Wedgwood firm acted on this intelligence and itself introduced a similar body (see page 261).

The standard printed mark is reproduced. On plates and dishes the

251

Plate 346. An impressed-marked 'Spode New Stone' tureen, cover and stand from a large dinner service decorated with a 'Japan' pattern. Tureen 14¼ ins. high. c.1820. Godden of Worthing Ltd.

mark is often found under the flange or edge, not in the centre. The impressed mark 'SPODES / NEW STONE' is also often found, as are the impressed initials 'N.S.', both of which date from c.1822. Copeland & Garrett succeeded from March 1833-47 (some Spode pieces will be found bearing a printed mark of this partnership), when the present firm of W.T. Copeland (& Sons Ltd.) was established. Copeland continued to 1970 when the style Spode Ltd. was adopted to underline the continuous link with the original Spode works and traditions — indeed Spode type stone china can be found with the name marks of Copeland & Garrett (1833-47) and of Copeland (1847-1970).

A standard reference book is *Spode and his Successors* by A. Hayden, 1924 — a work recently superseded by Leonard Whiter's tour-de-force mentioned earlier.

Staffordshire Potteries Ltd., Meir Park, Staffordshire, c.1964-present day.

This firm produce, under the registered trade name 'Kilncroft', a range of tablewares which are clearly marked with printed marks which include the description 'English Ironstone'.

Stevenson & Williams, Cobridge, Staffordshire, c.1825.

Printed marks incorporating the initials 'R.S.W.' or 'R.S. & W.' are believed to relate to the partnership between Ralph Stevenson and Williams, which is mentioned in a mortgage deed of 1825.

A fine tureen from a dinner service bearing the Royal Arms, the description 'ROYAL STONE CHINA' and the initials 'R.S. & W.' is illustrated in Plate 348, and a moulded-edge plate is shown in Plate 347.

Swift & Elkin, Longton, Staffordshire, c.1840-43.

This Staffordshire partnership produced 'Staffordshire Stone China' as well as normal earthenware. Printed marks include the initials 'S. & E.'.

Swillington Bridge, c.1820-50.

Recent excavations by Mr. Christopher Gilbert on the site of the Swillington Bridge pottery, some six miles south-east of Leeds, has

Plate 347. An unusual Stevenson & Williams 'Royal Stone China' plate bearing a printed Royal Arms mark. Diameter 9½ ins. c.1825. Godden of Worthing Ltd.

Plate 348. A rare Stevenson & Williams 'Royal Stone China' tureen, bearing a printed Royal Arms mark and the initials 'R.S. & W.' 12½ ins. high. c.1825. Godden of Worthing Ltd.

Plate 349. Representative pieces of a Stevenson & Williams 'Royal Stone China' dessert service. One plate reversed to show the Royal Arms mark with the initials 'R.S. & W.' Centre piece 14½ ins. long. c.1825. Godden of Worthing Ltd.

shown that this small Yorkshire pottery produced 'Ironstone China' and 'Opaque Granite China' during the 1820-50 period.

Good quality blue printed ware was made, as well as brown printed and enamelled earthenware. Excavated factory wasters show that an impressed crown mark was used, as well as a shield mark incorporating the words 'Opaque Granite China', the shield supported by a lion and a unicorn, an example of which is reproduced. The same basic mark, but with the initials 'W.R. & Co.', was used by William Ridgway of Shelton.

Blue printed Ironstone bears the printed mark with crown, reproduced. The discovery of these fragments on the site of the small, little-known factory suggests that other small Yorkshire potteries may well have made Ironstone ware.

John Tams (& Son) (Ltd.), Longton, Staffordshire, c.1875-present day.

John Tams worked the Crown Pottery at Longton from c.1875. Early marks incorporate the name 'J. Tams' or 'Tams' with a crown above and the description 'ROCK STONE'. Other marks incorporate the initials 'J.T.', often joined. Several marks incorporating the initials 'J.T.' with the descriptive term 'stone ware' are believed to relate to John Tams, and the name of the patterns — 'Orleans', 'Peacock', etc. — are also included. From 1903-12 '& Son' was added to the firm's style, and initial marks 'J.T. & S.' occur. From 1912 the style has been John Tams Ltd., but most marks include only the name 'Tams'.

George & Samuel Taylor, Hunslet New Pottery, Leeds, Yorkshire, c.1837-66.

William Taylor built the Hunslet New Pottery prior to 1823 and was succeeded by his sons George and Samuel in the late 1830s.

Various printed 'Ironstone China' marks, which incorporate the initials 'G & S.T.', probably relate to this partnership.

William Taylor, Hanley, Staffordshire, c.1860-73.

L. Jewitt, writing in *Ceramic Art of Great Britain* of William Taylor and the Pearl Pottery, Brook Street, Hanley, stated: ''In 1860 the works passed into the hands of William Taylor, who commenced making white Granite and common coloured and painted ware, but he discontinued, and confined himself to white graniteware for the United States and Canadian markets, of both qualities — the bluish tinted for the provinces, and the purer white for the city trade. He was succeeded in 1881 by Wood, Hines & Winkle...''

John Thomson (& Son), Glasgow, Scotland, c.1816-97.

John Thomson worked the Annfield Pottery, Glasgow, where a wide range of earthenware was produced, including stone ware. Printed marks include the initials 'J.T.' or 'J.T. & Sons' (from c.1865), sometimes with the name 'Annfield' or 'Glasgow'.

Thomas Till & Son(s), Burslem, Staffordshire, c.1850-1928.

Thomas Till & Son of the Sytch Pottery, Burslem, exhibited at the 1851 Exhibition and their ware included 'pearl white granite':

Albany shape dishes, baker and plates; pearl white granite.
Virginia shape set, teapot, sugar, cream [jug], cup and saucer, in pearl white granite.
Set of jugs, pearl white granite.
Albany shape soup tureen, complete, and sauce tureen, complete, white granite, gold bands...
Virginia shape, set tea cup and saucer and teapot, white granite, gold band.

At that period, 61 men, 34 women, 46 boys and 33 girls were employed. Till's various earthenware pieces are normally marked with the name in full.

George Townsend, Longton, Staffordshire, c.1850-64.

Printed marks occur showing the Royal Arms, the description 'Staffordshire Ironstone China' and the name 'G. Townsend'.

Turner, Goddard & Co., Tunstall, Staffordshire, c.1867-74.

The description 'Royal Patent Ironstone' occurs on marks with the Royal Arms and the name 'TURNER, GODDARD & CO.'

G.W. Turner & Sons, Tunstall, Staffordshire, c.1873-94.

This firm potted at the Victoria Works in High Street, Tunstall. Its printed mark has been reported on Ironstone products.

John Turner (Turner & Co.), Lane End, Staffordshire, c.1762-1806.

John Turner produced extremely fine earthenware — cream-coloured ware, Wedgwood-type jasper and basalt ware and, later, fine stoneware-type jugs, etc., with relief motifs — as well as porcelain. The standard reference book on John Turner and his ware is *The Turners of Lane End — Master Potters of the Industrial Revolution* by Bevis Hillier, 1965.

For the purposes of this book, the most important section of Turner's varied products is his 'patent' stone china-type body, which bears the painted mark 'TURNER'S PATENT' or the impressed mark 'TURNER'.

The abstract of the patent (No. 2367 of January 1800) is in the names of William and John Turner and reads:

A new method, or methods of manufacturing porcelain and earthenware, by the introduction of a material not heretofore used in the manufacturing of these articles. The material is known in Staffordshire by the names 'Tabberner's Mine

255

Plate 350. A superbly decorated 'Turner's-Patent' mug decorated with a rich dark-blue ground and finely gilt. Painted mark. c.1800-5. City Museum and Art Gallery, Stoke-on-Trent

Plate 351. The companion jug showing the finely painted scenic panel. Painted mark. 8½ ins. high. c.1800-5. City Museum and Art Gallery, Stoke-on-Trent

Rock', 'Little Mine Rock' and 'New Rock'. It is generally used as follows: ground, washed, dried in a potter's kiln, commonly called a slip kiln, afterwards mixed with a certain proportion of growan or Cornish Stone, previously calcined, levigated, and dried, a small quantity of flint similarly prepared is also added, but in different proportions, according to the nature of the ware, and the heat required in burning it.

The resulting ware bears the painted mark 'Turner's Patent' and, although the first of the stone chinas, it is often slightly translucent. Fine dessert services, mugs, jugs, bowls, etc., were made, the favourite pattern being a neat but bold formal floral pattern in the Chinese style (see Plate 356), similar in general effect to the later Mason 'Japan' patterns. Other rarer examples show finer styles of decoration (see Plates 350 and 351).

In 1803, John Glover and Charles Simpson joined the Turners; but

Plate 352. A rare impressed marked 'Turner' stone china-type plate decorated in the Oriental style. Diameter 9ins. c.1805. Godden Collection

Plate 353. A typical 'Turner's-Patent' oval centre piece decorated with a standard design. Painted mark. 12 by 8½ ins. c.1800-5. Mrs. Frank Nagington

Plate 354. A finely potted Turner dessert service centre piece decorated with an underglaze blue printed design. 13½ ins. long. c.1800-5. Geoffrey Godden, Chinaman

Plate 355. A rare 'Turner's-Patent' punch bowl, hand-painted in the style of the earlier Chinese imports. Painted mark. Diameter 10½ ins. c.1800-5. Geoffrey Godden, Chinaman

Plate 356. Representative pieces of a marked 'Turner's-Patent' dessert service showing typical shapes all painted with a standard Oriental-styled design. Painted mark. c.1800-5. Godden of Worthing Ltd.

Plate 357. A superb quality marked 'Turner's-Patent' sauce tureen, cover and stand after a Chinese shape (see Plates 1 and 3) and decorated after an Oriental original. Painted mark. Stand 7 by 5 ins. c.1800. Geoffrey Godden, Chinaman

the new partnership was of short duration, for in November 1804 John Turner withdrew, and in March 1806 the remaining partners dissolved their association. In July 1806 the Turners were declared bankrupt, and in June 1807 ''a large and elegant assortment of Earthenware and china, comprising the different articles...consisting of cream colour, china glazed blue edge, china glaze printed and painted, Egyptian black (basalt), Cane, Stone, Jasper, Pearl and Patent China...of Messrs. Turner & Co....'' was offered for sale.

According to tradition, Josiah Spode purchased the rights to the 'Turner Patent' body. However, no reference is made to it in the marks used by Spode on his own 'Stone China', which was probably a new variation of Turner's patent, using the basic raw materials with additions. For Spode's ware, see Spode entry.

Turner's-Patent.

Joseph Twigg & Bros., Kilnhurst Pottery, Yorkshire, c.1839-84.

Benjamin, Joseph and John Twigg of the Newhill Pottery near Swinton leased the Kilnhurst Pottery in 1839. Various types of earthenware were made some of which is marked 'TWIGGS' and some stone china was also produced. Various printed marks incorporate the initial 'T' sometimes with 'K P' for Kilnhurst Pottery, see *Yorkshire Pots and Potteries by H. Laurence* (David & Charles, 1974).

Venables & Baines, Burslem, Staffordshire, c.1851-53.

This short-lived partnership succeeded Mellor, Venables & Co. at Nile Street, Burslem, and produced some blue printed Ironstone-type ware. Marks incorporate the name or initials of the partnership. Venables, Mann & Co. (also termed J. Venable & Co.) succeeded c.1853-55.

Thomas Walker, Tunstall, Staffordshire, c.1845-51.

Thomas Walker worked the Lion Pottery at Tunstall. A good range of earthenware was produced, much of which was intended for the

American markets. Marks include the name 'T. WALKER' or 'THOS. WALKER'. In some instances, the place name 'Tunstall' was added to distinguish the ware from that produced by other potters of this name — Thomas Walker of Longton, c.1856-57 and Thomas Henry Walker of Longton, c.1846-49.

Edward Walley, Cobridge, Staffordshire, c.1845-56.

Edward Walley produced general earthenware, including Ironstone which bears the impressed mark 'Ironstone china. E. Walley'. Bold hand-painted designs were employed as well as printed patterns.

James Warren, Longton, Staffordshire, c.1841-53.

James Warren of the Victoria Works in the Longton High Street produced a general range of earthenwares including Ironstone-type wares. The printed marks include the name J. Warren. The subsequent partnership of Warren & Adams (1853-64) probably also produced Ironstone wares.

Washington Pottery (Staffordshire) Ltd., Shelton, Staffordshire, c.1946-present day.

This present Company of College Road, Shelton produces 'an international range' of Ironstone tablewares which is marked with the Washington Pottery trade name.

Wedgwood & Co. Ltd., Tunstall, Staffordshire, c.1860-present day (as Enoch Wedgwood (Tunstall) Ltd.)

This firm succeeded Podmore, Walker & Co. (q.v.) — a firm which had already used the name Wedgwood in its marks. Quotations from Jewitt's standard work *Ceramic Art of Great Britain* show the standing of the Company and its products in the 1870s:

> The works, which are very extensive, and give employment to six or seven hundred persons, occupy an area of about an acre of ground, and are among the most substantially built and best arranged in the pottery district. The goods produced are the higher classes of earthenware...The quality of the 'Imperial Ironstone China' — the staple production of the firm, is of remarkable excellence, both in body and in glaze, and the decorations are characterized by pure taste, artistic feeling, and precision of execution...they associate durability of quality in body and a perfect glaze with purity of outline in form, chasteness of decoration, and clearness and harmony of colour, adapting their designs and styles of decoration to the National tastes of the people in the various climes to which the goods are sent. One of the most successful of their original ordinary printed designs is the pattern known as 'Asiatic Pheasants', which has become so popular as to be considered one of the standard patterns of this country and the colonies. They also supply large quantities of ironstone china specially made for the use of ships, restaurants, hotels, etc....The Unicorn Works (as opposed to the Pinnox Works) is entirely devoted to the production of plain white granite ware for the American trade...

The 'Asiatic Pheasants' pattern referred to is shown in Plate 358. It was indeed popular, for I have seen the design and special 'Asiatic Pheasants' mark with the name or initials of more than twenty firms.

The Wedgwood firm continues to the present time, but with changes in its title. Owing to the confusion between Josiah Wedgwood & Sons Ltd., and Wedgwood & Co. Ltd., the latter was changed to Enoch Wedgwood (Tunstall) Ltd. in 1965.

The various marks incorporate the name 'Wedgwood & Co', and 'Ltd.' was often added from c.1900. The use of the '& Co.' (such as the

Basic Wedgwood & Co. mark, not to be confused with the simple 'Wedgwood' name marks used by Josiah Wedgwood & Sons Ltd.

Royal Arms device) distinguishes the marks from the one word 'Wedgwood' impressed into the ware made by Josiah Wedgwood & Sons Ltd. Standard descriptive names include 'Stone-Ware', 'Stone China', 'Imperial Ironstone China' and 'Patent Paris White Ironstone'. Sample marks are reproduced.

Josiah Wedgwood (& Sons Ltd.), Etruria (now at Barlaston) Staffordshire, c.1759-present day.

This famous firm should not be confused with Wedgwood & Co.

Plate 359. Representative pieces of a 'Wedgwood Stone China' dessert service, decorated with a typical design. Printed mark, with pattern number 1156. Comport 11½ ins. long. c.1827-35. Godden of Worthing Ltd.

Ltd. (see previous entry). Josiah Wedgwood & Sons Ltd. are mainly known for their fine coloured jasper ware with white relief motifs and for their fine cream-coloured or Queen's ware.

In 1818, experiments were begun to produce stone china to compete with Spode's successful body marketed under this name. A letter of 1817 from Josiah Bateman, Wedgwood's salesman, is quoted in the Spode entry, and this may have sparked off the experiments. Examples are plainly marked in underglaze blue 'WEDGWOOD'S / STONE CHINA' but examples are rarely found today. A dessert set with typical 'Japan' style design is illustrated in Plate 359. Factory records suggest that production of their 'Stone China' started in 1827 and ceased in 1861.

A.J. Wilkinson (Ltd.), Burslem, Staffordshire, 1855-1964.

Wilkinson (Ltd.), formerly Wilkinson & Hulme, produced good quality 'Royal Patent Ironstone' for the home and American markets from the 1880s onwards. Marks are full and self-explanatory.

The wording under the Royal Arms mark normally reads 'A.J. Wilkinson. England.'

Wood & Brownfield, Cobridge, Staffordshire, c.1838-50.

This partnership produced good quality earthenware, including 'Stone Ware'. Various marks incorporate the initials 'W. & B.'. W. Brownfield succeeded (q.v.).

Wood & Hawthorne, Cobridge, Staffordshire, c.1882-87.

This partnership produced white granite ware or Ironstone exclusively for the American market. The standard mark includes the description 'Ironstone china' and the names 'WOOD & HAWTHORNE, ENGLAND' beneath the Royal Arms.

John Wedg(e) Wood, Burslem and Tunstall, Staffordshire, c.1841-60.

This potter used misleading marks reading 'J. Wedgwood', as the example reproduced. The marks of Josiah Wedgwood & Sons Ltd. do not include the initial 'J'. John Wedg(e) Wood's marks sometimes have a slight space or dot between 'WEDG' and 'WOOD' but in some cases this distinction is not apparent.

Wood & Son(s) (Ltd.), Burslem, Staffordshire, c.1865-present day.

Wood & Son produced good quality general earthenware and Ironstone ware. Marks are clear and self-explanatory. From c.1907 '& Son' became '& Sons', and from 1910 'Ltd.' was added to the firm's official title but not to all marks. Sample marks are reproduced. The firm still enjoys a large export trade in Ironstone ware.

Wood Rathbone & Co., Cobridge, Staffordshire, c.1868.

Marked Ironstone from this short-lived company has been reported.

G. Wooliscroft, Tunstall, Staffordshire, c.1851-52 and 1860-64.

George Wooliscroft (also spelt Woolliscroft) potted at High Street and Well Street, Tunstall, during the 1851-53 period, and at the Sandyford Potteries, Tunstall, c.1860-64. Marks normally incorporate the name of the body — 'Ironstone', etc. — the pattern, and the potter's name.

Wrekin Ironstone Company, Shropshire, c.1815.

Michael Messenger in his catalogue of *Pottery & Tiles of the Severn Valley* (Remploy Ltd., London, 1979) illustrates a Mason's-type ironstone vase which he suggests may have been produced by the "little-known Shropshire factory of the Wrekin Ironstone Company which flourished c.1815''. This authority continues: "They are known to have made very close copies of Mason's Ironstone. . .and a number of pieces featuring this mark have occurred in Shropshire''.

The mark referred to is the impressed: 'IRONSTONE CHINA'.

John Yates, Fenton, Staffordshire, c.1784-1835.

John Yates produced a wide range of earthenware. The early examples would seem to have been unmarked, but ware of the 1820-35 period occurs with the mark 'J.Y. Warranted Stone China, Fenton'. The initials are believed to relate to this potter.

Plate 360. A blue-printed Ironstone platter or meat dish from a dinner service made at the Ynysmedw Pottery in South Wales. Printed mark as reproduced below, including the proprietor's name 'Williams'. 11¼ ins. long. c.1845-60. D. Harper, Esq.

Ynysmedw Pottery, Nr. Swansea, Wales, c.1840-70 + .

Recent excavations by Mr. D. Harper on the site of this little-known Welsh pottery have proved that its production included 'Ironstone' china. A blue printed platter is shown in Plate 360.

Marks include the impressed initials 'Y.M.P.' or 'Y.P.' or the name in full, 'YNISMEDW POTTERY. SWANSEA VALE' (note alternative spelling of Ynysmedw). Printed marks incorporate the name 'WILLIAMS' (c.1854-60) the initials 'L. & M.' (c.1860-70) or the initials 'W.T.H.', denoting the last proprietor, W.T. Holland, c.1870 + .

This last entry underlines the point that Ironstone-type ware was made by potteries large and small throughout the British Isles, and it was by no means limited to the Staffordshire potteries.

Registration Marks

Many items of English pottery (and porcelain) produced between 1842 and 1883 will be found to bear an impressed, or printed, upright diamond-shaped device containing in the centre the letters 'Rd'. Numerals and letters are contained in the inner angles of the diamond.

This device indicates that the basic shape or added design was registered at the Patent Office in London and was thereby protected from copying for an initial period of three years. Contrary to general opinion, it does *not* show the date of production of such articles but, when decoded, only the date of registration and therefore the *earliest possible* date of production. The date decoding key is also reproduced.

From January 1884, a new system of numbering consecutively registered designs was started: 'Rd. No.1.' in January 1884, 'Rd. No. 351202' in January 1900, etc. These registered numbers can be a most useful guide to dating later Ironstone and other ceramic designs.

Table of Registration Marks
1842-1883

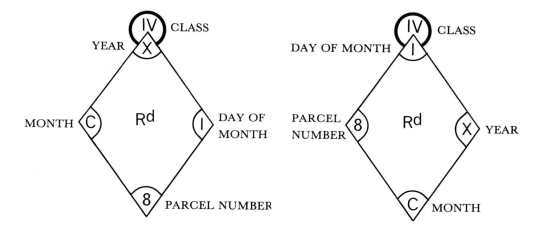

Above are the two patterns of Design Registration Marks that were in current use between the years 1842 and 1883. Keys to 'year' and 'month' code letters are given below.

The left-hand diamond was used during the years 1842-67. A change was made in 1868, when the right-hand diamond was adopted.

INDEX TO YEAR AND MONTH LETTERS

YEARS

1842-67
Year Letter at Top

A	= 1845	N	= 1864
B	= 1858	O	= 1862
C	= 1844	P	= 1851
D	= 1852	Q	= 1866
E	= 1855	R	= 1861
F	= 1847	S	= 1849
G	= 1863	T	= 1867
H	= 1843	U	= 1848
I	= 1846	V	= 1850
J	= 1854	W	= 1865
K	= 1857	X	= 1842
L	= 1856	Y	= 1853
M	= 1859	Z	= 1860

1868-83
Year Letter at Right

A	= 1871	L	= 1882
C	= 1870	P	= 1877
D	= 1878	S	= 1875
E	= 1881	U	= 1874
F	= 1873	V	= 1876
H	= 1869	W	= (March 1-6)
I	= 1872		1878
J	= 1880	X	= 1868
K	= 1883	Y	= 1879

MONTHS (BOTH PERIODS)

A	= December	G	= February	M	= June
B	= October	H	= April	R	= August (and 1st-
C or O	= January	I	= July		19th September,
D	= September	K	= November (and		1857)
E	= May		December 1860)	W	= March

Table of Design Registration Numbers Found on Ware from 1884

These numbers are normally prefixed by 'R^d N^o':

1-19753	registered in 1884
19754-40479	registered in 1885
40480-64519	registered in 1886
64520-90482	registered in 1887
90483-116647	registered in 1888
116648-141263	registered in 1889
141273-163762	registered in 1890
163767-185712	registered in 1891
185713-205239	registered in 1892
205240-224719	registered in 1893
224720-246974	registered in 1894
246975-268391	registered in 1895
268392-291240	registered in 1896

291241-311657 registered in 1897
311658-331706 registered in 1898
331707-351201 registered in 1899
351202-368153 registered in 1900
368154-385087 registered in 1901
385088-402912 registered in 1902
402913-424016 registered in 1903
424017-447547 registered in 1904
447548-471458 registered in 1905
471486-493486 registered in 1906
493487-518414 registered in 1907
518415-534962 registered in 1908

This system is continued to the present time.

Unidentified Marks

The ornate version of the **pre-Victorian Royal Arms** mark occurs on very fine quality Ironstone China, often decorated with extremely colourful designs. The wording below the Royal Arms reads 'IMP^d. [Improved] IRON STONE CHINA, Stoke Works'. The use of the word Ironstone suggests a date after 1813, but the identity of the manufacturer has not as yet been discovered. William Adams had works at Stoke (as well as at Tunstall) from 1811-30, and he may be regarded as a possible producer of the fine early Ironstone ware which bears this printed mark. These same ornate Arms, with the Prince of Wales' feathers above and the motto 'Ich Dien' below, are shown on page 200, and the same ornate design occurs with the words 'Genuine Folch's Stone China' (see entry for Folch).

The wording '**Britannicus Dresden China**' occurs printed in underglaze blue on good quality Ironstone-type ware of the 1820 period, but the maker has, as yet, not been identified, see Plate 361.

Many examples of English earthenware can be found with ornate printed marks including the name '**F. Primavesi (& Son)**', with various addresses — Cardiff, Swansea, etc. This was a firm of retailers and shippers, not manufacturers.

The name marks of hundreds of retailers may be found on nineteenth century English ceramics which were made to their special order. The names and periods of the more important retailers are given in my *Encyclopaedia of British Pottery and Porcelain Marks,* 1964. Primavesi operated from c.1850-1915; '& Son' would seem to have been added to marks from about 1860.

Plate 361. The as yet unidentified mark 'Britannicus Dresden China', shown with other pieces from an Ironstone-type ware dessert set of the 1820 period. Godden of Worthing Ltd.

The wording **'Real Stone China'** occurs on printed marks with crown above (see example). It would appear to have been first used by Hicks, Meigh & Johnson (c.1822-35) but can also occur on ware made by John Ridgway in the 1830s.

Blue printed marks incorporating the description **'Tonquin China'** occur on good quality Ironstone-type ware of the 1820 period (see Plate 362). The name of the manufacturer is, as yet, not known.

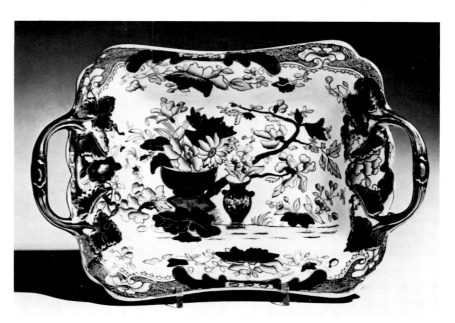

Plate 362. A dish bearing the printed mark 'Tonquin China'. c.1820. Godden of Worthing Ltd.

No ware has so far been discovered with the name **'Wrekin Ironstone China'**; but newspaper advertisements mention Wrekin or

Shropshire Ironstone china, which suggests that it was produced before Mason's introduced their Patent Ironstone.

The Wrekin is a hill in Shropshire — a prominent landmark visible for many miles — and it would appear that Wrekin Ironstone was of Shropshire manufacture. Many potteries were in the neighbourhood of Coalport. In November 1816 T. Brocas, the Shrewsbury retailer, advertised in the *Salopian Journal* "...Wrekin Ironstone which they have sold for many years, and which lately has been so highly approved of..."; and in November 1815, Thomas Brocas begged "leave to observe there lately being an amazing improvement in the British Manufacture of china, both in material, shape and pattern," he now has by him "a number of tea and breakfast services also Table [Dinner] services of the WREKIN or SHROPSHIRE IRONSTONE CHINA, etc..." See also page 262.

Details of many of the small British manufacturers can be found in L. Jewitt's *Ceramic Art of Great Britain* (J. Virtue & Co., 1878, revised edition 1883). The basic marks and working periods of many potters are recorded in my *Encyclopaedia of British Pottery and Porcelain Marks* (Herbert Jenkins Ltd., 1964). Some details of scenic patterned English Ironstone-type ware are given in Sam Laidacher's Anglo-American China, Part II (privately published in the U.S.A., 1951), but there are some errors of attribution and dating.

The British potters were not left entirely alone to enjoy the North American market for their popular Ironstone and granite ware. The marks used by many American producers are given in C. Jordan Thorn's *Handbook of Old Pottery and Porcelain Marks* (Tudor Publishing Co., New York, 1947) and R.M. & T.H. Kovel's *Dictionary of Marks — Pottery and Porcelain* (Crown Publishers Inc., New York, 1953). Many American marks follow the standard English mark forms in style (even including versions of the British Royal Arms!) and the ware can consequently be mistaken for British Ironstone.

Appendix

Catalogues of Mason's Stock Sold in 1818 and 1822

1818 SALE CATALOGUE

A

CATALOGUE

OF

A MOST VALUABLE AND EXTENSIVE STOCK

OF

ELEGANT AND USEFUL

CHINA

SUITED FOR DOMESTIC PURPOSES

OF ENGLISH MANUFACTURE

Recently consigned from the Manufactory for actual sale, and highly deserving the attention of Persons of Fashion and Private Families.

It comprises

a large assortment of complete Table and Dessert services, composed of strong and serviceable material, painted in imitation of the rich Japan and other Oriental Patterns; Breakfast, tea and coffee equipages, ornamental Dejeunes and Vases for flowers and essence, including about Twelve of noble size, suited to fill niches or Recesses in Drawing Rooms, superbly ornamented.

Which will be sold by Auction

BY MR. CHRISTIE

at his Great Room, Pall Mall,

on Tuesday, December 15th, 1818

and two following Days, at one o'clock

(N.B. Few lots would appear to have been sold. Prices have been inserted against those few lots and these originate from the auctioneer's master, priced, catalogue. The original spelling has been retained where the meaning is clear. Some duplicated lots have been deleted from the original listing, as have been the non-Mason items such a glass and some unhelpful descriptions, for example — ''twenty-six pieces, various'', but the original lot numbers have been retained.)

FIRST DAY'S SALE

TUESDAY, DECEMBER 15th, 1818

punctually at one o'clock

1 Two taper candlesticks, coloured and gilt, and 2 cabinet pitchers

2 One toy ewer, bason, jug, and mug, and 2 tall taper candlesticks, roses and gilt

3 Two toy cups and saucers, japanned and gilt

4 Two Dresden pattern jars, 2 square essence burners; and 2 toy jars

5 One table service, India pheasant pattern, viz. 18 dishes in sizes, 2 soup tureens, covers and stands, 4 sauce ditto, 4 square vegetable dishes, 1 sallad ditto, 1 fish ditto, 72 table plates, 24 ditto soup and 24 pye ditto

6 Two square Chinese jars and covers. £1.3.0.

7 One coffee pot, antique pattern and shape

8 Two hexagonal antique beakers

9 Two handsome tulip cups and saucers, and 2 match pots

10 Two tall jars and covers, richly ornamental and gilt

11 Two elegant mitre shaped jars and covers, sumptuously gilt

12 One desert service, Mogul pattern, viz. 1 centre piece, 12 fruit dishes, 2 cream tureens and stands, and 24 plates. £5.18.0.

13 One breakfast tea and coffee service, corn flower sprig and gold lines, viz. 12 bowls and saucers, 12 tea cups and saucers, 15 coffee cans, 12 breakfast plates, 1 tea pot and stand, 1 salt box, 1 cream ewer, 1 pint bason, 2 bread and butter plates, and 2 butter tubs and stands

14 One toy ewer, bason, jug and mug for a cabinet

15 Two chimneypiece jars. 16/-

16 One table service, exact quantity as Lot 5, Chinese landscape pattern

17 Two cabinet cups and saucers, a toy ewer, bason, jug and mug

18 One Dejeune service, antique forms and ornamented. £3.8.0.

19 One desert service, old Japan pattern, blue, read, and gold, exact quantity as Lot 12

20 Two costly beakers, a la Chinoise

21 Two jars and covers, Chinese forms, richly enamelled and gilt

22 One table service, exact quantity as Lot 5, blue and gold border

23 One handsome sideboard jar, dragon handles and sumptuously gilt

24 Two rose and apple jars and covers, octagonal bronze and gold

25 Two square caddies

26 Two ornamental groups of flowers and gold

27 One antique coffee pot

28 Two tulips and stands, cabinet, and two square scent boxes. £1.4.0.

29 One table set, exact quantity as Lot 5, table and flower pot pattern

30 Two costly jars, a la Chinoise, beautifully pencilled, and gilt

31 One desert service, exact quantity as Lot 12, gold rose japanned and gilt, antique forms

32 One breakfast tea and coffee service, exactly as Lot 13 (only in lieu of butter tubs, 2 covered muffin plates) sprig and gilt

33 Two tea caddies, groups of flowers and gold lace border

34 One table service, exact quantity and pattern as Lot 5

36 Two taper candlesticks, toy ewer, bason, jug and mug, 2 lavender bottles, 2 flower beakers, and 1 cabinet teapot. £2.12.6.

37 Two dragon octagonal beakers

38 One desert service, plain Japan, exact quantity as Lot 12. £12.12.0.

39 One Italian formed jar, or vase, biscuit of elegant workmanship

40 One table service, exact quantity as Lot 5, old Japan pattern, in green, pink, mazarine, red, and richly gilt

41 One breakfast tea and coffee set, exact quantity as Lot 13, French ground, Dresden sprigs, and gold

42 One Trentham bowl

43 One splendid dragon jar, a la Chinoise

44 Two costly beakers

45 One watering can and 2 flat formed bottles. £1.2.0.

46 Two Chinese jars. £1.3.0.

47 One desert service, gold rose, exact quantity as Lot 12

48 One table service, blue and gold

49 One octagonal rose and apple jar

50 One breakfast tea and coffee set, white and gold, embossed and coloured sprigs, exact quantity as Lot 32

51 One table service, exact quantity and pattern as Lot 5

52 Two cabinet jugs and mugs and 2 flower beakers

53 One foot pail. £1.1.0.

54 Ditto and slop jar. £2.2.0.

55 One table service, exact quantity as Lot 5, basket Japan

56 Two bell jars, lion's heads

57 Two 3-handled fluted vases

58 Two hexagonal tea caddies. £2.10.0

60 Two low fluted jars

61 One fine octagon vase, a la Chinoise

62 One Table service, exact quantity as Lot 5, India gold jar pattern

64 Two card candlesticks, 2 tall ditto, Dresden pattern, and 2 baskets

65 Two tall hexagonal embossed jars and covers

66 Two small griffin octagonal jars

67 Two cabinet jugs and mugs

68 One table service, richly japanned in red, blue, green, and gold, exact quantity as Lot 5

70 Two low bat-head ornaments. 18/-

71 Two hexagonal beakers

72 Two lavender bottles, 2 low bat-head ornaments, 2 beakers, and 2 cabinet coffee biggins. £2.5.0.

73 Two antique jars and covers

75 Two sugar caddies

76 One desert service, gold thorn, exact quantity as Lot 17

77 One breakfast tea and coffee set, ditto, vine embossed, exact quantity as Lot 18

78 Two pot pourri jars. £1.1.0.

80 Two small antique bottles

81 One table service, landscape, Japan, slightly gilt, exact quantity as Lot 5

82 Two lavender bottles, 2 ranunculus pots, and 2 card candlesticks
83 Two rounds jars, of rich pattern
85 Two toy churns, 2 Dresden pattern jars, and 2 toy cups and saucers
86 Two tripods, 2 coffee biggins
88 Two flower vessels, colour and gold. 10/-.
89 Two tall Roman shaped jars. £1.0.0.
90 Two toy churns, lavender bottles, 2 candlesticks
End of the First Day's Sale

SECOND DAY'S SALE
WEDNESDAY, DECEMBER 16th, 1818
at one o'clock precisely

91 One cabinet ewer, bason, jug and mug, 2 ditto, coffee biggins
92 Two Chinese beakers
93 Two three-handled dragon jars, fluted, richly coloured and gilt
94 One desert service, Indian figure pattern, exact quantity as Lot 12. £4.14.6.
95 One table service, India pheasant, japan, slightly gilt, exact quantity as Lot 5
96 Two dolphin-head bowls, rich in colours and gold
97 Two pot pourries
98 Two cabinet teapots
100 Two rose-handled bell-shaped jars, bronze and gold
101 One table service, exact quantity as Lot 5, richly coloured figure pattern
102 Two three-handled jars
103 Two watering cans, 2 low bottles and stoppers. £1.7.0.
104 Two octagon jars. 14/-.
105 Two curiously formed vases, of antique shape, elegantly enamelled and gilt. £3.7.0.
106 One desert service, landscape Japan as Lot 12
107 Two small antique bottles, 2 toy cups and saucers
108 One table service, blue pheasants with gold border, exact quantity as Lot 5
109 One elegant sideboard jar, damaged
110 Two ink stands, 2 tulip cups and stands
111 Two Dresden cans and stands, 2 ditto cups, etc.,
112 One table service, blue Chinese landscapes, exact quantity as Lot 5
113 Two large beer jugs. 9/6.
114 Two small Dresden pattern cups
115 Two garden flower pots and stands
116 Two small octagon jars, 4 card candlesticks, 2 ink stands
117 Two elegant beakers and covers, a la Chinoise
118 Two antique coffee pots
119 Two Trentham bowls, highly finished
120 Two 3-handled Dragon vases. £3.8.0.

121 One table set, richly finished in colour and gold, exact quantity as Lot 12

122 One desert set, rock and rose japan and gilt, exact quantity as Lot 12

124 Two bell shaped jars

125 Two lavender bottles and 1 cabinet ewer, bason, jug and mug

126 Two watering cans

127 Two tall covered jars

128 Two low open jars

129 A table service, mandarin pattern in colours and gold, exact quantity as Lot 5. £15.15.0.

130 Two beer jugs

131 One desert service, pheasants, in colours and gold, exact quantity as Lot 12

132 One table service, red mazarine, and richly gilt, exact quantity as Lot 5

133 Two Dresden pattern tulips and stands, 2 ditto, cans and stands, and 2 flat formed bottles. £1.4.0.

134 Two large bottle-shaped perfume jars. £6.6.0.

136 Two small hexagonal bottles. 9/-.

137 Two beer jugs

138 Two tall octagonal embossed Chinese covered jars

139 Two low fluted open jars, a la Chinoise

140 Two low jars and covers. 9/-.

141 Two small octagonal jars and covers, red, blue and gold

142 Two Lizard-handled vases. 18/-.

143 One table service, of costly manufacture, in colours, mazarine and gold, exact quantity as Lot 5

144 Two fine large bottles, ornamented, a la Chinoise

145 One breakfast, tea, and coffee set, Parisian sprigs and gold lines, exact quantity as Lot 13

146 One desert service, gold rose pattern as Lot 12

147 Two essence burners, 2 lavender bottles, and 4 paint cups

148 Two open jars

149 Two singularly formed jars, a la Chinoise

150 Two low Dolphin vases

151 One table set, old India Japan pattern, exact quantity as Lot 5

153 Ditto, blue, red, and gold, ditto

155 Two beakers

156 Two tall hexagonal beakers

157 Two curiously formed beakers, a la Chinoise

158 Two small round jars and covers. 10/-.

159 Two ditto octagon jars and covers

161 Ditto, rich Japan pattern, in colours and gold, as Lot 9

162 One breakfast tea and coffee set, french sprigs, and gold lines, exact quantity as Lot 18

163 One Dejeune set, red and gold

164 Two small round jars and covers, and 2 cabinet cups and saucers

165 Two porter mugs

166 Two sugar caddies

167 One ewer and bason, and 2 cabinet cups and saucers
168 One table service, India grass-hopper pattern, in colours, and slightly gilt, exact quantity as Lot 5
169 One desert service, Japan, red purple and gold, exact quantity as Lot 12
170 One breakfast tea and coffee set, sun flower and gold, exact quantity as Lot 13
171 One drawing room lions head perfume jar, and 4 toy Dresden pattern cups and saucers. 12/-.
175 Two jars, colours and gold
176 Two jardiniers and stands. 13/-.
177 Two antique formed coffee pots
178 Two watering cans, rich pattern, 2 small round jars and covers
179 Two rich lizard-handled jars. 18/-.
180 Two Etruscan jars
181 Four chamber candlesticks
182 Two square scent boxes, 2 toy churns
183 Two perforated jars
184 Two lizard jars. 10/6.
185 One desert service, India gold vase pattern, as Lot 12
186 Four jugs for beer. 17/-.
187 One fine perfume jar, a la Chinoise
End of Second Day's Sale

THIRD DAY'S SALE
THURSDAY, DECEMBER 17th, 1818
at one o'clock precisely

189 Two match pots, 2 Lizard handled vases, 2 ink stands
190 Two rich beakers, 2 toy pitcher jars, 2 handled embossed essence burners
192 Two handsome ornaments, a la Chinoise
193 Two rich tea caddies
194 Desert service, India flower basket Japan exact quantity as Lot 12
195 Breakfast tea and coffee set, coloured sprigs, gold lines, exact quantity as Lot 13
198 A table service, of rich Mogul pattern in colours and gold border, exact quantity as Lot 5
199 One desert service, gold rose Japan in colours and gold, exact quantity as Lot 12
200 One costly Hall jar, elegant Chinese designs
202 One table service, pattern and quantity as Lot 5
203 Two caddies, flowers and gold
204 Two pot pourris, small
205 Two Lizard-handled jars
206 One table service, Pagoda pattern in mazarine and gold, as Lot 5
207 Two fluted open jars
208 Two coffee biggins, toy size
209 Three handsome octagonal jars

210 Two small octagonal dragon-handled bottles
211 Two beakers, handsome patterns
212 One desert service, India grasshopper pattern
213 One breakfast tea and coffee service, quantity as Lot 18, sprigs, gold lines
214 Two vase-shaped ink stands
215 Two elegant Trentham bowls
216 One table service, rose and rock pattern, a la Chinoise, richly gilt, quantity as Lot 5
217 Two caddies, mazarine colours and gold
218 Two flower horns
219 Four wafer cups
220 Two square essence boxes
221 Two toy churns
222 One elegant toilet ewer and bason, antique forms and pattern
224 One table service, old Japan pattern, red purple and gold, quantity as Lot 5
225 One very large dolphin-headed bowl, richly embellished in colours and gold, damaged
226 Two watering cans, colours and gold
227 Two toy pitchers
228 One sideboard jar, dragon handles, sumptuously gilt
229 One desert set, Chinese thorn pattern, in colours and gold
230 Two rose and apple handled octagonal perfume jars
231 Two dolphin-headed bowls
232 One table service, India water-melon Japan, and richly gilt, quantity as Lot 5
233 Two beakers and covers, rich, in Mazarine, enamel and gold
234 Two handled open top fluted jars
235 Two lizard-handled vases
236 Two flat bottles
237 One breakfast tea and coffee set, French sprigs and gold border, quantity as Lot 13
238 One table service, Mogul pattern, enamelled and gilt, quantity as Lot 5
240 One table service, blue India pheasant (pattern and quantity as Lot 5)
241 Two antique pattern coffee pots
242 Two cabinet ink stands
243 One table set, gold jar pattern, gold border, quantity as Lot 5
244 Four card candlesticks
245 Two handsome vase inkstands
246 Two cabinet tea kettles
247 Two cabinet coffee biggins
248 Two flower horns
249 One table set, India figure pattern, as Lot 5
250 One breakfast tea and coffee set, grasshopper pattern, 85 pieces
251 Two open perfume bowls
252 Two Etruscan jars for pastiles
253 One desert set, flower basket pattern

254 One table service, richly finished in mazarine, green and gold; quantity as Lot 5
255 Two strawberry jars and covers
256 One fine hexagonal hall jar and cover, enamelled in compartments, and sumptuously gilt
257 Two Pan's head ornaments, landscapes in compartments of Mazarine, and splendidly gilt
258 Two cabinet tea pots
259 One desert service, Chinese subject, in compartments of Mazarine and gold
260 Two scollopt scent jars
261 Two three handled fluted jars
262 Two water bottles
264 Two watering pots
265 Two elegant dragon head octagonal jars
266 Two octagonal embossed jars and covers
267 One table set, India pheasant pattern in colours
268 Two round jars and covers
270 Two Chinese beakers, richly ornamented
271 Two oak-leaf low vases and covers
272 One richly executed jar, Chinese subjects, on Mazarine ground
274 Four toy cream stands
275 Two cabinet pitchers
277 Two griffin-handled vases
278 Two embossed jars and covers
281 Two octagonal rose and apple jars for perfume
282 Two curious antique formed jars, handsomely gilt
283 Two octagonal jars and Covers
284 One ditto embossed jar and cover

1822 SALE CATALOGUE

THE VALUABLE & EXTENSIVE
STOCK OF CHINA
OF THE LATE
MR. MASON,
PATENTEE AND MANUFACTURE OF THE
IRON STONE CHINA,
AT NO. 11, ALBEMARLE STREET.

A
CATALOGUE
OF THE
ENTIRE ASSEMBLAGE OF USEFUL & DECORATIVE
PORCELANE,
OF RICH AND ELEGANT PATTERNS;
comprising
SEVERAL HUNDRED
DINNER, DESSERT, BREAKFAST AND TEA SERVICES;
JUGS, EWERS, BASINS,
DISHES IN SETS, BOTH OPEN AND COVERED;
PLATES IN DOZENS, OF EVERY SIZE:
NOBLE ORNAMENTAL JARS & EWERS,
superbly gilt and beautifully enamelled;
AND
A GREAT VARIETY OF CABINET ORNAMENTS,
OF THE MOST TASTEFUL AND ELEGANT FORMS.
WHICH WILL BE SOLD BY AUCTION

BY MR. PHILLIPS,

ON THE PREMISES
AT NO. 11, ALBEMARLE STREET,
ON FRIDAY, the 14th day of JUNE, 1822,
And following Day, at Twelve for ONE precisely,
BY ORDER OF THE EXECUTORS,
WITHOUT RESERVE.

May be viewed Four Days preceding the Sale, and Catalogues had on the Premises; at the Auction Mart, and at Mr. Phillips, 73, New Bond Street.

NOTICE

This Sale will commence every Day PRECISELY at ONE, on account of the number of Lots in each Day.

FIRST DAY'S SALE
TUESDAY, the 4th Day of JUNE, 1822
commencing at one o'clock precisely

The Description of the various Pieces composing the Dinner, Dessert and Tea Services, will be found on the largest or principal Piece in each Service.

Lot		Reserve
1	Twenty-four jars and covers	12/-
2	Two blue and white pheasant toilet suites, 16 pieces	10/-
3	Six ditto jugs, and a toilet suite, dragon pattern	10/-
5	A tea and breakfast set, 56 pieces	16/-
6	Four antique shape jugs	14/-
7	A tea service, 43 pieces	20/-
8	Two match boxes and 3 paper cases, mazarine ground	30/-
9	A dejeune, gold edge, japan	42/-
10	Two broth basins, covers and stands and 2 porus wine coolers	24/-
11	Five jugs from the antique and 5 kitchen jugs	16/-
13	Two card racks and 2 violet baskets	30/-
14	A dinner service, dragon pattern, 142 pieces, as per label on tureen	9gns.
15	A pair of wine coolers, gilt mask heads and ornaments	42/-
17	A pair of jars, Chinese landscape and figures	25/-
18	A pair of essence jars, gilt and painted in birds and flowers, faulty	30/-
20	A breakfast service, neat sprig, 100 pieces	90/-
21	Two large jugs, gold plaid and flowers	30/-
22	Eleven meat, 12 soup and 5 pie plates	42/-
23	A Stilton cheese stand and cover, and 3 trays	20/-
24	A pair of hexagon vases, gilt Chinese building, figures, flowers and moths	55/-
25	A pair of ice pails, covers and liners, gilt and painted in flowers	60/-
26	Six basins, covers and stands, painted in flowers	42/-
27	A DINNER SERVICE, in boquet, 142 pieces, as per description on tureen	12gns.
28	A wine cooler, gilt and japanned flowers	30/-
29	A breakfast service, dragon pattern, 69 pieces	90/-
30	Two ink stands, green ground and flowers, gilt	24/-
31	Six jugs, formed from the antique	16/-
32	Four basins, covers and stands, gilt edge	20/-
33	A ewer and basin, Indian sprig, gilt edge	20/-
35	A pair of jars and covers, japanned flower and gilt ram's heads and edges	70/-
36	A supper service, centre and 4 quadrants and covers, japanned flower, gilt	80/-
37	Six jugs, pheasant and flowers from the antique	14/-

38	A ditto toilet suite, 8 pieces, and a tea set painted in flowers	30/-
39	A dessert service, gilt and painted in flowers, centre, 12 compotiers and 24 plates	150/-
40	A large chamber jar and cover, blue landscape and a foot pan	30/-
41	A pair shaped jars and covers, japanned and gilt flower	100/-
42	Three jugs from the antique, fancy pattern	30/-
44	A pair of hand candlesticks with extinguishers and glass shades	42/-
45	A pair of biscuit vases, with bandeau of flowers and glass shades	35/-
46	A suite of three ditto with shades	45/-
47	A DINNER SERVICE, gilt and ornamented with flowers, 142 pieces, as described	30gns.
48	A handsome tea set, 44 pieces 'Very high indeed' auctioneer's comment written in catalogue	9gns.
49	A toilet suite in flowers, 8 pieces and a glass caraft and tumbler, fluted	55/-
50	A small ewer, basin and pair of candlesticks with glass shades	30/-
51	A DINNER SERVICE, rich japan pattern; sumptuously gilt, 142 pieces	£35.
52	A pair of Grecian form essence bowls, with handles, sumptuously gilt	£6.
53	A pair of blue essence bottles, 2 inkstands, wafer cup and cover and 4 glass shades	35/-
54	A pair of handsome urns on pedestals, richly gilt and glass shades	40/-
55	A NOBLE LOFTY JAR with cover, surmounted with griffins and blue ground, beautifully enamelled in birds and flowers	9gns.
56	An essence cup and cover, pair of square bottles and a breakfast and tea set, blue border	65/-
57	A chamber slop pail and cover, painted in flowers, gilt edges and ornaments	40/-
58	A porous wine cooler and 9 jugs, formed from the antique	16/-
60	A lofty ESSENCE JAR and cover dragon handles, and top painted in flowers	63/-
62	A dessert service, blue and gold flower border	190/-
63	A chamber suite of 9 pieces, caraft and tumbler	50/-
64	A DINNER SERVICE, peacock and flowers, 142 pieces	£14.
65	A suite of 4 jugs in flowers	30/-
66	A tea set, white and gold, 45 pieces	20/-
68	A dessert service, blue birds and flowers, 43 pieces	130/-

69	A DINNER SERVICE, hexagon shape, blue birds and flowers, 142 pieces	11gns.
70	A pair of shaped jars and covers, gilt and painted flowers	40/-
71	A pair of flower urns, richly gilt and painted and 2 glass shades	35/-
72	A pair of handsome essence jars and covers, large hexagonal, gold plaid	30/-
73	A pair of blue sprinklers, gilt handles, embossed figures and glass shades	40/-
74	A DINNER SERVICE, rich old japan pattern, containing 142 pieces, as described	25gns.
75	A ditto DESSERT SERVICE, 43 pieces	6gns.
76	A pair of jars with dragon handles	35/-
80	A pair of match cases, Dresden flower and glass shades	20/-
81	A centre piece, fruit basket, radish tray, 2 sallad bowls, mustard, pepper, argyle and egg beater	26/-
82	Two chamber services, 16 pieces	32/-
83	A DINNER SERVICE, Dresden sprig, 142 pieces, as described	25gns.
84	A ewer and basin, enamelled moths and flowers, and 8 jugs, blue bird and flower	30/-
85	A set of five Grecian shape urns, painted in birds and flowers, sumptuously gilt and 5 shades	130/-
87	Twenty-two meat, soup and dessert plates, Dresden flower and gold edge	40/-
88	A DINNER SERVICE, blue bird and flower, containing 142 pieces, as described	190/-
89	A dessert service, blue sprig, 43 pieces, ditto	5gns.
90	Four jugs from the antique, enamelled border and flowers	10/-
92	A dejeune, festoon flowers and sprig	15/-
93	Two pink jars and covers	20/-
94	A DINNER SERVICE, blue birds and flowers, contents, 142 pieces, as described	190/-
96	A tea set, same pattern, 45 pieces	7gns.
97	A pair of broth basins, covers and stands, japanned blue compartments	30/-
98	A pair of hexagon FLOWER POTS and stands, mazarine ground and gold edge	5gns.
99	Two jugs from antique designs	16/-
100	A breakfast service, painted sprig, 30 pieces and 12 plates, melange	40/-
101	A ragout dish, cover and liner, a steak ditto, an ice butter tub, butter tub, and a pickle stand	50/-
102	A supper service, richly gilt, 10 pieces	70/-
103	Two ice pails, covers and liners, grasshopper and flowers, gilt edge	42/-
105	Twelve jugs and covers, blue birds, etc	30/-

107	A chamber slop pail and cover, blue birds and flowers	16/-
108	Four antique form jugs, grasshopper pattern	11/-
109	Two fruit baskets, on feet	40/-
110	Three mugs, gold plaid, and shaving box, red rose, etc.	20/-
111	Five large jugs, embossed flower	15/-
112	Two japanned jars, dolphin handles	35/-
113	A DINNER SERVICE, dragon pattern, contents, 143 pieces, as described	9gns.
114	A rich japan DESSERT SERVICE, 43 pieces	8gns.
117	A DINNER SERVICE, hexagon shape, grasshopper pattern, 143 pieces, as described	15 ? gns.
119	Pair of rich jars and covers, sumptuously gilt	30/-
120	Twelve melange plates	18/-
121	Twelve ditto, various rich patterns	18/-
122	A rich gilt and japan toilet service, 8 pieces	63/-
123	A DINNER SERVICE, Tourney sprig, 143 pieces, as described	11gns.
124	Two ewers, gilt and japan flower, formed from the antique	20/-
125	A breakfast service, white and gold, 30 pieces	30/-
126	A broth basin, cover and stand and chamber slop pail and cover	24/-
127	A handsome essence jar, green ground and flowers and 2 match cases in landscapes	63/-
128	Two blue and white chamber sets, 16 pieces	35/-
130	A potatoe dish and cover, 5 potting pots and an eggstand with 6 cups	12/-

End of the First Day

SECOND DAY'S SALE
WEDNESDAY, the 5th Day of JUNE, 1822
commencing at One o'Clock precisely

Lot		Reserve
131	Thirteen blue jugs, in sizes	30/-
132	Two blue chamber sets with carafts and tumblers	40/-
134	Twelve white preserving jars and covers	32/-
135	A dejeune, Bourbon sprig	30/-
138	Two Stilton cheese stands and 2 fluted top wine coolers, willow	40/-
141	Six coloured jugs and 12 mugs	27/-
142	Two ice pails, richly gilt (1 cover faulty)	37/-
143	A table set, willow	190/-
146	Three paper cases and 2 scent pots, mazarine	20/-
147	Three rich India pattern jugs	25/-
148	Two wine coolers, elegantly gilt	42/-
149	A breakfast service, 42 pieces	70/-

150	A breakfast and tea service, 93 pieces	50/-
151	Two chamber sets, japan, with caraft and tumbler	60/-
152	A table set, grasshopper, gold knobs	£16.
153	A ditto, flower pattern (not Ironstone)	£7.
154	Two porous wine coolers, 2 ditto butter tubs and 24 glass wines	36/-
156	A dessert service, japan	105/-
160	A supper set, rich japan, gold edge	38/-
161	Three jars, mazarine and gold chased figures, with shades	105/-
162	A breakfast set, Chinese sprig, 77 pieces	60/-
163	Two chamber sets, white, with carafts and tumblers	28/-
164	Two large flower pots and stands, mazarine	80/-
166	A set of lunch plates, Tourney sprig, gold edge	30/-
167	A pair of ice pails, japan	60/-
168	A table service, Chinese Figures, gold edge, as described	£18.
169	A very richly gilt tea service	190/-
172	Six hunting jugs and 5 mugs	24/-
173	Three jugs, japan	20/-
174	Two antique coffee pots, with glass shades	35/-
175	One fine hexagonal hall jar	150/-
176	Six broth bowls, covers and stands	35/-
177	Twenty-four rich melange plates	50/-
178	Two antique jars	42/-
180	Two pastille burners, with glass shades	55/-
181	A breakfast set, coloured flowers, 61 pieces	75/-
182	A table service, japan, richly gilt	23gns.
183	A blue supper set	25/-
190	One superb square very large hall jar, mazarine and Indian devices	17gns.
191	A tea set, japan, 57 pieces	84/-
192	A chamber set, green border, enamelled, with caraft and tumbler	15/-
193	A Trentham plaid jar	35/-
194	Seven mugs, hunting, and 24 glass tumblers	25/-
195	Two toy ewers and basins, mazarine with shades	27/-
196	Two shell pen trays, 2 hand candlesticks and 2 glass shades	24/-
197	A dessert service, roses and gold edge, 41 pieces	6gns.
198	Two porous wine coolers and 2 butter tubs	20/-
202	Forty-eight lunch plates	30/-
203	Two chamber sets, blue, with carafts and tumblers	40/-
204	A supper set, blue	30/-
205	A table service, blue	190/-
206	A dessert service, Dresden flowers, 37 pieces	7gns.
207	Two ice pails, flowers in compartments, on blue border, richly gilt	4gns.
208	Two elegant vases, with shades	40/-

209	Two flower pots and stands, japan, with shades	31/6
210	Three ragout dishes, pans and covers, white	60/-
211	A breakfast set, Indian dragon, gold edge, 94 pieces	110/-
212	A table service, white	6gns.
216	Eight jugs, blue, and 4 covered ditto	30/-
217	Six jugs, gold jar pattern	25/-
218	Twelve breakfast cups and saucers, white and gold	30/-
219	An elegant chamber service, with caraft and tumbler	60/-
220	Six very rich plates	52/-
221	Two elegant griffin jars, painted in fruit and flowers, sumptuously gilt	6gns.
224	Forty-eight lunch plates, various	30/-
225	Two broth basins, covers and stands, japan, and 4 soup plates, rich melange	30/-
226	A table service, japan, gold edge	£25.
227	A dessert set, japan, ungilt	6gns.
228	An oval set, japan, gilt, with mahogany tray	52/-
233	A tea set, coloured flowers, 45 pieces	30/-
234	A breakfast and tea service, India sprig, 111 pieces	84/-
235	A chamber service, Chinese figures, with caraft and tumbler	25/-
237	Twelve plates, richly painted, with various arms and crests	60/-
239	Seven handsome dessert plates, melange	35/-
240	A splendid Neapolitan vase, painted by S. Bourne	£30.
241	Two hexagon vases, mazarine (1 faulty)	10/-
244	Twelve blue mugs and 12 horns	25/-
246	Five club top jugs and 6 stone mugs	25/-
247	Twelve lunch plates, blue bell japan, and dish and cover	25/-
248	Two vegetable dishes for hot water	60/-
249	Four chocolate cups and stands, and 4 odd dishes	20/-
250	Twenty-two lunch plates, gilt Japan	25/-
251	A lunch set, of basket pattern, gold edge, 68 pieces (plates not gilt)	96/-
252	Two chimney vases, Chinese pattern	20/-
253	Two ditto, japanned	25/-

End of the Second Day

THIRD DAY'S SALE
THURSDAY, the 6th Day of JUNE, 1822
Commencing at One o'Clock precisely

Lot		Reserve
262	One foot tub and 1 slop jar, blue	20/-
263	Two ice pails, blue, and 2 wine coolers, white	25/-
266	Two blue large flower pots and stands	40/-
268	A breakfast set, Tourney sprig, gold edge, 54 pieces	63/-
269	A ditto, japan, 22 pieces	35/-
270	Two bottles, mazarine, white figures with shades, and 1 centre jar	63/-
271	Nine hunting mugs	12/-
272	Two vegetable dishes, japan	30/-
273	A table service, white	6gns.
274	A ditto, blue	9½gns.
275	A ditto, blue japanned	12gns.
276	A melange breakfast and tea service, 73 pieces	70/-
277	Three cheese stands and 1 vegetable dish for hot water, japan	42/-
278	Two new form blue chamber sets with carafts and tumblers	40/-
281	One large sideboard bowl, Indian pattern	105/-
282	Two richly gilt ice pails	80/-
283	Three jugs, japan	25/-
284	A supper set, richly gilt	60/-
288	A set of three vases, fruit and green ground, with shades	75/-
289	Two match pots, roses on black ground and 1 antique coffee pot, with shades	32/-
290	A japanned table service, grasshopper	£14.
292	Thirty-five lunch plates, rich brown and gold border	90/-
294	A very rich ragout dish and cover	50/-
295	A table service, blue	£9.10.0d.
296	A breakfast service, blue, 87 pieces	40/-
298	A large hydra top jar, mazarine birds and flowers	9gns.
299	Two Chinese jars and covers	no price
300	Four toy spouted mugs, rich japan, and 2 candle-sticks, tourney and shade	35/-
301	Two candlesticks, flowers and orange ground, with shades	40/-
308	A rich japan table service	£25.
309	A very beautifully painted landscape dessert service, by S. Bourne	£30.
311	A breakfast service, green scroll and gold border, 77 pieces	5gns.
312	A dejeuner, Indian garden	50/-
313	Two chamber sets, green leaf border, with carafts and tumblers	35/-

314	A ragout dish and cover, and 2 vegetable dishes for hot water, gold jar pattern	42/-
316	Six beautiful plates	35/-
317	Four hexagon jugs, mazarine and gold bands	50/-
318	Six broth basins and stands, grass hopper japan	24/-
319	A blue table service, willow	9½ gns.
320	Twelve species of useful articles, willow	18/-
324	A richly gilt table service, gold tops	£25.
325	A table set, Tourney sprig	£20.
326	Two vases, mazarine, and 1 centre ditto, with shades	63/-
327	Two vases, Views in Rome	4gns.
329	A very beautiful Italian formed vase, painted by S. Bourne, superbly gilt and burnished	35gns.
330	Sixty-nine sundry pieces, peacock japan	90/-
332	Two large myrtle pots and stands, mazarine	84/-
333	Two candlesticks, buff ground, with shades	40/-
341	A Chinese jar, white, figures on mazarine	30/-
344	A breakfast service, green ground, gold edge, 52 pieces	£5.
345	Five stone jugs and 6 mugs	25/-
348	A table service, gilt japan	£26.
349	A ditto, common japan	£14.
351	A tea set, Bourbon sprig, 45 pieces	25/-
352	A breakfast and tea service, white and gold, 11 pieces	6gns.
353	Two hexagon tall jars and covers, japan	42/-
354	Eight mugs and 8 ditto japan	£6.16.0d.
355	Three jugs, corbeau grounds	32/-
356	Two ice pails, peacock japan	40/-
359	Eight jugs, blue, and 6 mugs	25/-
360	Two wine coolers and 2 ice pails, blue	25/-
361	Five punch bowls, blue	30/-
362	A table set, enamelled sprigs	14gns.
363	A table service, Chinese characters on mazarine ground	£40.
364	A breakfast service, dragon pattern, 70 pieces	55/-
365	A tea service, richly japanned, 45 pieces	6gns.
367	Three small vases with shades	35/-
368	A pagoda vase, japan	£5.10.0d.
377	Two card racks, mazarine	20/-
378	Four rich broth basins, covers and stands	32/-
379	Two very rich chocolate cups and stands	30/-
380	Three cheese stands and 6 bakers, rich japan	40/-
381	Eight hunting jugs	24/-
382	Two chamber sets, gold jar, with carafts and tumblers	£2.10.0d.
387	Two fruit baskets, japan	42/-
388	Six jugs, gold jar and 4 ditto grasshopper	26/-
389	Six mortars	30/-
390	Seventeen ice plates, japan	50/-

End of the Third Day

FOURTH DAY'S SALE
FRIDAY, the 7th Day of June, 1822
commencing at One o'Clock precisely

Lot		Reserve
391	Two vegetable dishes for hot water, 2 cheese stands and 6 bakers, grasshopper japan	28/-
392	One ragout dish and cover and 2 vegetable dishes for hot water, japan	30/-
394	Nine jugs and 4 covered ditto, blue	30/-
395	Two small hexagon bottles, mazarine, with shades, and 2 small candlesticks, red ground, with ditto	27/-
396	A breakfast set, bourbon sprig, 54 pieces	30/-
405	Two lotus porous coolers and 12 glass fluted and diamond border tumblers	48/-
406	A tea set, white and gold, 45 pieces	50/-
407	Two chamber sets, green border, with carafts and tumblers	45/-
410	Two soup tureens and stands, rich brown and gold border	70/-
412	A trentham jar, japan	25/-
413	A set of 5 vases, painted shells and landscapes, red ground	8gns.
414	A table service, japan	11gns.
415	A ditto, peacock japan	12gns.
416	A dessert service, gold jar japan	80/-
418	A square supper set, rich japan	50/-
420	One chamber set, Indian paintings, with caraft and tumbler	30/-
422	Two vegetable dishes and 4 bakers, rich japan	63/-
426	One dragon jar	84/-
427	A splendid hall jar, mazarine and Oriental device	12gns.
428	Four cabinet pieces	12/-
429	Two rich toilet ewers and basins	63/-
430	Four broth bowls and stands	28/-
435	A table service, very richly japanned hexagon tureens, gold burnished tops	£26.
443	Nine stone jugs and 12 goblets	24/-
445	A tea service, coloured sprigs, gold edge, 45 pieces	38/-
446	A dessert service, rich japan, gold edge	7gns.
447	Six beautiful plates	30/-
449	Two fruit baskets and stands, japan	30/-
450	Three Indian sprig jugs	63/-
452	A pair of ice pails, very richly japanned	63/-
453	Twenty-four lunch plates, enamelled	12/-
454	Six bakers, rich japan	15/-
455	Two hexagon vegetable dishes for hot water and 6 bakers nosegay	30/-

459	Two tall Chinese jars	15/-
460	Two small Indian pattern tea pots, pair vases, and glass shades	30/-
461	An Italian formed vase, superior painting, richly burnished and finely modelled	18gns.
462	A breakfast set, Indian coloured sprigs, 70 pieces, gold edge	35/-
463	A chamber service, very richly japanned, with carafts and tumblers	42/-
466	A tea service, red and gold border	30/-
467	A small breakfast service, japanned, 33 pieces	105/-
468	A ditto, ungilt, 68 pieces	63/-
470	Two foot pans, blue	20/-
471	Two ditto	20/-
474	A rose and apple jar	42/-
475	Five two-handle vases, enamel sprig, on mazarine ground	50/-
476	Six beautiful plates	40/-
480	Two ice pails, japan	42/-
481	A hexagon temple jar	28/-
482	Six bakers and 3 cheese stands	25/-
483	Two vegetable dishes for hot water and a 22-inch dish, japan	63/-
484	A coloured table service	12gns.
485	A handsome table service, rich Indian devices, hexagon tureens	£21.
486	A table service, bourbon sprig	12gns.
488	A pot pouri, ram's head, mazarine	42/-
489	Two Indian flower jars, mazarine	42/-
492	Three paper cases, beautifully painted and glass shades	42/-
493	A tea set, brown and gold border	80/-
494	A ditto coloured wreath, gilt, and 12 breakfast cups and saucers	73/-
503	Two white ice pails and 2 blue coolers	20/-
504	Six jugs and 3 covered ditto, blue, and 24 liquere glasses	35/-
505	A shell ink stand, red ground, 1 toy watering can, and 2 tea pots	32/-
506	Four square canisters, japan, with shades	40/-
507	Two ditto and a shell ink stand	20/-
509	A shaving box and 2 violet baskets, Dresden flower	20/-
511	A ditto, willow, japanned and richly gilt (only one tureen)	16gns.
514	Thirty-three preserving jars, white	50/-
518	Two hexagon jars and covers, japan	21/-
519	A tea set, white, 45 pieces	15/-
520	A ditto, yellow and gold border, 45 pieces	25/-

End of the Fourth Day

FIFTH DAY'S SALE
SATURDAY, the 8th Day of JUNE, 1822
Commencing at One o'Clock precisely

Lot		Reserve
523	Two mantle jars, mazarine	?40/-
524	One soup tureen, 4 bakers and 2 vegetable dishes for hot water, Mogul japan	?40/-
526	One tea set, gilt japan, 49 pieces	50/-
527	A Bourbon sprig breakfast set, 87 pieces	80/-
536	A breakfast service, red and gold, 74 pieces	no price
537	A table service, japan	no price
538	Two jars, sprigs, on mazarine	no price
539	A fine hall jar, Oriental design	no price
540	Four baskets, Dresden flowers, and 2 square bottles	25/-
544	One chamber set, basket japan, with caraft and tumbler	20/-
545	Two sets, green leaf border	30/-
546	Six bakers, 4 boats and stands and 2 cheese stands, jar pattern	28/-
547	A tea service, green ground	70/-
548	A dessert, richly gilt Indian pattern	147/6
550	A breakfast service, roses and gilt, 72 pieces	94/6
551	A breakfast service, blue, 100 pieces	30/-
552	A chamber service, japanned and gilt, with caraft and tumbler	25/-
554	A table service, birds, gilt	7gns.
558	A dragon vase and cover, Indian devices	73/6
560	A highly finished tea service, 45 pieces	9gns.
567	Eleven jugs, Indian form	22/-
568	A large sideboard bowl	4gns.
570	Two paper cases, raised figures on mazarine	15/-
571	Two Indian formed jars and shades	4gns.
567	A very rich dessert service, Oriental style	10gns.
569	A breakfast service, after the Chinese manner, 94 pieces	6gns.
570	A tea service, blue and gold border	4gns.
571	A small breakfast service, melange, 60 pieces	
572	A very rich pair of ice pails	
573	Six finely pencilled plates	
575	Twelve melange plates and a fine round dish	
576	Two match cases, delicately finished, with shades	£3.10.0d.
577	Two beautiful antique coffee pots, with shades	£3.13.6d.
580	Eighteen preserving jars, white	20/-
582	A dinner service, nosegay pattern	£12.
584	A toilet ewer and basin, rich pattern	20/-
585	A flower bowl, mazarine and delicate sprigs	30/-
586	Two exquisitely painted satyr goblets	£5.
591	A breakfast service, enamelled roses, 77 pieces	3gns.
599	Five rich mugs, various	20/-

Lot		Reserve
600	Twenty lunch plates	20/-
602	Two potatoe dishes and covers, and 1 vegetable dish for hot water, japan	no price
603	A rich dessert service	£9.19.6d.
604	A tea service, white and gold border	£2.10.0d.
605	A rich tea service, 45 pieces	£7.
606	A table service, highly gilt, etc.	£22.10.0d.
611	Two wine coolers, richly japanned	£2.
612	A small lunch service, blue and gold edge, 27 pieces	no price
613	Two octagonal jars, Chinese	no price
614	A conservatory bowl	no price
615	Two Indian bottles with shades	no price
616	A mazarine toilet, ewer and basin, with shades	no price
617	Four small flower pots and stands, mazarine and delicate sprigs	no price
625	A hall jar, lion head handles	£2.10.0d.
626	A table service, enamelled and gilt in the Oriental manner	£22.10.0d.
627	A very highly japanned chamber service	45/-
628	A breakfast service, Chinese coloured sprigs, 116 pieces	90/-
629	A tea set, sprigs and gold	no price
630	A small tea set, melange, 30 pieces	no price
631	Twelve white jugs	no price
632	A two-handled Etruscan formed flower vase, highly finished in flowers and gold, with shade	no price
641	A pagoda vase, for vestibule	no price
642	Two very rich water jugs	no price
643	Four mugs, richly gilt	no price
644	A trentham bowl	no price
647	Two very rich chocolate cups and covers	no price
648	Three large and 2 small dishes, and 1 drainer, coloured	no price
649	Twelve stone jugs, of two shapes	no price
650	Two chamber sets, jar pattern	no price

End of the Fifth Day

SIXTH DAY'S SALE
MONDAY, the 10th Day of JUNE, 1822
Commencing at One o'Clock precisely

Lot		Reserve
651	A tea set, white and gold	35/-
652	A breakfast set, yellow and gold border, 64 pieces	70/-
655	Four mortars and 2 porous wine coolers	30/-
660	Two chamber services, gold jar pattern	35/-
661	Twelve melange breakfast cups and saucers	18/-

666	Two chocolate cups and saucers and 7 useful pieces of table ware	27/-
669	Two fruit baskets and stands, Oriental designs	35/-
670	Three paper cases, rich, with shades	35/-
671	Two octagon jars	63/-
672	Twelve beautifully finished plates, various	80/-
673	Two serpent handled jars	42/-
674	Two vases, green ground, fruit and shades	84/-
678	A table service, richly coloured and gilt, hexagon tureens	£26.
680	A square supper service, finished japan	70/-
681	A small breakfast set, 30 pieces	30/-
682	A chamber service, richly gilt	35/-
684	A table service, green ground, Dresden border	15gns.
686	Two handsome jars and covers	50/-
689	A table service, blue	9gns.
691	A splendid hall jar, from an improved Indian model	16gns.
692	Two delicate vases, with shades	24/-
693	Four japan candlesticks, mazarine	16/-
694	A very richly finished tea set, 45 pieces	8gns.
695	An Indian pattern breakfast service, 77 pieces	30/-
701	Four candlesticks and extinguishers, mazarine japan	15/-
702	Two large flat candlesticks, mazarine, with shades	42/-
703	Two handsome mantle jars, with shades	45/-
704	Four rich jugs	35/-
705	A table service, coloured hexagon tureens	17gns.
706	A small breakfast service, 28 pieces	42/-
709	A dessert service, blue foliage	3gns.
710	Two beautiful painted goblets	4gns.
711	Four delicate cabinet pieces	24/-
716	Two porous coolers and 4 mortars	30/-
718	A tea set, dragon and gold border	36/-
719	A breakfast service, coloured sprig, 47 pieces	35/-
720	A table service, blue	9gns.
721	A ditto, rich japan	25gns.
722	Two toilet ewers and basins, and 2 chocolate cups, rich	30/-
723	Seven dishes, rich japan	30/-
728	Six highly wrought plates	60/-
729	Six soup ditto	50/-
730	Two fruit baskets and stands, rich	35/-
731	Two sugar bowls, covers and stands, japanned	24/-
738	An elegant flower vase, with shade	42/-
740	A chamber service, green leaf border	20/-
741	A table service, nosegay pattern, hexagon tureens	12gns.
743	Six compotiers	20/-
744	Seven bakers, rich japan	30/-
745	Two vegetable dishes for hot water, a ragout dish and cover and 2 bakers, coloured	40/-

746	One 20-inch gravy dish, 1 cheese stand and 1 vegetable dish for hot water	25/-
750	Two two-handled low vases, with shades	40/-
751	One toilet ewer and basin	21/-
752	Five scent jars and covers	42/-
753	Two large flat candlesticks, mazarine with shades	42/-
754	A hall bowl	42/-
756	A table set, plaid japan, richly gilt	£30.
758	A breakfast service, japan, 54 pieces	105/-
760	A square supper set, Indian pattern with border	40/-
761	Two chamber services and gold jar	40/-
762	A small melange breakfast set, 31 pieces	23/-
763	Two cream bowls and covers, gold thorn	18/-
771	A table set, brown border	73/-
772	A dessert set ditto, 4 chamber sets ditto, with carafts and tumblers	70/-
774	A tea set, dragon gold edge	35/-

End of the Sixth Day

SEVENTH DAY'S SALE
TUESDAY, the 11th Day of JUNE, 1822
commencing at One o'Clock precisely

Lot		Reserve
781	Twelve jars and covers	16/-
783	Two porous wine coolers and 2 butter tubs	15/-
785	Ten jugs from the antique	23/-
793	Two sprinkling bottles, 2 cups and covers, moths on mazarine ground with glass shades	30/-
795	A pair of toy chamber candlesticks and 2 buckets with glasses	23/-
796	A breakfast set, dragon, 43 pieces	50/-
798	A tea service, painted in flowers	no price
801	Two chamber suites, blue and white	30/-
802	A tea set, painted in roses, 45 pieces	no price
803	A dessert service, painted and gold flower, 43 pieces	8gns.
805	A shell ecritoire and pair of match cases, blue and gold	32/-
806	Ten mugs, embossed hunting figures	20/-
807	Twelve broth basins and stands	30/-
808	Six punch bowls	25/-
809	A pair of toy hand candlesticks, a pen tray, and sprinkling pot, gold edges and flowers	25/-
813	A chamber suite, blue and gold edge	20/-
814	A DINNER SERVICE, blue and white	9gns.
815	Twelve fruit dishes	12/-
816	A pair of blue bottles, raised flower, an ink cup and canister and 4 glass shades	28/-
817	A pair of ice pails and 2 baskets and stands	25/-

818	A tea set, blue border, 45 pieces	30/-
819	A chamber set, japan gold edge	30/-
822	Twelve breakfast cups and 12 saucers, roses and gold edge	30/-
826	Two vegetable dishes and covers and a steak ditto	25/-
827	Two blue essence bottles, 2 wax hand candlesticks, gilt and painted flower, 2 inkstands and 4 glass shades	35/-
828	A chamber suite, japan flower	25/-
829	Eight broth basins and stands	20/-
831	A pair of handsome vases, richly gilt and painted in flowers, and 2 blue bottles in birds and glass shades	30/-
832	A rich tea set, japan flower, 33 pieces	6gns.
833	A breakfast service to match, 54 pieces	9gns.
837	A costly DESSERT SERVICE, exquisitely painted in SELECT VIEWS, by S. Bourne, enriched with burnished gold	35gns.
838	Ten jugs, embossed flowers and figures	23/-
839	A handsome DINNER SERVICE, painted in roses	18gns.
840	A DESSERT DITTO, japan and gilt flowers, 43 pieces	£8.
842	Two neat essence bottles, gold sprig, and 2 jugs with glass shades	35/-
850	A handsome japan and gilt DINNER SERVICE	£21.
851	A dessert service, blue and gold border	9gns.
852	Two blue essence bottles, small sprig, 2 hand candlesticks, a pot pouri and cup and cover	25/-
855	A handsome DESSERT SERVICE, painted in boquets, relieved by sea green and gold devices	15gns.
856	A pair of handsome jars, with glass shades	28/-
857	An ice pail, japan, and 1 ditto barbeaux	30/-
858	Two vegetable dishes and covers, 2 cheese stands and 4 bakers	25/-
859	A handsome ecritoire and 2 essence bottles	25/-
862	A pair of toy jars, gilt and painted in flowers, and a violet basket painted in landscapes	25/-
863	A pair of handsome ice pails	37/-
865	Twelve breakfast cups and saucers, India sprig	21/-
866	A NOBLE VASE, formed from the antique, beautifully painted in landscapes and figures, by Bourne, and sumptuously gilt	£21.0.0d.
867	A pair of ornaments in the style of the Portland vase, and shades	50/-
868	A pair of neat jars and covers	40/-
872	A violet basket, painted in a landscape, a toy jug, an ink stand and sprinkler	20/-
873	A pair of handsome candlesticks, painted in flowers and glass shades	30/-
875	A pair of jars, neat sprig, on blue ground	63/-

878	A pair of jars, painted in landscapes and glass shades	40/-
879	A handsome TABLE SERVICE, japanned	13gns.
880	A pair of beakers, painted in flowers, and a japan vase	20/-
881	A NOBLE ESSENCE JAR, painted in flowers, on celests ground, relieved by burnished gold	20gns.
882	A pair of reading candlesticks, Dresden flower, a pen tray and an ink stand with glass shade	30/-
883	A handsome jug, painted in landscapes and hunting subject	42/-
887	A handsome ESSENCE URN, blue ground, enriched by moths, flowers and gilt decorations	84/-
888	A ditto, its companion	84/-
889	Two ice pails, rich japan	84/-
894	A coffee ewer, richly gilt, from the antique, and glass shade	25/-
896	A breakfast set, India sprig, 44 pieces	50/-
897	A pair of flower pots and stands, painted in moths, and an accurate sun dial with glass shades	25/-
898	Six handsome dessert plates, sumptuously gilt	36/-
899	A pair of neat reading candlesticks, with glass shades	25/-
901	Two violet baskets, 2 hand candlesticks, gilt and painted in flowers and 2 sprinkling pots	30/-
903	A pair of blue jars, raised figures, on blue ground and glass shades	40/-
904	Two toy jugs and a sprinkler, a japan flower, 3 glasses and 4 toy candlesticks	40/-
905	A toy ewer and basin, painted in landscapes, 2 pair of candlesticks and glass shades	25/-
907	Six punch bowls	20/-
908	A breakfast set, 41 pieces, blue flower	35/-
909	Three japan jugs, gilt edge	24/-
910	Twelve breakfast cups and saucers, small sprig	20/-
919	A soup tureen and cover, Japan	12/-
920	Four delicate cabinet pieces and shades	27/-
925	Four Plaid Japan dishes and drainers	105/-
926	A tea service, 99 pieces, blue sprig	75/-
930	Six cups and 7 saucers in roses, 6 breakfast ditto and muffin & cover	20/-

End of the Seventh Day

EIGHTH DAY'S SALE
FRIDAY, the 14th Day of JUNE, 1822
commencing at One o'Clock precisely

Lot		Reserve
932	Two vegetable dishes and steak ditto with covers and liners, for hot water	28/-

933	Two chamber suites, blue and white	30/-
937	Eight breakfast and tea cups and saucers, 2 plates, tea pot and sugar basin, rich mazarine pattern	4gns.
941	An ewer basin and slipper, japan	15/-
952	Nine jugs, 4 covered ditto and 3 mugs	35/-
954	A breakfast set, yellow and gold, 89 pieces	£9.
957	Twenty-one hexagon shape blue jugs	45/-
958	A pair of vases and covers, mazarine, 1 faulty	30/-
959	A dessert service, colour japan	4gns.
960	Two chamber suites, blue and white	30/-
964	A pair of hexagon essence jars, painted in flowers, and a glass shade	3gns.
966	A tea set, India sprig and gold edge	60/-
967	A japan vase and shade	30/-
968	Two vegetable dishes and steak ditto, with covers and liners	28/-
970	A DINNER SERVICE, coloured japan	14gns.
972	Two rich cabinet cups, covers and stands, painted in landscapes and shade	70/-
973	A japan ewer and basin, soap and brush trays	20/-
975	Two pastil burners with glass shades, and 2 match cases, mazarine	42/-
977	A breakfast set, dragon, 62 pieces	46/-
978	A sprinkling can, 2 shell candlesticks and 3 egg cups	20/-
981	An essence jar, painted in flowers on green ground, and glass shades	31/6
984	Five ornamental vases	46/-
986	Three handsome paper vases with glass shades	40/-
987	Two vegetable dishes, covers and liners, and a steak ditto	28/-
989	A pair of japan reading candlesticks and 2 paper cases, birds on green ground	42/-
991	A vase and 2 match cases, mazarine, and glass shades	46/-
992	A breakfast set, coloured and gold sprig and edge, 52 pieces	5gns.
995	Two candlesticks, 2 vases, and 2 paper cases, mazarine glass shades	40/-
997	A lofty ESSENCE JAR, dragon handles, japan flower and gilt ornaments	70/-
1001	An essence bottle, 2 vases, 2 scent pots, and 3 glass shades	46/-
1003	A breakfast set, blue border, 73 pieces	46/-
1004	Two scent bottles, 2 candlesticks, 2 hexagon bottles, and 4 glass shades	35/-
1007	A scent bottle, 2 ditto pots, and 2 paper cases and glass shade	25/-
1008	A noble square ESSENCE JAR and COVER, Mazarine ground, enriched with flowers, etc.	20gns.

1010 A TABLE SERVICE, green border	15gns.
1012 Two hexagon jugs, 2 ditto bottles and 2 taper candlesticks, and 4 glass shades	40/-
1013 A breakfast and tea set, Tourney sprig, 73 pieces	73/6
1016 A handsome NEAPOLITAN VASE, formed from the antique, beautifully painted in landscapes, enriched with burnished gold, by S. Bourne	15gns.
1017 Six essence bottles and covers, 2 paper cases, in landscapes, and 6 shades	40/-
1018 A NOBLE CISTERN, japan flowers and gilt dolphin handles	10gns.
1022 Five scent bottles, 3 match cases, painted in landscapes, with 2 shades	52/6
1024 Two vegetable dishes and steak ditto, with covers and liners	28/-
1025 Twenty-four tea cups and 24 saucers, and basins	23/-
1028 Two essence bottles, toy tea pot, 2 ink stands, 2 paper cases in landscapes, and 7 glass shades	50/-
1029 A pair of handsome vases	46/-
1030 A DINNER SERVICE, coloured japan	£20.
1033 Two match cases, birds on green ground, 2 jars and covers, a bottle and 2 vases, with glass shades	46/- 46/-
1034 A handsome tea set, rich japan, 41 pieces	69/-
1038 Three paper cases, landscapes, a bottle, an inkstand, and 4 shades	50/-
1039 A LOFTY JAPAN ESSENCE JAR and COVER, with gold enrichments	8gns.
1043 Two wafer baskets in landscapes, 2 bottles and shades, 3 cups and saucers, and 2 glass shades	40/-
1044 Two vegetable and 1 steak dishes, with covers and liners	28/-
1046 Two ewers and basins, japan	35/-
1047 A breakfast set, dragon pattern, 86 pieces	30/-
1048 Twelve breakfast cups and 12 saucers, barbeau gold edge	30/-
1049 Three ornamental vases and covers	60/-
1053 Twelve breakfast cups and saucers, tea, sugar and milk pot	25/-
1054 A tea set, japan, 21 pieces	10/-
1057 Two toy jugs and shades, 3 paper cases and shades	35/-
1058 A toy ewer and basin, and 3 flat candlesticks and 3 shades	28/-
1059 A handsome ewer and basin, India sprig	20/-

End of the Eighth Day

NINTH DAY'S SALE
SATURDAY, the 15th Day of JUNE, 1822
Commencing at One o'Clock

Lot		Reserve
1062	Three breakfast cups and saucers, 2 plates and a butter tub	8/-
1063	Three vegetable dishes and a steak ditto, with covers and liners	30/-
1066	A breakfast set, barbeau, gold edge, 50 pieces	60/-
1071	A steak dish and 2 vegetable dishes, with covers and liners for hot water	23/-
1072	A breakfast and tea set, barbeau sprig, 106 pieces	70/-
1073	Four large beakers, green dragon	25/-
1074	A pair of reading candlesticks and shades	40/-
1076	Three violet baskets, a wafer box, vase and 2 churns	15/-
1077	A roll tray, potatoe dish, 2 nappies, and bowl	14/-
1078	Two jars and covers, and 2 vases, green dragon (1 faulty)	40/-
1079	Six ewers and basins, and 6 slippers, blue	30/-
1080	A DINNER SERVICE, Tourney sprig	13gns.
1081	A ditto, blue and white (1 soup tureen)	£6.
1082	Two jars and covers, a cup and saucer, and 3 vases	30/-
1086	A DINNER SERVICE, embossed, blue foliage (no soup tureens)	15gns.
1089	Two japan vases, and a paper case	25/-
1095	Two mummy jars, and 2 octagon vases	40/-
1096	An ink stand, 2 wafer baskets, and 2 candlesticks and shades	30/-
1097	Two card racks, and 2 incense burners, mazarine	46/-
1098	Two vases and covers, and 2 jars and covers	40/-
1099	Four large bottles, dragon	40/-
1102	Four vegetable dishes and 3 small ewers and basins	40/-
1104	An ink stand, 2 canisters, 2 candlesticks and shades	35/-
1107	Six ewers and basons, and 6 slippers, white	60/-
1108	Two vases and 4 bottles, dragon	40/-
1109	A tea set, barbeaux sprig, gold edge, 43 pieces	40/-
1112	Two jars and covers, and 2 vases	£2.
1113	Pair of ice pails, rich japan	3½ gns.
1114	Forty-eight cups and saucers and 24 basins, blue	28/-
1115	Six ewers and basins, and six slippers, blue	30/-
1119	Six ewers and basins, and 12 mugs and jugs	23/-
1123	Forty-eight cups and saucers and 24 basins, blue	30/-
1124	A rich japan DINNER SERVICE	£21.
1128	A very rich breakfast set, fawn and gold, 72 pieces	9½ gns.

1130	Six ewers and basins, and 6 slippers	30/-
1133	A handsome TABLE SERVICE, blue, enamel and gold border	£20.
1139	A pair of ice pails, richly coloured and gold border	90/-
1140	Two hexagon soup tureens, 4 sauce ditto, 4 dishes and covers, rich japan, and 2 salad bowls, flower and gold decoration	25gns.
1142	A breakfast set, barbeau sprig, 42 pieces	35/-
1143	Two card racks and 2 incense burners, mazarine	30/-
1146	A pair of ice pails, rich japan	70/-
1147	Four vegetable dishes, and 3 small ewers and basins	35/-
1148	Two vases and covers, and 2 jars and covers	40/-
1150	A splendid japan DINNER SERVICE	£42.
1153	Six ewers and basins, and 4 slippers, white	42/-
1173	A table service, blue birds	£9.
1189	Six handsome chimney ornaments	60/-
1190	A DINNER SERVICE, blue and white	£9.

End of the Ninth Day

THE REMAINDER OF THE
STOCK OF CHINA
OF THE LATE
MR. MASON
PATENTEE AND MANUFACTURER OF THE IRON
STONE CHINA
AT NO. 11, ALBEMARLE STREET.
A
CATALOGUE
OF THE
ENTIRE ASSEMBLAGE OF USEFUL & DECORATIVE
PORCELANE,
OF RICH AND ELEGANT PATTERNS;
COMPRISING
SEVERAL HUNDRED
DINNER, DESSERT, BREAKFAST, & TEA SERVICES;
JUGS, EWERS, BASINS,
DISHES IN SETS, BOTH OPEN AND COVERED;
PLATES IN DOZENS, OF EVERY SIZE;
NOBLE ORNAMENTAL JARS & EWERS,
Superbly Gilt and beautifully Enamelled;
AND
A GREAT VARIETY OF CABINET ORNAMENTS,
OF THE MOST TASTEFUL AND ELEGANT FORMS,
The extent, Variety, and great Value of this Stock afford the most
advantageous opportunity to the public to provide themselves with
Porcelane of every class, and of peculiar strength, for which the Iron
Stone China has long been distinguished.
WHICH WILL BE SOLD BY AUCTION
BY MR. PHILLIPS,
ON THE PREMISES,
AT NO. 11, ALBEMARLE STREET,
On THURSDAY, the 20th day of JUNE, 1822,
And Two following Days, at Twelve for ONE PRECISELY,
BY ORDER OF THE EXECUTORS
WITHOUT RESERVE

FIRST DAY'S SALE
THURSDAY, the 20th day of JUNE, 1822
Commencing at Twelve for One o'Clock precisely

Lot		Reserve
1	Twelve breakfast cups and saucers and 12 tea ditto, earthenware	10/-
2	Twenty-four breakfast cups and saucers and 2 milks, earthenware	12/-
4	Five hunting jugs, stone	12/-
5	Twelve mugs, iron stone	14/-
6	Seven ditto, stone devices	12/-

8	Six antique jugs, iron stone	15/-
9	A pair of Chinese formed jars	52/-
10	A fine pot pourie	30/-
13	A table service, blue, iron stone, 142 pieces (2 soup tureens, covers and stands, 4 sauce ditto, 18 dishes, 1 drainer, 4 ragout dishes, 1 salad, 60 plates, 18 soup, 18 dessert)	£9.
14	Two rich fruit baskets and stands	30/-
17	Two match cases, an antique coffee pot and 2 shades	36/-
18	Five jugs from a beautiful Chinese original	30/-
19	Two chocolate cups and stands, very rich	18/-
20	Two pair of Chinese beakers	36/-
26	A pair of well painted vases	42/-
29	Two highly finished candlesticks and shades	24/-
31	Two match cases, and shades, mazarine	22/-
32	A breakfast service, japan colours and gold, 22 pieces	£8.
33	A pair of rich ice pails	£3.10.0d.
36	Two rich caddies and shades	42/-
37	A pair of beautiful hexagon flower pots and stands	£3.10.0d.
42	A beautiful flower bowl, mazarine	18/-
48	A breakfast set, 52 pieces	40/-
49	A lofty hall jar	7gns.
50	A dinner set, blue and white earthenware, 142 pieces	6gns.
51	A set of 3 vases and shades	36/-
52	A breakfast set, 6 large and 6 small cups and saucers, 6 cans, 6 plates, 6 eggs, 1 slop, 1 cream, 1 roll tray, 2 dishes, and 2 cake plates	63/-
54	Two vases, landscapes, and crimson grounds	30/-
55	Two khan dragon beakers	30/-
56	A pair of rich chamber candlesticks and shades	30/-
59	A pair of card cases, mazarine and white embossed figures	24/-
64	A fine dragon jar	4gns.
65	A table service, basket pattern, 142 pieces	14gns.
66	A set of 5 jars	50/-
68	Four jugs and 5 mugs, stone	18/-
69	Four antique jugs, corbeau	£1.
70	Gold edge, 6 breakfast cups and saucers, 6 cups and saucers, 6 coffee cups, 6 egg ditto, 6 plates, 2 large ditto, 1 tea pot, and stand, and 1 sugar and cover	£2.18.0d.
72	Two very rich vases	£3.10.0d.
77	A pair of essence burners, mazarine	32/-
79	Three handsome vases, painted in landscape, and shades	4gns.
80	Two vases, flies, on mazarine, and shades	28/-
84	One handsome japan vase and shade	£1.

Lot		Reserve
85	Five vases and covers, japan	£2.
92	A handsome japan bowl	30/-
93	Two vegetable dishes and 1 steak dish	38/-
96	Six breakfast cups and saucers, 6 plates, 6 egg cups, and 1 muffin plate and cover, ditto	36/-
98	Two rich cups, covers and stands, painted in landscapes and shades	58/-
102	Two vegetable dishes, rich japan	50/-
103	Six beakers and 3 cheese stands, ditto	50/-
106	Two vases and covers, green dragons	30/-
107	Four rich jugs, corbeau	20/-
108	Three paper cases, rich landscapes	30/-
109	Two ewers and basins, and 2 slippers, blue	25/-
110	Two bottles, mazarine, and shades, and 2 baskets, landscapes	27/-
112	A pair of ice pails, rich border	£4.10.0d.
113	One essence pot, mazarine, and 3 cabinet cups and saucers	28/-
120	Two vegetable dishes and 1 steak ditto, blue	28/-
122	Two paper cases, landscape, and 2 essence bottles and 4 shades	30/-
123	One toy tea pot, 2 inks and 3 shades	24/-
124	A dragon pattern earthenware breakfast set, 92 pieces	37/-

End of the First Day

SECOND DAY'S SALE
FRIDAY, the 21st Day of JUNE, 1822
Commencing at One o'Clock precisely

Lot		Reserve
131	Three ewers and basins, and 3 slippers, white	30/-
133	Two foot pans, white	25/-
134	Two dozen blue earthenware cups and saucers, 2 tea pots, 4 basins, and 2 milks	15/-
137	A square supper set, 8 pieces, snipe pattern	40/-
139	Two vegetable dishes, and 1 steak ditto, blue	25/-
141	A dessert service, India landscape, 43 pieces	£4.
145	Eight baking dishes in sizes, peacock	16/-
147	Two candlesticks, japan, and 2 paper cases, birds	25/-
148	Three paper cases, painted birds, and shades	40/-
149	Six breakfast cups and saucers, 6 plates and 1 milk pot, India coloured, and gold sprigs	50/-
152	A pair of vases and covers, mazarine	35/-
153	Two hexagon bottles, 2 ditto jugs, and 2 taper candlesticks and 4 shades	36/-
154	Four breakfast cups and saucers, 4 plates, 4 egg cups, and 1 muffin plate, yellow and gold	50/-
155	Two hexagon vases and covers, dragon	30/-
161	A square supper set, willow japan, 12 pieces	78/-

162	Two bottles, and 2 scent pots, enamelled	22/-
163	Two vegetable dishes and 1 steak ditto, blue	25/-
167	Two handled vases, mazarine, and shades	24/-
168	Two vases, mazarine, and 2 essence bottles, japan and glass shades	30/-
174	Two Spanish vases and covers, japan	44/-
175	A tea set, sprigs and gold edge, 46 pieces	50/-
181	A dessert set, red and gold rose, 43 pieces	£8.10.0d.
183	Four tea cups and saucers, 4 coffee cups, 2 plates, and 2 egg cups, yellow and gold	28/-
184	Two small bottles and 2 essence ditto, mazarine and shades	27/-
188	A handsome antique jug	23/-
189	A very rich tea set, 45 pieces	8gns.
190	A very rich coloured and gilt table service, 142 pieces	£35.
194	A rich antique vase	35/-
195	Two Spanish vases, coloured and gilt	30/-
196	A paper case, and 2 small jugs, mazarine and shades	20/-
198	A pair of vases and covers, green dragon	15/-
199	A handsome antique jug	20/-
202	Two baskets and stands, japan	50/-
203	Two tall hexagonal bottles, mazarine	35/-
204	Four flower pots and stands, mazarine	63/-
206	Two bottles, India figures and landscape	30/-
207	Two three-handled vases, mazarine	60/-
208	Two vases, views in Rome	80/-
209	Three vases, painted in landscape	70/-
211	A vase, painted in shells	50/-
212	A tea set, rock pattern, 41 pieces	50/-
213	Two tall jars and covers, dragon	15/-
214	Twelve custard cups and covers, basket pattern	14/-
217	An ewer and basin, and brush tray, handsome japan	46/-
219	A shell ink stand, and 2 paper cases, flower border	23/-
220	A table service, peacock, japan, 87 pieces	£8.10.0d.
221	A dessert set, japan, 43 pieces	8gns.
225	A handsome antique ewer, japanned and gilt	25/-
226	A pair of flat candlesticks and extinquishers, mazarine	25/-
227	A tea set, gold border, 44 pieces	50/-
231	Two vases and 2 beakers, green dragon	30/-
232	A large essence jar, japanned and gilt	42/-
234	Two bottles, 2 vases, and a watering pot, mazarine	30/-
236	Two buckets, 2 ink stands, and 2 flat candlesticks	23/-
237	Two handsome vases and shades	28/-
239	A dejeune, coloured sprigs	35/-

301

245	Five punch bowls, blue	30/-
246	A breakfast set, blue, 54 pieces	23/-
247	Four broth basins, 3 pudding ditto, 5 mugs, and 2 boats, blue	23/-
248	Four candlesticks, 2 small ewers and basins, and 2 broth basins, blue	23/-
249	Two vegetable dishes and 1 steak ditto, blue	25/-
250	Three small vases, and an essence pot, flowers	18/-
251	A caddy, candlestick, jug, mazarine, and ink stand	15/-
252	Six ewers and 6 basins, blue earthenware	23/-
253	A breakfast set, blue sprig, 36 pieces	28/-
256	Twenty-four tea cups and saucers, 2 tea pots, 2 milks, and 4 basins, blue earthenware	14/-
257	Two vegetable dishes, 2 small ewers and basins, and 4 mugs, white	23/-

End of the Second Day

THIRD DAY'S SALE
SATURDAY, the 22nd Day of JUNE, 1822
Commencing at One o'Clock precisely

Lot		Reserve
262	One potato dish, 3 hot water plates, 7 bakers, and 3 pudding basins, white	22/-
263	Six ewers and basins, blue earthenware	15/-
266	Two vegetable dishes, and 1 steak dish, blue	24/-
268	Three jugs, japan flowers and gold edge	21/-
269	One chamber set, gold jar	31/-
270	A table service, blue, 87 pieces (1 soup tureen, cover and stand, 2 sauce ditto, 2 covered vegetables (or ragouts) sallad, 13 dishes, 36 meat plates, 12 soups, 12 sweets)	£5. 0.0d.
271	Twelve jugs, blue earthenware, and 12 cups and saucers	14/-
273	Six breakfast cups and saucers, 1 muffin plate and cover, flowers, and 6 cups and saucers, roses	21/-
278	Eighteen tea cups and saucers, 2 milks, 4 basins, and 1 tea pot, blue earthenware	10/-
281	Twelve custard cups and covers, grasshopper	14/-
284	A tea set, rich japan pattern, 45 pieces	£6. 6.0d.
285	Three beakers, mazarine sprigs	16/-
286	Two bottles, ditto and white flowers	24/-
287	Two Grecian shape vases, flowers and green ground with shades	63/-
289	A handsome two-handle vase, mazarine and shade	42/-
292	Two handsome satyr vases, painted in landscapes and shades	90/-
295	Two candlesticks, green, and flowers with shades	28/-
296	A handsome one handled vase, fruit and green ground	30/-

297	Two hexagon vases, japan, with shades (1 faulty)	42/-
298	A handsome japan dessert set, 43 pieces	14gns.
299	A pair of ice pails, ditto	90/-
300	A table service, blue, 87 pieces	£5. 0.0d.
302	Two rich vases, fruit and green grounds	50/-
305	A handsome Trentham bowl	24/-
307	A small ewer and basin, 2 toy watering cans and 2 shell candlesticks	27/-
311	A pair of four-handled vases, mazarine	42/-
312	Two Spanish vases, mazarine	42/-
313	A breakfast set, rock pattern, 94 pieces	8gns.
314	A pair of urns, beautifully painted in landscapes, and glass shades	48/-
315	A pair of vases, mazarine, and shell ecretoire and 2 glass shades	48/-
316	A pair of flower pots and stands, painted in birds, with glass shades and two match cases	28/-
317	A pair of jars, japanned, flower and dragon handles	24/-
319	A pair of green dragon beakers	21/-
321	A dessert service, japan, birds and flowers, 43 pieces	£5. 0.0d.
323	Four jars and beakers, green dragon	60/-
324	Pair of hand candlesticks and extinguishers, and 2 bottles flowers on mazarine ground	28/-
326	A rich blue and gold ewer and basin with glass shade	38/-
327	A pair of ditto essence burners, and 2 cups and covers	30/-
329	A blue and gold coffee ewer and 2 tea canisters	26/-
332	Two flat candlesticks and extinguishers, 1 toy ewer and basin, 2 essence bottles and 5 shades	38/-
333	A chamber set, rich japan	70/-
336	Two broth basins, covers and stands, rich japan	28/-
337	Two hexagon vases and covers, mazarine	42/-
338	Two rich candlesticks and extinguishers, and 1 small vase, japan	28/-
339	A dejeune, rich japan	50/-
341	Six plates, birds and shells on gold border	30/-
342	Two match cases, mazarine, and shades	18/-
344	Two Satyr vases, flowers and red ground	63/-
345	Two beakers and covers, Chinese pattern	20/-
346	Pair of ice pails, flowers and blue border	5gns.
347	A table service, blue sprig and gold edge, 142 pieces	15gns.
349	Two bottles and 1 beaker, green dragon	20/-
352	A breakfast set, yellow and gold, 47 pieces	90/-
353	Four breakfast cups and saucers, 4 coffee cups and saucers, and tea pot, blue and gold, and flowers	60/- 60/-
354	Two coolers, plaid Japan	50/-

357	A supper set, 5 pieces, and tray, rose japan	63/-
359	Two bottles and covers, and paper case, japan	21/-
360	Two candlesticks, japan, and 1 antique vase	26/-
364	A rich flat candlestick and extinguisher, and a pair small bottles, mazarine	12/-
368	Four oval dishes and covers, blue	22/-
369	Four antique jugs, corbeau	20/-
371	A breakfast set, Bourbon sprig, 77 pieces	50/-
375	A breakfast set, blue border, 32 pieces	20/-
377	A supper set, blue, 9 pieces	21/-
378	A breakfast set, coloured and gold sprigs, 25 pieces	50/-
380	A table service, blue, 87 pieces	£5.
381	A breakfast set, dragon, 62 pieces	48/-
384	Two vegetable dishes, peacock pattern	42/-
386	Eight beakers, blue	16/-
387	Twenty-four tea cups and saucers, dragon, earthenware	8/-
388	Twenty-four ditto, blue earthenware	8/-
389	Twelve jugs, blue earthenware	12/-

FINIS

THE LAST PART OF THE
STOCK OF CHINA
OF THE LATE
MR. MASON
PATENTEE AND MANUFACTURER OF THE IRON
STONE CHINA
AT NO. 11, ALBEMARLE STREET
A
CATALOGUE
OF
THE REMAINING STOCK
OF USEFUL & DECORATIVE
PORCELANE,
OF RICH AND ELEGANT PATTERNS:
COMPRISING
DINNER, DESSERT, BREAKFAST, & TEA SERVICES;
JUGS, EWERS, BASINS,
DISHES IN SETS, BOTH OPEN AND COVERED;
PLATES
AND A
VARIETY OF CABINET ORNAMENTS,
OF THE MOST TASTEFUL AND ELEGANT FORMS.

The Extent, Variety, and great Value of this Stock afford the most advantageous opportunity to the public to provide themselves with Porcelane of every class, and of peculiar strength, for which the Iron Stone China has long been distinguished.

WHICH WILL BE SOLD BY AUCTION
BY MR. PHILLIPS.
ON THE PREMISES,
AT NO. 11, ALBEMARLE STREET,
ON FRIDAY, the 28th day of JUNE, 1822
And following Day, at Twelve for ONE precisely,
BY ORDER OF THE EXECUTORS

May be Viewed One Day preceding the Sale, and Catalogues had on the premises; at the Auction Marts; and at Mr. PHILLIP'S, 73, New Bond Street.

FIRST DAY'S SALE
FRIDAY, the 28th Day of JUNE, 1822
Commencing at One o'Clock precisely

Lot		Reserve
1	Twelve white jars	24/-
4	Twelve ditto mugs	7/-
5	Two ditto ice pails	16/-
7	Twenty-four cups and saucers, 2 pint and 2 half pint basins, blue earthenware	10/-
8	Six jugs, blue iron stone	18/-

9	Twelve ditto, blue earthenware	13/-
12	A breakfast set, 36 pieces	28/-
13	Eight stone figured jugs	20/-
15	Two porous wine coolers and 2 butter tubs	18/-
16	A Stilton cheese stand	44/-
17	A pair of fruit baskets, rich japan	18/-
18	A breakfast set, 37 pieces	28/-
21	A pair of Indian beakers	28/-
22	A pair of blue iron stone coolers	14/-
25	A pair of mantle ornaments	28/-
28	A dessert service, Indian landscape	4gns.
30	A table set, blue, 87 pieces	6gns.
32	A breakfast set, japan, 22 pieces	48/-
33	A pair of vases, painted in landscapes, and shades	42/-
38	A very finely japanned jug	31/-
39	A pair of mazarine myrtle pots and stands	84/-
41	A rich pot pourie	36/-
46	Seven stone figured mugs	18/-
47	A pair of ice pails, blue iron stone	36/-
48	A pair of chinese flower vases	60/-
50	A table set, 142 pieces, Tournay, gold edge	28gns.
51	Four rich jugs	28/-
53	Two chamber sets, blue, iron stone	30/-
56	A pair of water jugs, mazarine and broad gold edge	32/-
57	Two green beakers	36/-
58	A rich pagoda formed hall jar	6gns.
60	A table set, 142 pieces, Tournay	12gns.
61	A tea set, white and gold, 45 pieces	2gns.
63	A pair of elegant vases	120/-
65	Two vegetable dishes and a steak dish, blue iron stone	25/-
67	A pair of fruit baskets and stands, japan	32/-
68	A pair of mantle jars	34/-
75	Two card racks and a pen tray	30/-
77	A set of 5 ornaments	44/-
78	One flower bowl and shade	30/-
79	A supper set, richly japanned and gold edge, 12 pieces	£3.10.0d.
82	A rich toilet ewer and basin with shade	34/-
83	A pair of ice pails, japanned	£3.10.0d.
84	One water jug, neatly pencilled	36/-
86	A pair of wine coolers, rich japan	50/-
87	One pot pourie, rich japan	36/-
88	A dessert service, beautifully painted in flowers and green ground	18gns.
89	Twenty-four plates, carnation, gold edge	36/-
93	Twelve custard cups	18/-
95	A pair of flower jars and shades	£3.10.0d.

97	Two ewers and basins, green border	26/-
103	A chamber set, green border	27/-
107	Two mantle jars	63/-
108	Twelve jugs, blue earthenware	14/-
109	Twenty-four breakfast cups and saucers, 2 pint basins, cream, 1 tea pot, dragon earthenware	21/-
112	Two punch bowls, blue iron stone	15/-
114	Two broth basins and stands	10/-
115	Two punch and 2 pudding bowls, blue iron stone	11/-
116	Six ewers and basins, blue earthenware	24/-

End of the First Day's Sale

SECOND DAY'S SALE
SATURDAY, the 29th Day of JUNE, 1822
Commencing at One o'Clock precisely

Lot		Reserve
133	A breakfast set, 55 pieces, dragon, iron stone	30/-
140	Four composition mortars and pestles	10/-
141	A table set, 87 pieces, blue, iron stone	£5.10.0d.
145	A chamber set, green border	27/-
147	A chamber service, green border	27/-
149	Two vegetable dishes, and 1 steak ditto, blue, iron stone	25/-
152	Six ewers and basins, blue earthenware	24/-
160	A table set, 87 pieces, blue iron stone	6gns.
163	Two vegetable dishes and 1 cheese stand, richly japanned	60/-
164	Two beautiful caudle cups and shades	84/-
165	A dessert service, Indian flowers, rich	£8.10.0d.
166	A set of 3 rich jars	58/-
167	Two bottles and 2 match cases, ditto	30/-
170	A table set, 142 pieces	15gns.
171	A white iron stone dessert set, 43 pieces	40/-
172	An ink stand and 2 wafer cups with 2 shades	28/-
173	Two vegetable dishes and 1 steak dish, blue iron stone	25/-
176	Three match cases and shades	30/-
178	Two richly painted flower baskets and 2 lavender bottles and shades	27/-
189	A breakfast set, enamelled, 31 pieces	18/-
190	A table set, 142 pieces, rich Japan pattern	21gns.
191	A pair of candlesticks, Japan	16/-
192	A chamber service, ditto	24/-
193	Six very rich dessert plates	30/-
195	A dessert service, Pekin sprigs	10gns.
196	Three jugs and 2 mugs, figured stone	10/-
197	Three flower baskets, enamelled china	16/-
198	A pair of Chinese vases and covers	63/-
199	A very fine hall jar, mazarine hydra top	9gns.

207	A pair of Chinese jars	50/-
210	A table set, 87 pieces, grasshopper, hexagonal tureens	£9.10.0d.
211	A breakfast set, 42 pieces, red and gold	78/-
214	A breakfast set, richly jappaned, 42 pieces	60/-
215	Three cabinet pieces	17/-
216	A rich chamber service	£3.10.0d.
218	Eighteen tea cups and saucers, blue earthenware	8/-
220	A table set, 87 pieces, rich japan	12gns.
221	Two wine coolers, blue iron stone	20/-
225	A handsome mantle jar, beautifully painted in shells	50/-
226	Twenty-four cups and saucers, blue earthenware	11/-
230	A table set, 87 pieces, mandarine	£9.10.0d.
231	A pair of very richly painted goblets	£4.10.0d.
232	A pair of candlesticks and shades	48/-
233	A pair of cabinet jars and a vase	18/-
234	Eight rich plates, arms	40/-
242	Two beautifully painted candlesticks	28/-
243	A fine flower bowl and shade	£3.10.0d.
246	Four broth basins and stands, blue iron stone	20/-
253	A pair of rich broth basins and stand	12/-
255	Two toilet ewers and basins, and a candlestick, ditto	24/-
256	Two vegetable dishes, blue	20/-
257	A pair of porous wine coolers	16/-

FINIS

Photographic Credits

Plate numbers are listed beside the names of individuals or organisations who have provided illustrations for this book.

Mrs. G. Allbright, 247
L.J. Allen, 217-219
R.G. Austin, 100, 187, 207, 226, 239, 257, 263; Col. Pl. 3

Miss K. Baker, 261
W. Baker, 306
Dr. and Mrs. G. Barnes, 97
Beaverbrook Art Gallery, 138
Bonhams, 229, 278
A.M. Broad, 29, 233

E.H. Chandler, 20, 43, 64, 131, 133, 228
Chichester Antiques, 274
Christie's, 123, 141, 323, 339, 342
A.M. Cuthbert, 147

W. Davidson, 119, 120
Delomosne & Son Ltd., 230

J.K. des Fontaines, 252

Mrs. Y. Eldridge, Col. Pl. 8

William P. Firth Antiques, 74

G.A. Godden, 144-145, 200, 273, 307, 352
Geoffrey Godden, Chinaman, 6-8, 12-15, 21-23, 25-27, 30, 32, 34-36, 38, 39, 42, 45, 46, 51, 53, 55, 62, 77, 78, 81, 83, 84, 87, 89, 91, 95, 96, 98, 101, 107, 118, 121, 124, 125, 146, 160, 161, 163, 167, 172, 176, 204, 205, 223, 225, 268, 326, 328, 329, 338, 354, 355, 357; Col. Pls. 4, 11
Godden of Worthing Ltd., 2-5, 9, 10, 16-18, 41, 44, 50, 60, 61, 66, 70, 73, 75, 76, 79, 80, 88, 92, 94, 104-106, 110, 113-117, 122, 130, 132, 136, 142, 143, 148-154, 158, 164-166, 168, 170, 175, 177, 179-182, 184, 185, 188-191, 193-195, 199, 203, 206, 208, 209, 212, 222, 224, 227, 234, 236, 241, 244, 246, 254, 255, 260, 266, 269,

Bibliographic Note

Many general reference books give some information on the Masons and their products but in general these brief accounts are of very little help to the serious collector.

The standard reliable books are:

The Masons of Lane Delph by Reginald G. Haggar, Lund Humphries, London, 1952.

The Illustrated Guide to Mason's Patent Ironstone China by Geoffrey Godden, Barrie & Jenkins, London, 1971.

Mason Porcelain & Ironstone 1796-1853 by Reginald Haggar and Elizabeth Adams, Faber & Faber, London, 1977.

In addition valuable papers have been published in the Transactions of the English Ceramic Circle:

Miles Mason, by Reginald G. Haggar, vol.8, part 2, 1972.

Thomas Wolfe, Miles Mason and John Lucock and the Islington China Manufactory, Upper Islington, Liverpool, by Alan Smith, vol.8, part 2, 1972.

C.J. Mason, Pattern Books and Documents, by Reginald G. Haggar, vol.9, part 3, 1975.

In addition Reginald G. Haggar contributed a very helpful paper, *Miles Mason and Others,* to the Journal of the Northern Ceramic Society, vol.3, 1978-79.

Other relevant material may be found in John Vivian Goddard's work *The Mason Family and Pottery* first published in 1910 and in Alfred Meigh's unpublished manuscript *The Masons of Lane Delph* completed in 1937.

The Price Guide to 19th and 20th Century British Pottery by D. Battie and M. Turner, Antique Collectors' Club, 1979 will be found to include several illustrations of Mason and Mason-type wares with guidance as to their market values.

Magazine articles on the Masons include:

Mason's Ironstone China, by Stanley W. Fisher, Country Life, 29th December, 1955.

Mason's Patent Ironstone China, by G. Godden, Spinning Wheel (U.S.A.), September, 1972.

Miles Mason's Teapots, by G. Godden, Collectors Guide, August, 1975.

Miles Mason's Breakthrough, by G. Godden, Art & Antiques Weekly, 13th March, 1976.

Mason's Patent Ironstone China, by Teresa Sackville-West, Antique Collector, September, 1978.

For information on Mason's contemporaries, in particular those who produced Ironstone-type wares, the reader is referred to Llewellynn Jewitt's nineteenth century masterpiece — *The Ceramic Art of Great Britain* (Virtue & Co., London, 1st edition 1878, 2nd edition 1883 and later reprints), or to my revised edition of that work — *Jewitt's Ceramic Art of Great Britain 1800-1900* (Barrie & Jenkins, London, 1972). My standard work, the *Encyclopaedia of British Pottery & Porcelain Marks* (Barrie & Jenkins, London, 1964) will be found to give basic details of the many potters who emulated Mason's Patent Ironstone China.

Mrs. E. Collard's *Nineteenth Century Pottery & Porcelain in Canada* (McGill University Press, Canada, 1967) helps us to understand the vast export market which the Masons and their contemporaries had built up for these durable useful Ironstone-type earthenwares. American market-wares are also covered in Jean Wetherbee's book *A Handbook of White Ironstone.*

For those wishing to learn about the Chinese porcelains, which in many cases served as prototypes for the Mason wares or inspired the traditional designs, I would direct your attention to my recent book *Oriental Export Market Porcelain and its influence on European Wares* (Granada Publishing, 1979).

Other source material drawn upon in the preparation of this book — such as the original sale catalogues, are acknowledged in the text.

Apart from these printed sources there is available a tape-recorded talk with illustrated booklet showing in group poses the pieces discussed. This talk is available from Geoffrey Godden, 17-19 Crescent Road, Worthing, West Sussex, BN11 1RL at £5, post free in U.K.

All serious collectors of Mason should endeavour to join the Mason Collectors' Club which apart from holding interesting meetings also publishes (for members only), a newsletter containing information on new discoveries, etc. The Secretary is Mrs. Elizabeth Jenkins, 27 Roe Lane, Newcastle, Staffordshire, although there is a waiting list for membership. The club held an exhibition at the City Museum and Art Gallery, Stoke-on-Trent in 1974 and issued an interesting catalogue entitled *The Masons of Lane Delph.*

Index

Sale items from the Appendix are not included in this index, but references to individual sale items in the main text have been indexed.